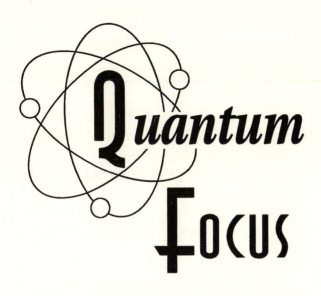

Quantum Focus

**The Quick, Mind-Powered
Total Program
For Self-Development,
Healing and Happiness**

Here's what the experts are saying about Quantum Focus!

A remarkable self-help book designed to enhance one's relationship with oneself, others and the universe . . . helpful to individuals who suffer from physical and/or emotional problems as well as those who simply want to get more out of life.
> Michael B. Schachter, M.D., President, Foundation for the Advancement of Innovative Medicine (FAIM).

An excellent resource for anyone with chronic illness or just interested in health. It teaches practical skills for a range of disorders. I highly recommend it.
> Frank Lipman, M.D., Internal Medicine, Stress Medicine. Director, Eleven Eleven Wellness Center, NYC.

"Quantum Focus" presents the interrelationship between mind, body and spirit with precise clarity, making it a "must read" for anyone.
> Dr. Patricia Trowbridge, D.C.H., R.N., N.L.P.

A helpful guidebook for those ready to start on the journey of self-empowerment.
> Bernie Siegel, M.D., Author LOVE, MEDICINE & MIRACLES

One of the more insightful and useful books on the subject — clearly a valuable tool. I highly recommend it.
> Gary Null, Ph.D., Alternative Health Educator, Documentarian and Award-Winning Investigative Journalist.

This empowering book enables the reader to discover their hidden assets within. It is chock-full of exercises designed to break through barriers . . . A beautiful work.
> Jillian La Velle, President, International Association of Counselors & Therapists.

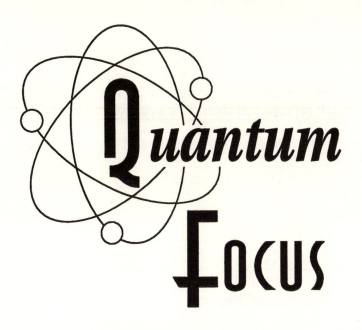

Quantum Focus

The Quick, Mind-Powered Total Program For Self-Development, Healing and Happiness

MICHAEL ELLNER, Ph.D.
RICHARD JAMISON, Ph.D.

New York

The intent of this book is solely informational and is in no way meant to be taken as nutritional or medical prescription. Please consult a health professional should the need for one be indicated.

Copyright © 1997 by Michael Ellner, Ph.D. and
Richard Jamison, Ph.D.

Instant Improvement, Inc.
210 East 86th Street
New York, NY 10028

Cover Design — Sam Magee
Editor — Roberta Waddell
Book Design — Gigantic Computing
All Rights Reserved

No part of this book may be reproduced by any mechanical, photographic, or electronic process, or in the form of a phonographic or other recording, nor may it be stored in a retrieval system, transmitted, or otherwise copied for public or private use other than for "fair use" without the written permission of the publisher.

Printed in the United States of America

Library of Congress Cataloging-in-Publication Data

Ellner, Michael.
    Quantum Focus : the quick mind-powered total program for self-development, healing, and happiness / Michael Ellner and Richard Jamison.
       p. cm.
   Includes index.
   ISBN 0-941683-35-4
   1. Self-efficacy. 2. Change (Psychology). 3. Mind and body. 4. Mental healing. I. Jamison, Richard. II. Title.
BF637.S38E44 1997
158--dc21   97-5115

Contents

Introduction 11
Acknowledgements 15

Chapter 1. The Background of Quantum Focus 17

Chapter 2. The Basic Exercise 31
    The Quantum Focus Basic Exercise — Part One 34
    The Basic Exercise – Part Two 36

Chapter 3. Controlling Your Body 45
    Increasing Hand Temperature Exercise 47

Chapter 4. Reconnecting With The Spirit 49
    Reconnecting with the Spirit Exercise 54

Chapter 5. Emotional Stability 59
    Emotional Stability Exercise 65
    The Cleansing Sleep Exercise 67

Chapter 6. Relieving Dis✴stress 69
    The End-of-Dis✴stress Exercise 75

Chapter 7. Finding Your Life's Purpose .... 85 ✓
    Discovering Your Life's Purpose Exercise 88

Chapter 8. Increasing Self-Esteem 91
    Self-Esteem Exercise A 97
    Self-Esteem Exercise B 99

Chapter 9. Achieving Self-Forgiveness 103
    Forgiveness Exercise 104

Chapter 10. Healthier Finances 107
   Healthier Finances Exercise 110

Chapter 11. Conquering Anxiety 115
   Anti-Anxiety Exercise 117

Chapter 12. Setting and Obtaining Goals 125
   The Goal-Setting Exercise 127

Chapter 13. Rising And Shining 131
   Exercise One 133
   Exercise Two 133
   Exercise Three 134

✓ **Chapter 14.** Programming Your Dreams 139
   The Exercise 141

Chapter 15. Overcoming Agoraphobia 145
   Method One Exercise 148
   Method Two Exercise 149

Chapter 16. Overcoming Claustrophobia 151
   Desensitization Exercise 152

Chapter 17. Overcoming The Fear Of Driving 155
   Desensitization Exercise 156
   Dream Driving Exercise 158

Chapter 18. Overcoming Fear Of Death 161
   Eternal Source Exercise 163

Chapter 19. Overcoming Fear Of Heights 167
   Overcoming The Fear Of Heights Exercise 169

Chapter 20. Overcoming Fear of Water 173
    More Imagery & Affirmations 175

Chapter 21. Overcoming the Fear of Flying 177
    I Can Fly Exercise (or The Peter Pan Principle) 181

Chapter 22. Overcoming The Fear Of Failure 189
    The No More Failure Exercise 192
    Dream Exercise 193

Chapter 23. Overcoming The Fear Of Success 197
    Overcoming the Fear of Success Exercise 201
    Dream Exercise 202

Chapter 24. Overcoming The Fear Of Public Speaking 205
    Overcoming the Fear of Public Speaking Exercise 210
    Dream Exercise 212

Chapter 25. Overcoming the Fear of Change 215
    Desensitization Exercise 218
    Dream Exercise 220

Chapter 26. Stop Smoking Comfortably 223
    Stop Smoking Exercise 1 225
    Stop Smoking Exercise 2 226

Chapter 27. Taking Absolute Control Over Your Weight .. 229
    Getting Rid of Unwanted Weight Exercise 234
    Gaining A Few Pounds Exercise 240

Chapter 28. Losing the Nail-Biting Habit 243
    Freedom From Nail-Biting Exercise 246

Chapter 29. Staying Healthy 249
   The Quantum Focus Shake Exercise............................ 255
   Young "Old Age" Exercise 259
   Perpetual Healing Exercise 261
   Every Day In Every Way Exercise................................ 263

Chapter 30. Eliminating Headaches and Migraines........... 275
   Common Headache Cure/Relief Exercise 277
   Migraine Headache Control 278
   The Ultimate Migraine Control 279

Chapter 31. Eliminating Aches and Pains........................... 281
   Pain Management Exercise 1 — Floating Away 283
   Pain Management Exercise 2 — Dropping Off 285

Chapter 32. Painless Childbirth 287
   Painless Childbirth Exercise 289

Chapter 33. Overcoming Allergies 293
   Overcoming Allergy Attacks Exercise......................... 295

Chapter 34. A Better Sex Life 297
   Better Sex Exercise 299

Chapter 35. Overcoming Frigidity 301
   The Exercise 302
   Affirmations and Quantum Focus Imagery 302

Chapter 36. Overcoming Impotence 305
   The Exercise 306

Chapter 37. Enhancing Creativity.. 309
   Creativity Enhancement Exercise................................ 312

Chapter 38. Inner Child Care 317
    The Magic Smile Exercise 318

Chapter 39. Learning Faster 321
    Faster Learning Exercise — Phase One 324
    Faster Learning Exercise — Phase Two 326

Chapter 40. Remembering More 333
    The Memory Conditioner 334
    The Memory Conditioner Exercise 1 335
    The Memory Conditioner Exercise 2 335
    The Memory Conditioner Exercise 3 336

Chapter 41. Better Golf 337
    Better Golf Exercise 340

Chapter 42. Better Tennis 345
    Better Tennis Exercise 345

Chapter 43. Better Bowling 349
    Better Bowling Exercise 350

Chapter 44. Better Relationships 353
    Better Relationships Exercise 356

Chapter 45. Better Communication 361
    Better Communication Exercise 364

Chapter 46. Your Quantum Future...Inner Peace & Bliss .. 367

Appendix A Overcoming Insomnia 371
Appendix B Remembering Your Dreams 377
About The Authors 379
Index 381

Dedicated to

Alexandria Lynn Trowbridge-Ellner,
Sheila English Jamison

and the memory of

Kiki Ellner
S. A. Adiv
Michael E. Cohen
Cliff Kali Goodman
Felicity Mason
Quique Palladino
Tim Pettifer
John Michael Williams

Introduction

Quantum Focus is a unique, powerful, personal-success program that teaches you to concentrate your mind's full power like a laser beam. It goes beyond meditation, visualization and self-hypnosis to help you turn your fantasies into realities after as little as 30 days of practice.

Anyone can use Quantum Focus for their mental, emotional, physical and spiritual gain, growth and balance. It will give you the ability to create sudden, extensive life changes that you desire and consciously decide to create.

Quantum Focus was originally developed to aid people facing life-threatening and catastrophic illness. It was designed to help them discover, initiate and increase their own inner healing abilities and skills while developing their control of the creative healing process. Because the original audience for Quantum Focus often did not have the luxury of time, the method had to be designed so that it could be quickly and easily learned . . . more quickly and easily than any other approach.

Quantum Focus is an ability with which we are all born, but too often allow to be turned off before we have even become aware of its presence. It is not in any way conventional psychology, psychotherapy, medicine or any other usual approach to living, staying healthy or healing. You will see very few similarities between Quantum Focus and any of these modalities. It is based, and focuses on, each individual's abilities, never their perceived "disabilities."

We are confident that every reader of this book has every inner resource necessary to recharge and re-create themselves in terms of breaking out of their self-imposed limitations. The first few chapters will help you to turn on the process again, and aid in transferring this knowledge to your creative, intuitive brain *automatically*.

Quantum Focus works from the inside out. The imagery and exercises in the book are designed to help you learn how to commune and communicate with yourself at your highest levels. Learning to center yourself in your being leads to a higher self-activation process that promotes a higher quality of life. The combined result is a rapid integration and internalization of the Quantum Focus process.

Subsequent chapters then deal with how to apply your Quantum Focus abilities to solve a variety of problems. It can be used in an untold number of situations. The examples in the book are merely that: examples. They are included to get you off to a good start in using Quantum Focus to improve your life and health. However, Quantum Focus in your hands is limited only by your imagination. Once you have used it several times to solve real-world challenges, you will easily extend your successes into any areas you wish to apply your Quantum Focus skills.

Quantum Focus is also a novel way of experiencing the world. Quantum Focus practitioners learn to unleash and take advantage of powers the average person never even recognizes exist, let alone learns to use. We call it psychosociospiritual science because it originates at, and emanates from, the points where spirituality and science meet, the very crossroads of metaphysics and physics.

There is an audiotape to supplement the text. While this tape is not essential to mastering Quantum Focus, many people find that it facilitates the process and makes learning Quantum Focus even faster and easier. For those who choose to use this tool, instructions for when and where to use it are included in the chapters where it applies.

It is important to realize before you start that you will not be able to understand everything that is said on the tape. Quite to the contrary; the two simultaneous messages will overload your conscious mind's ability to process information. You will find your conscious mind will follow one voice or the other, maybe switching back and forth from time to time – and maybe eventually just kind of spacing out entirely. This is the normal response to this technique. In fact, for the side dealing with better sleep, the object is to space out so much that you fall asleep.

The unconscious mind, however, will hear and process both tracks simultaneously with ease. This simultaneous processing will help you to open new channels within your mental mechanisms that effectively speed your Quantum Focus mastery. (The use of headphones or sitting between two stereo speakers while using your tape will accentuate the effect and accelerate the process even more.)

Quantum Focus techniques have helped people to help themselves with a variety of challenges, including many in the medical arena. However, we are not physicians and our text is not meant to be taken as medical advice. When dealing with any potential medical challenge, either rule out medical problems first or, if a medical condition is confirmed, use these techniques in conjunction with your physician's advice and care. The techniques can complement your chosen medical care, and possibly catalyze and speed your recovery, but they are not intended as substitutes for medical treatment.

We commend you for your desire to improve your life and commend you even more for actually doing something about making things happen. Quantum Focus may be the first recorded "user's manual" for the human mind. If not the first, Quantum Focus is certainly the easiest to use. We truly believe you will be able to reap the many benefits we have seen our clients experience and the many benefits we are experiencing for ourselves.

One of the nicest benefits of Quantum Focus is its self-sustaining nature. After you have given it the initial push, the process will become automatic. So, relax and enjoy your new-found skills and abilities, and a better, more rewarding life.

With peace, love, hope and joy,

M.E. & R.J.

Acknowledgements

Although the authors developed Quantum Focus into the technology it is today, it is truly the culmination of many years of experience by many people. We would like to acknowledge all of those people who influenced us, from whom we have learned and who helped us successfully incorporate some of their techniques and ideas into our own. Many of these people were present during the early development of Quantum Focus, and lent their thoughts, ideas, comments and criticisms to it.

This list includes, but is not limited to, the following: early collaborators David Frederick and Bud Weiss; Sheila Jamison, for the Life Mapping techniques she shared; H. Jane Ruskin, for her inspiration and insight; Rosemary Barone, Dr. David Bellizzi, Dr. George Bien, Dr. Al Bottari, Dannion Brinkley, Scott Bruner, Dr. F. R. Buianouckas, Dr. John Cardino, Dr. Deepak Chopra, Dr. Anthony Cimino, Dr. Andrew Cort, Dr. Dwight Damon, Anthony DeMarco, T. DiFerdinando, Dr. Larry Dossey, Dr. Peter Duesberg, Sister Lucille Durso, Elsom Eldridge, Dr. Milton Erickson, J. M. Ellner, Dr. John Gatto, Dr. Sheila George, B. and S. J. Gilbert, Louise Hay, Ed Hightower, Dr. Bill Horton, Dr. John Hughes, Maria C. Isotti, John Jacobsen, Dr. Richard Johnson, Tony King, Steve and Jill LaVelle, Fred Leidecker, Dr. Larry LeShan, Sol Lewis, Ed Lieb, Dr. Frank Lipman, Charlotte Louise, Roxanne Louise, Ed Martin, Dr. Ormond McGill, Dr. Raymond Moody, Dr. Gary Null, M. Dennis Paul, Dr. Loel Ressler, Tony Robbins, Dr. Ernest Rossi, Tony and Arlene Sabino, Dr. Michael Schachter, Barry Seedman, Dr. Bernie Siegel, Dr. Carol Sommer, Dr. Anne Spencer, R. M. Stetson, Charles Tebbetts, Ernest Telkemeyer, Patricia and Pat Lynn Trowbridge, Oscar Turrentine, Anna Vitale, Dr. E. Arthur Winkler, Arthur Worrell and Richard Zarro, all of whom either directly or indirectly enriched Quantum Focus through their own work, questioning and teachings.

Last, but certainly not least, we would like to extend a special thank you to John Burns who created, performed and donated the special music on the *Quantum Focus* tape. He also patiently recorded the authors and professionally mixed the spoken and musical tracts for the tape.

While we worked to make our list comprehensive (and it certainly appears to be so), we have undoubtedly omitted some names which deserve to be on it. We extend our apologies in advance to any such individuals.

Chapter 1

The Background of Quantum Focus

"Cultivation of the mind is as necessary as food to the body."
CICERO

Where Are We Going?

Eric is a hardworking, hard-playing financial planner. One of your authors met him and his wife socially, and we quickly struck up a friendship. Eric always seemed easygoing and unemotional and usually appeared happy. One evening a few years later, we found ourselves in the quiet corner of a social gathering. Eric looked beat and he told me he was really feeling down and hopeless because, after a year of therapy, his depression was increasing instead of decreasing. He felt his anxieties were getting the best of him.

I explained to him I had a technique that helped people tap into their inner resources and recharge themselves. I explained that I felt, in his case, I could help him turn himself around in a matter of minutes, and that he would notice the shift first thing when he awoke in the morning. I also assured him that we could do my Quantum Focus work right where we were without attracting any attention. We could use the privacy we were already enjoying in the corner of the large room we were chatting in.

You Gotta Have Heart

Having nothing to lose, but with little expectation of anything happening, he let me guide him into an enhanced state of consciousness. I then told him, although our conversation may have seemed common in many ways, he was preconditioned for something quite extraordinary taking place deep inside him. I told him that the combination of imagery and feelings we were using at a time when he was at one with himself — body, mind and spirit — was helping him put his heart into the matter and, in my humble opinion, all he needed was some heart.

The "session" lasted about three minutes. We split up and began to resocialize. About a half-hour later we said good night. I received the following letter three weeks later.

> "Much to my surprise, but as you predicted, our two minute QUANTUM FOCUS session succeeded. I am no longer experiencing the anxiety or depression that a few weeks ago could make me feel fatalistic and prevent me from working or getting up in the morning. Each day I'm amazed at how I can rise in the morning and start the day. A year's worth of therapy did not create such quick and effective results, much less approach the cost-effectiveness of your results.
>
> "I was and am willing to consider and experiment with almost any idea that improves quality of life, and in turn teach these principles to others, but I was and still am at a loss to explain this good fortune. My habits are healthier and the quality of my experiences is fuller, more motivating and satisfying. I also still suspect that other external and internal factors may have contributed to my new-found mental health, but the

bottom line is that I believe that what you did, and/or helped me to do, worked. Both my wife Andrea and I thank you! I am in your debt.

Sincerely,
Eric

We share this case with you because you have something in common with Eric. You too have been preconditioned for success and all you need to get "magical" and practical benefits is to put your heart into the Basic Exercise.

You've Got A Head Start

The fact that you are reading this book suggests you already hear the calling or feel the tugging or have some other sense of something missing in your life. This is a very common experience in our society today. This sensation is complex. It comes from more than your head; it originates from much deeper in your gut. Perhaps it is from your mind, perhaps from your spirit or "soul." But it is your head's conscious decision to do something about that which brings you to here.

A Key Factor

Our work with people with life-threatening illnesses (like Cancer and AIDS) has taught us that these situations are often *turning points* for these people rather than the *points of no return* they often understand them to be. As they become aware of the lack of an inner-life, the people who generally do the best physically are those who also discover a strong desire for spiritual reunion. This shift from outer to inner consciousness appears to be one of the most important factors in the healing process. It often acts as a powerful stimulant to the inner healing abilities which lay deeply buried in our subconscious or unconscious minds.

Quantum Focus was originally designed to meet the special needs of these people. It was developed with the intent of helping them to create their *own* spiritual pathways. It also had to be fast, practical and easy to learn as many of these people had no time to spare. To meet these objectives, Quantum Focus draws on a wide range of healing systems that use the powers of imagination and belief to empower healing and promote spiritual awakenings.

Although we will explore the theory and philosophy behind many of these, our focus is always on their practical application; that is, how do I do this to make it work for me? The most useful and effective parts of each of these systems have been extracted from them and incorporated into Quantum Focus in a way that makes it the fastest and most powerful program of its kind.

Discovering Your Way

The good news is that you do not need to be facing a life-threatening illness or catastrophic situation in order to rediscover, learn to use and reap the benefits of traveling your very own personal path. Quantum Focus is about helping all people reconnect to their inner life, and recognizing what it truly means to be awake in their waking life. We have found the Quantum Focus approach to spirituality to be exceptionally useful when working with people to achieve a wide array of goals and objectives. More than just its apparent boost to the self-improvement process, it seems to fill a need within us all and empower us to reach down within to harness and focus even more of our latent power.

At The Heart Of The Matter

Please keep the terms "spiritual" and "religious" separate in your mind. To some readers, they may be truly synonymous, but it is not necessary to be religious in order to be spiritual. We use the word spirituality to represent the essence of what religion would be if we could strip religion of all the man-made rules it imposes on others and which are imposed on it. Spirituality is a very personal, and often private, thing. It refers to your individual relationship(s) to whatever higher power you acknowledge and/

or to others and/or to the universe as a whole. It calls forth terms like God, Universal Consciousness, Brotherhood, Oneness and Higher Self. Only you can know what is right for you. Quantum Focus urges, encourages and helps you find and follow *your* path.

The Quantum Moment

The Quantum Moment — that is, **right now** — is where and when it's all happening. But instead of living in this glorious moment, most of us miss it completely as we mull over the past or worry about the future. In what is best described as a mechanical (i.e. automatic) response to the awesome power of the present moment, we habitually switch on the auto-pilot and head for those mental hills. To make matters worse, we are generally unaware that what we are missing is the most important moment in our lives! Thankfully, a moment later another glorious moment comes along, ready and willing to serve anyone who masters it. Oops! Missed another one. It won't wait for its master. But here comes the mother of all moments. Oh no. Missed again. Better luck next time.

Mental Martial Art

We like to think of Quantum Focus as a mental martial art. Although from the very first lesson, there would be many benefits from learning the process itself, mastery is essential for profound benefits to manifest. This is not unlike the difference between "meditating" and "meditation". Specifically, the Master meditates while the student thinks about meditating. With mastery of the basic Quantum Focus exercise, you can begin to expect profound benefits within 30 days of serious lighthearted practice.

Inner movement is essential to initiating outer change. Doing the "work" creates a Quantum fluctuation within your universe, thus initiating the process. It will also create within you an expectation for success. This in turn causes you to act and behave in a manner most likely to achieve your goal. It is the same law that runs all the behaviors you always seem stuck with. (The ones you explain away with, "It's just the way I am".) Remember Jamison's Law: "You get what you expect...at least in the subconscious and unconscious parts of your mind." When you spend your time worrying about the future, you are mentally rehearsing and preparing for that particular future. When you constructively plan for a better or more desired future and focus on living in the now, you are rehearsing and preparing for that future.

So if you don't like what you're getting now, it makes sense to reprogram a constructive expectation into the deepest levels of your being. We discovered that one sure way to give the process practical value is to make people aware of how they can speed things up internally and slow things down externally so they can experience the peace of mind and excitement only to be found in the present moment.

Life Is A Highway

In many ways, people live their lives the same way they drive their cars. Most of the time we are so lost in our thoughts that, instead of being in the driver's seat of our lives and taking full advantage of the many awesome powers operating within us, we are driving on auto-pilot. We are somewhere else in our minds altogether (and $5 will get you $10 it's in the past or in the future). Perhaps we are just out to lunch — the point being that, more often than not, we are unconsciously driving our cars and our lives.

So Who *Is* Driving?

His/her name is "Auto-Pilot". It works something like this: Although an individual may be intoxicated, that individual can be unaware of their intoxication, feeling perfectly capable of driving safely. Most drunken drivers are shocked to find out that they're intoxicated. Similarly, although you may have no awareness of it, Timmy or Tammy Auto-Pilot steps in when you step out. You may be shocked to discover how many things you are doing without being fully aware of them. But you and Auto-Pilot cannot both occupy the same space (the driver's seat) at the same time. Thus, Timmy or Tammy *only steps in when you step out*. When you are present, Auto-Pilot cannot be, which implies that a way to stay off Auto-Pilot is to be present yourself. (This, for the record, is Ellner's Rule.)

As we well know, this being on auto-pilot can be painful and dangerous. But it's not only dangerous to us. It is dangerous to everybody we share the road of life with. The mind operates in such a way that everything we believe, think, breathe, see, hear, taste, remember, feel, etc. simultaneously — and usually unconsciously — becomes our understanding and experience of that reality.

There are many hidden meanings. Hence arises the ancient Far Eastern belief that we are never angry about what we think we are angry about. The anger is merely a symptom of an underlying problem. We truly shape our reality to fit our perceptions and expectations. The mind simply creates what we program it to create via our deepest desires and expectations.

Unfortunately, in most cases, our deepest desires and expectations are unknown to us *consciously*. In fact, the best way to assess the current situation is to take a good look around you. Are you happy? Are you at peace? Are you healthy? Are you doing what you want to do with your life? Do you know what you want to do with your life? Are you prosperous? Are you in a healthy relationship? Do you want to be? Overall, is your current situation what you want?

This power we hold to create our life situations is why it is a good idea to know that we are always creating. We can create either that which we want or that which we do not want. When we are unaware of this power, we run the risk of creating that which we do not want.

Retaking Control

When you experience peace of mind, being in the present is as natural as being in your body. So instead of either being bummed about your past or bummed about your future, you could be living (and creating) the great life *right now*. Alas, peace of mind, it seems, is but a rare experience for most of us. So not only are we missing all the action of the moment, but with every destructive image, thought, feeling, association, etc. we are also subconsciously programming ourselves for disaster. Quantum Focus is about re-establishing our awareness of being in the moment and standing on the firm, flexible foundation of being present.

Fast But Foolproof

Keeping in mind that we developed the Quantum Focus experience to meet the needs of people who felt very pressured about not having enough time, we developed a fast and powerful program consisting of *personal empowerment* and *self-improvement*. Combined, these modalities are irresistible simply because they use the very same pathways your unwanted behaviors now travel. That is, you already have the power to create. It is *what you are now creating* that is the problem, not your ability to create.

When a person is programmed to believe that they have a short fuse, no matter how hard they try, they will have a habit of losing their temper. In this area of their life, they feel totally out of control. But the habit has an underlying set of programs and conditioning. If the person were to change this conditioning, they would get a very different response to the same stimulus. Once the constructive programming replaces the destructive programming, it's automatic!! You count to ten and smile before responding, and you love the results.

It's Just That Easy

Here's a quick illustration of the process at a superficial level. Suppose you are driving your car in the fast lane about ten miles per hour over the speed limit. Someone races up behind you and begins blowing their horn. There is no room to move right comfortably and you feel you are already going fast enough, so you keep on going as you have been. They keep tailgating and blowing the horn. Then they cut off a car to their right and speed up next to you. As soon as they can get the back of their car up to the front to yours, they jump in front of you, cutting you off. How do you feel? Most of us are pretty hot! This results from our deeply held beliefs and subconscious programming.

But now add to this scenario that this car gets off at the next exit, which happens to be for the local hospital. You see the driver race up to the Emergency Room entrance, fling open the door, run around the car, fling open the passenger's door, lift a baby — obviously very young, unconscious and bleeding profusely — and race into the hospital at a full run. How do you feel now? The acts on the highway didn't change. Your perception did, and this connected you to a different set of programs and conditioning. What a difference this made.

This is what Quantum Focus can do for you. All we ask is that you practice the exercises, do the activities and, from now on, view your past with a healing heart while you watch the constructive possibilities flow into your future.

The practice also helps you make the most of your inner programming by helping you cultivate constructive thinking and weed out destructive thinking. Remember Ellner's Rule, *they can't both occupy the same place at the same time*. Amazingly, in our direct experience, learning to be centered within oneself and in the moment at hand is in itself one fine way to cultivate peace of mind as well as make all kinds of wonderful changes in our lives — spiritual, mental, emotional and physical.

Going Back To Basics

Now here is where the basic Quantum Focus exercise comes in. Once you begin to master the basic exercise, you will be able to tune in to the moment or make better use of the "hang time" when you are out of the moment. When you initiate your Quantum state of mind and choose to Focus on your "in"tention or "at"tention, you are bringing all the powers of the mind to bear. So be in the moment when you can, and if you are not in the moment, be sure you are creating constructively. Keep Mr. or Ms. Auto-Pilot from filling in these moments destructively.

The book's chapters are organized so you can improve your life in increasing ways and magnitude as you develop your Quantum Focus skills and abilities. The different chapters give you the opportunity to center yourself in your being and *re*-create your past while positively influencing your future in a number of different situations. All the while, you will be learning to master the technique so that you can then apply it to any of the challenges you may face in life. The imagery, suggestions, metaphors, activities and stories in this book are designed to help you do exactly that: make Quantum Focus an automatic process. This, dear reader, is the spirit of Quantum Focus.

It All Starts Here . . .

As you can easily tell from the approach we take to making life truly wonderful, we believe that the ultimate solutions to its challenges lie predominantly in the mind. Still, we are very practical in our approach to improving our lot. We stress the mental aspects of improving our lives over all else because many people are either unaware of them at all or unaware of their importance in reaching their goals.

Even when we do all the "right things" at the physical level, it is the environment in the mind that most often limits how successful these physical things turn out to be. So, unless appropriately and effectively addressed, the mental aspects we stress in this book can sabotage the best of efforts in other areas.

We want to help you incorporate this perspective into your life. Thus, we hope, you will quickly eliminate many, if not all, of these barriers. If you do not address them, they might otherwise keep you from achieving — despite the hardest work at the physical level — the things you want to achieve.

. . . And Can Be Helped Along

Here is another thought you will want to consider in adopting this more liberating perspective and the power (or empowerment) that comes with it. While we envision ourselves going through our lives both happy and healthy, this does not mean that either of your authors crosses streets without looking both ways first. It would be foolish not to do as many different things to ensure our health and happiness as we can comfortably handle.

To this end, we have included the equivalent to looking both ways before crossing the street in various chapters throughout the book. These are usually rather simple steps you can take to increase the speed or magnitude of your results. You might want to consider taking some of these additional steps towards making your life a magnificent experience. While these are usually physical in nature, consider them analogous to this situation.

A Practical Example

You want a better job. So you do your Quantum Focusing to find one. You incorporate all the most useful things you can think of. You learn of an absolutely great position, one that is so suited to you that they could have saved time and space by simply writing your name in the job description. You imagine applying for that position and really impressing the screener. You get an interview and see yourself shining in that interview. Of course, they offer you the job, and at a higher pay level than you had originally hoped for. Then you imagine yourself being even better at this new job than you had ever before hoped to be. You picture your interactions with your colleagues creating a great respect for you and your abilities. You visualize making all kinds of connections that will help take you to the next few positions after this one.

This is typical of the Quantum Focus work to align the universe with your desires and your actions with your desired goals. It creates a Quantum fluctuation within the universe that begins the process. It also will create within you an expectation for success. This will in turn cause you to act and behave in a manner most likely to achieve your goal. Remember this about life and expectation: *You don't always get what you want in life, but you do pretty much get what you expect* . . . at least in the subconscious and unconscious parts of your mind. It makes sense, therefore, to program that positive expectation into the deepest levels of your mind.

In Mysterious Ways

All that is consistent with the purpose and value of Quantum Focus. Here's the point of doing other things that help your goal to come about. While your Quantum Focus programming may very well lead to someone offering you a new job without your actually going out to look for one, *it is reasonable to expect that reading the want ads and answering those that appeal to you will speed the process.* It may be that your Quantum Focusing was responsible for putting the exact position you imagined into those ads in the first place. It would also be reasonable to accept that the universe may consider it has fulfilled its part of the deal at this point. It has presented you with exactly what you wanted. Now it is up to you to do your part. They say God works in mysterious ways. When God is working to help you, why not give him or her all the help you can?

You've Got To Buy A Ticket

We know intentions and mental processes can influence the material world. For example, Robert Jahn, Ph.D. and Brenda Dunne, Ph.D., researchers at Princeton University's Engineering School, have scientifically shown people's thoughts affecting the mathematical output of computers. (You may want to keep this in mind the next time you're experiencing a somewhat less than perfect day in front of your computer.) Among the lessons we learn about using our mental abilities to put our lives on our own paths and create the kind of lives we want, it is useful to remember an ambitious young man named Albert. Albert learned all about the influence of intentions and thoughts, and about using his mental ability to create in the physical world. His first objective was money. (This might hold true for many of us until we begin to center ourselves and discover what is really important. So, let's not pass any judgment on Al.)

Albert mentally programmed winning the lottery. As he had learned to do, he then began acting as though it had already happened, thus exhibiting and strengthening his expectation. He signed a lease on an expensive foreign sports car. He put down a deposit on an elegant new home in an exclusive neighborhood. He signed a contract for a 40 foot cabin cruiser. Later that week, he sat down in front of his new big-screen television set (also bought on credit) to watch the drawing of the winning numbers. "Sixteen", called the hostess who was pulling the numbers. "Twenty-two", she continued. "Forty-one, twelve, fifteen" and "seven".

Albert was horrified. He didn't win. He was facing absolute ruin. Not only was he unable to pay for the things he had committed to, he might even go to jail for misrepresenting his ability to pay when he signed the contracts and left deposits. At the very least, his deposits — representing all the money he had in the world — would be forfeit. "Why?", he moaned. "Why didn't you make me the winner?" "What kind of universe is this? I did everything I was supposed to do. I visualized. I planned. I acted as though it had already occurred. I built up my positive expectations." A thundering voice reverberated, "Albert, I am happy to help you. Next time, though, at least buy a ticket!"

You can consider the additional actions or ideas we include as buying a ticket, looking both ways before you cross the street, or any other way you wish that reminds you to do whatever it is that will help bring you the results you want.

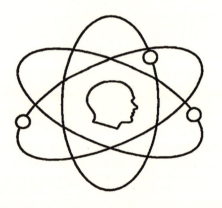

Chapter 2

The Basic Exercise

"The Kingdom of Heaven is Within."
JESUS OF NAZARETH

It All Begins Inside…

As you learn to move in and out of Quantum Focused states of enhanced consciousness, you are coming into contact with your greatest gift: the many and awesome powers of presence of mind. Throughout the ages certain groups of people were aware of, and teaching and practicing the art of being in the moment. In this work we are teaching you how to rediscover the art and science of this practice. You will be both surprised and amazed to discover how much this simple act can change your life.

Note, though, that "simple" doesn't necessarily mean "easy". The simplicity often fools people into thinking there is nothing to it, or that they can just do it from the start without any practice. As we repeatedly emphasize, however, mastery requires practice. With practice, Quantum Focus then truly becomes as easy as it first appears. Without practice, you may get some limited results, but you won't get the full benefit of the process. Think of it this way. Because the practice is easy and because, in this instance, practice really does make perfect, do your easy practice! You can count on the world of Quantum Focus opening to you automatically.

In the simplest terms, you are going to learn how to shift into states of enhanced consciousness, intentionally and at will. In these special states, people (and you) easily demonstrate significantly greater control over both mental and physical functions. Quantum Focus was engineered to take you way beyond guided meditation, visualization and self-hypnosis. It was designed to give you the ability to consciously shift sequentially into what we call "Real Time", "Heal Time" and "Zeal Time" while giving you the tools to change your past and influence your future. In essence, you will learn states that will enable you to throw off those invisible chains that bind you to your past, many of which you may not even now know are present and constraining your life, and open the door to your bright future.

These states include a wide range of outward appearances, from wide awake and alert to profoundly entranced. In them, physiological changes which reflect a much healthier state of being are automatically attained. The chapters *Stress* and *Staying Healthy* explore some of these changes in detail. You will be astounded by the degree to which you can consciously and/or deliberately affect your body's functioning.

But for the Quantum Focuser, all of this is just the tip of the iceberg. So while you add new meaning to your life, increase your self-esteem, overcome pain and fears, eliminate unwanted habits, bring new zest to your love life, sleep better and put your dreams to work for you, the hidden benefit is that you will rediscover the inner peace and bliss that comes with spiritual growth.

The Foundation

Just like the multiple states of water (solid, liquid and gas), human consciousness exists in many states. Quantum Focus operates in the most useful of these. We call these states Quantum Consciousness. It is of the utmost importance to master the basic Quantum Focus state before you pursue and expect significant results from the more advanced exercises. Of course you will still obtain some benefits right away, but because achieving them depends on being in Quantum Consciousness, you will be much more successful by mastering the first step before you take the second. Remember that houses built on rock stand far stronger than those built on sand.

Being, Doing, Becoming

This is the Basic Quantum Focus technique. It is only one of several techniques you will be using to shift into Quantum States at will, but it is the foundation for those that follow. Thus, it is important that you practice this exercise regularly. It is easy and fun, and it can become automatic very quickly.

The "keys to the kingdom of Quantum Focus" are *a relaxed body, a quiet mind* and *a positive expectation*. Let's start with a positive expectation. This is as easy as accepting that something will happen when you practice the exercise. You don't need to figure out now just what will occur. Make up your mind only that something will happen and that, in some way, it will be a positive experience. So now, find a suitable place to begin your personal adventure into the wonderful world of Quantum Focus.

Getting Started

For those who are learning to enter the Quantum Focus state without the audiotape, read and learn the following section well enough to guide yourself through the exercise from memory before you begin to practice the exercise. Don't worry if you don't get it exactly right the first few times. It will get progressively easier with practice. Your objective is to capture the feel of the exercise for now. The exact wording will unfurl itself with future readings and practice.

If, as do many people who are just beginning, you find it helpful to play soft music in the background when you are practicing, please feel free to do so. Choose something gentle and comfortable, perhaps classical or New Age. Then, just take your time with the exercise and allow the feelings to move gently throughout your body with the music. Remember, there is no hurry. It may take you anywhere from 15-30 minutes to complete the exercise when you first begin practicing. This is fine. As you continue to practice, you will find you will naturally access the Quantum State more quickly and easily.

[TAPE INSTRUCTION: If you are using the Quantum Focus audiotape, start side A now.]

The Quantum Focus Basic Exercise
Part One

With the intention of becoming deeply relaxed, sit or lie down, gently close your eyelids and take two or three long, deep, calming breaths. Feel yourself drawing in peacefulness with each relaxing breath and exhaling all your problems, worries and concerns with each out breath. You are off to a very good start.

Now think about your inner mind taking over this experience and, as you do, make mental contact with the bottoms of your feet. Now move your attention to your feet . . . then slowly to your ankles . . . then slowly to your calves and shins. Notice what this mental contact feels like.

Now, bring your attention gently to your thighs and slowly up through your genitals, pelvis and hips. Notice how they become heavy with relaxation as you focus your awareness on them.

And now move your attention into your solar plexus and abdomen. As you become aware of these parts of your body relaxing, slowly bring your attention to your chest and lungs, thinking that your breathing is free, easy and automatic.

Now bring your attentions to your heart and think to yourself, "My heartbeat is steady, strong and calm", and this is the heart of the matter. Notice that the lower parts of your body are becoming warm and heavier with every breath you take. And while your body is becoming heavier and more deeply relaxed, you are becoming lighter and feeling higher with each breath. Very good! Let yourself just sit, relax and enjoy that for a while.

Now move your attention slowly to your fingers, hands, wrists, arms and upper arms. Bring your attention into your entire back and up into your shoulders and neck.

And now into your face and head so that you have an inner sense of your whole body from the bottom of your feet to the top of your head. Holding that awareness, we want you to now focus your attention on your eyelids and think about your eyelids becoming totally relaxed. Imagine how happy and heavy your eyelids are becoming . . . so heavy . . . so relaxed. That's it.

Continue to focus on your eyelids while the rest of your body just fades out of your awareness. Your whole body is so relaxed and at rest . . . that's it . . . all your nerves, all your muscles becoming loose and limp as they continue to relax and fade further and further away.

And as you move deeper and your body feels heavier, you feel higher and lighter. . .and become even more relaxed. And you begin to feel a sense of enthusiasm for what you are doing. You become more and more in tune with your inner mind. Ask it to lead you deeper and deeper in this experience . . . and just stay with it.

You may feel a sense of being in some favorite place where you are relaxed. Perhaps it will appear to be a warm tropical isle; maybe it will feel like a cool green forest; or maybe just the sound of soothing music lights up your relaxed mind. Perhaps it is just the new awareness of the presence of nothingness that fills your mind with a pleasant emptiness. Sometimes, it's nice to just sit and enjoy that for a while.

As you drift and drift, you become more and more aware of new possibilities. Allow yourself to bask in the good feelings and sensations and you begin to open to a whole new way of seeing yourself and the world you live in. Feel the excitement and peace that can bring.

And now, very slowly, permit your attention to gently return to a fully conscious and aware state. Let your inner mind guide you back to the present, to the here and now. . . feeling at peace, energized and completely alert.

VERY GOOD!

Making It Routine

Once you have mastered the *"Art of the State"* (that is, when the above exercise leads to an almost automatic relaxation when you so much as *intend* to relax), it is time to proceed to Part Two of the Basic Exercise. Part Two makes it possible for you to use the Quantum Focused state during your routine day with ease and facility.

The Basic Exercise
Part Two

In this exercise, please sit on a chair with feet flat on the floor, your spine erect and your hands at your sides or in your lap. Please keep your eyelids open and your eyes unfocused; that is, staring blankly into space without actually looking at anything, just as you might do in a daydream, as you begin to consciously connect with yourself as a *bodymindspirit* sitting in a chair and becoming aware of the self-initiated relaxation process. Mentally scan your body slowly, and passively let yourself relax completely. Simply focus your attention on the process of letting go.

Now slowly open up your attention to everything around you . . . extend your sense of hearing so you are aware of the sounds inside and outside you. Be aware of every sound, near and far, and even the silence beyond. Extend your sense of feeling in a similar manner. Become aware of all your exposed skin and the different sensations of air on your forehead, the back of your neck and your hands. Permit your eyes to receive color and form without classifying or categorizing whatever it is that comes to your eyes. Simply note the shapes and colors. Notice, too, any aromas that may surround you as you seek them out. Perhaps you may even observe a sensation of taste as you continue to expand your senses.

As soon as you feel good with this part of the Basic Exercise, practice it standing up. After a few days practicing this sitting and standing, begin to attempt walking. Keep your attention on every step you take (that is, consciously feel your feet when and where they contact the ground as you walk) and be fully aware of the basic movements and shifts in support. Very good!

Next, use this exercise before beginning each activity of the day . . . i.e., wake up and do the exercise for 2 minutes. Before showering, do the exercise for 2 minutes. Similarly, before shaving, brushing your teeth, getting dressed and eating your breakfast, do the exercise for 2 minutes and bring your conscious intent into your activities. As you continue your day, notice the stop and start of all your activities and commit to going into a waking here/now

Quantum Focused state. Bring this into the very heart of all your actions.

Now, as you begin this practice in your ordinary day-to-day activities, become aware of how you actually slip from the enhanced state of consciousness into the ordinary state of consciousness you find yourself in before your next activity.

A helpful exercise is to sit quietly and count from one to ten over and over again . . . 1, 2, 3, 4, 5, 6, 7, 8, 9, 10, 1, 2, 3, 4, 5, 6, 7, 8, 9, 10 — over and over again. Be very gentle with yourself when you notice you've gone above 10, i.e., 11, 12, 13, 14,15, etc. The thing is, it takes a great deal of concentration skill to repeat 1 through 10 over and over without losing your concentration and continuing to count to eleven, twelve and beyond. We highly recommend this practice until you can repeat it for five minutes without overcounting.

Getting The Most Out Of Your Practice

A very powerful way to enhance your life is to start developing your power imaging skills and abilities as quickly as possible. Spend 30 seconds viewing your Power Image every time you practice shifting into a Quantum Focus State.

Your Power Image

What is a Quantum Focus Power Image? A Quantum Focus Power Image is a moving mental picture in which a person watches themselves move from where they are to where they want to be. It's like fine-tuning the mental imagery equivalent to "every day in every way I am getting better and better."

The power of the Quantum Focus Power Image is that it enables people to make sweeping changes without wasting time on content. In other words, once you master the basic exercise, all you will have to do is be able to see yourself moving quickly from where you are to where you wish to be while in a Quantum Focus state. The key to this is becoming centered in your being and concentrating on your Power Image several times a day for the last 30 seconds of your of your 2 to 3 minute practice sessions.

Creating Your Power Image?

In Quantum Focus a mental picture is worth a zillion words. We are convinced that flashing on a Power Image — one that programs you to see yourself improving daily in every way imaginable — for about 30 seconds at *any* time, is the most powerful way to inspire that improvement (with the exception of practicing the Power Image while Quantum Focusing). In short, your Power Image is a crystal clear image of yourself exactly as you dream yourself to be. When you follow any of the other exercises in this book with a Power Image of yourself, you are not only increasing the benefit of the exercise but are also improving yourself in a more holistic fashion.

Unexpected Benefits

On more than one occasion, clients have reported having a specific image flash into their mind's eye while they were fine-tuning their Power Image. For example, Alice is an independent, intelligent and a highly-stressed woman. She was referred to the authors by one of her doctors who told her that learning to manage her stress would improve the quality of her life. During our initial session, Alice said she could never drive in the city. Since she lived in New York City, this was somewhat of a problem for her.

Noticing how even the image of her driving in the city stressed her, we mentioned in passing that soon she might feel so relaxed and confident she would be able to see herself driving anywhere. After she learned to shift into Quantum states, it was suggested to her that she experiment with different images that might translate into self-healing. She was also instructed to work on a Power Image that would reflect her "non-treatable" condition going into remission. In a creative moment, while switching from her healing imagery to her Power Image, a very personal and powerful healing image flashed in her mind's eye.

Alice began utilizing her Power Image every time she did her Quantum Focus stress management exercises. Within 60 days, all her doctors noticed improvement. Alice's positive expectations are becoming stronger every day. She is an excellent candidate for a total remission because, at her deepest levels, she now believes that the greatest healing power of all is inside her. She totally trusts that healing happens when all the essential spiritual, emotional and physical nutritional requirements for healing are met. She is finally learning not to sweat the small stuff which diminished her pleasures, increased her discomfort and fueled her condition. She is rediscovering herself as a person and is breaking free of former limitations. Most pointedly, she is now taking driving lessons. The healing is happening.

What You Can Expect

The combination of both parts of the exercise (part one plus the graduated steps of part two) will greatly enhance your entire life as you gain awareness of the powerful state of being in the moment (being here/now), and you sharpen your concentration. *The power of your attention and the increased power of learning to focus your attention are the ultimate benefits of your Quantum Focus practice.*

The various exercises will help you improve the quality and experience of your life and, at the same time, increase your Quantum Focus skills and abilities. You can use these enhanced skills to overcome all types of challenges which present themselves in your life.

We have devoted many chapters in this book to surmounting specific obstacles. Begin with the areas that will be beneficial to you personally. After you have successfully handled a few of these areas, you will have internalized the essence of how to approach any difficulty life may put in your path. Use the principles you have learned to structure specific solutions to any of these difficulties you want to overcome. *You can only win when you practice Quantum Focus!*

Understanding Follows Practice

Know also that the universal laws and metaphysical tenets that will bring you closer to both the understanding and the full use of your higher powers will become clearer and clearer as you practice Quantum Focus. They will make more sense and will become more a part of you during the next several weeks of practice.

Once you have internalized the technique, that is, once you have practiced it enough to do it easily and naturally without feeling as though you were "forcing" it, here is what happens. In essence, you will make several automatic shifts in consciousness whenever you even intend to Quantum Focus. Your practice will have made each shift into a conditioned response that requires little more than your intention and the time and place to carry it out.

Real Time

As you begin, your bodymind shifts first into what we refer to as Real Time . . . the *moment* . . . right **now**. You are centered in your being. Your body is relaxed. You are peaceful in mind and flowing in spirit. Your attention is focused far and wide, fully opened and focused outward. You experience time as it occurs. This is mastering the moment.

Heal Time

From Real Time, you may easily shift into Heal Time if your intention for Focusing includes a goal that would be best handled from this state of consciousness and you desire to do so. (We can hear you asking, "Why else would I be doing this?" The answer is that once you become accustomed to just "hanging out" in the moment, you will find yourself doing that a lot simply because it is such a great place to be!) Heal Time is the hypno-meditative state of mind in which you are able to give your images viability and amplify the intensity of your feelings. This is the ideal time/space in which to develop your self-healing skills and abilities. It is here you can best heal your past and breathe life into your dreams for tomorrow.

In Heal Time you are relaxed in body and peaceful in mind and flowing in spirit, just as in Real Time. However, now your attention and focus are concentrated and turned inward. Remember that in Real Time your attention was focused outward. In Heal Time the viability of our images and the intensity of our feelings are naturally amplified by the enhanced state of mind that Quantum Focusers work with. In Heal Time you can heal your wounds and breathe life into your fantasies, turning them into realities. In Heal Time, time itself is slowed. Research on the rates of oxygen consumption in meditative and normal states of consciousness by Herbert Benson, M.D., at the Harvard Medical School, has shown that 15 minutes spent in this deep state of consciousness gives you the equivalent of between one and two hours of rest.

Here are some examples of how you can use Heal Time to improve your life or health.

The Quantum Focus Shuffle

Let us suppose you have a project of some kind that you want to work on. You shift into Heal Time and, in your mind, review all the things you think are going for the project and all the things going against your project. Now in your mind let your subconscious mind shuffle the *fors* and *againsts* until it feels that you have some creative solutions and approaches to the project bubbling deep inside you. Trust that some truly interesting ideas will just pop into your mind in the next few hours or days. They may come as dreams, flashes of insight (*aha's*) or even seemingly as the result of logical thought and reasoning.

The Quantum Focus Blast

Think of something going on in your life with which you are not happy. Shift into Heal Time and mentally view whatever is troubling you. See it clearly in your mind's eye. Now feel it intensely. Be with it for a moment, and now take a deep yawn, close your eyes and imagine all the powers of your mind are concentrated into a powerful beam like a laser beam. Now blast the picture immediately, replacing it with a new image, the one you consider to be the happy ending.

Future Focusing

If your mind's eye can vividly see it, you can be it! Whenever you find yourself thinking about the future in any negative or uninspiring way, shift into Heal Time and re-focus on what you wish to create or influence. Practice creating vivid images of what you want and when you want it.

Zeal Time

When you want to extend your powers beyond this point, move on to Zeal Time. In Zeal Time, you are centered in your being and in the moment. On the inside you are peaceful and at ease. Everything is sharp and clear. Things seem to be happening at a very high but manageable speed. On the outside, everything seems to be in some kind of slow motion. Everything is larger than life, and has its own logic. You are easily able to see and comprehend that logic to the extent that it is useful to do so. You are vitally alive and aglow as you remain centered in your being with your attention opened far and wide.

As you continue to practice and rack up successes in shifting into Real Time and Heal Time, and making the most of these states, you will begin to automatically begin shifting into Zeal Time whenever it is beneficial for you. Just be with it. Enjoy it and think to yourself how easily you can interact, in any way you wish, with this slow moving external world. Think to yourself, "I can enter Zeal Time by just reimagining the deep feeling of being centered in my being and by being mentally in tune with my body as the full force of my attention opens outward. Life is great.

You bring this state with you as you reenter the everyday world, at least to the best ability of those around you to determine. Now, things just flow more smoothly for you. Everything seems easier than before. You are creating one of those days when everything you do is just right, sort of a modern day Midas Touch, except with control Midas never had. You are creating an experience that generates a true zeal for life itself; the kind of day when we stop what we are doing, take a deep breath and think to ourselves, "What a great day to be alive!" (You may also hear this state referred to as "flow" or "being in the zone.")

In chapter 3, we will learn how to harness the special power available in the Quantum States you are now accessing, and focus it on a specific objective.

Chapter 3

Controlling Your Body

"Imagination is more important that knowledge."
ALBERT EINSTEIN

Practice Having Fun

Practicing Quantum Focus will be deeply rewarding, relaxing and transforming. It provides a very special and needed nourishment for spiritual growth as well as for mental and physical wellbeing. Researchers (like Dr's Herbert Benson and Joan and Myrin Borysenko of the Harvard Medical School's New England Deaconess Hospital) are able to observe psychological and physiological changes that indicate these Quantum States are indeed healthier as well as more productive than other states of consciousness.

Time Tested

The Basic Exercise has passed the test of time with flying colors. The ancient Egyptians, Greeks, Romans and Asians each used their own versions of Quantum Focus to empower, heal and promote spiritual growth. So give yourself a mental pat on the back, and continue to practice shifting into your Quantum Focus States.

As you master going into the deeply centered and fully balanced state of bodymindspirit we call Quantum Focus, we will begin to enhance your self-enrichment program further. This is done through the use of imagery and affirmation.

How Long To Mastery?

You can look forward to some deep stirrings happening inside of you as you "work", in the Quantum States, with the Basic Exercise. Many people experience these sensations in as little as three weeks. A few others require a little longer, sometimes as long as twelve weeks of regular practice before they detect the spiritual awakenings. (Your audiotape can hasten the process.)

But remember, the small, still voice inside you speaks ever so subtly. You must quiet the collection of other thoughts and voices that normally run through your mind on a daily basis in order to hear the quietest one. And while the usual collection of thoughts tells you many things, it is the quietest thought that holds the truth. Practice is both preparation and listening. So practice, practice, practice . . . and be prepared for some outstanding results.

Building Basic Skills

The easy-to-learn techniques of Quantum Focus help balance left- and right-brain activity, and this balance adds to the superior results practitioners achieve. So let's begin to learn to focus our imagination while in the Basic Quantum Focus State. Prepare to enter the Basic State and then go through the following exercise while you are deeply relaxed. You will experience your body doing something once considered impossible.

This exercise will teach you how to deliberately raise the temperature of your hand. Get a small thermometer, one which lets you easily hold the bulb in your closed fist. Now close your fist *gently* around it. Don't squeeze tightly. You want to surround the bulb with your fist so it is making contact with your skin. You want to avoid straining or introducing muscle tension. Now wait a minute or two to allow the temperature to equilibrate. Then note the temperature.

Now — still holding the thermometer bulb in your gently closed fist — find a comfortable place to sit, close your eyes and slowly repeat the following to yourself for 20 minutes:

[TAPE INSTRUCTION: You can use side A to guide you into the Quantum Focus state. Keep your tape player near enough that you can *stop the tape before it guides you back up*. Once you have stopped it, do the exercise below and then bring yourself back to the present.]

Increasing Hand Temperature Exercise

"It is a very warm day. The sun is shining brightly. There is almost no breeze whatsoever. It is a very lazy day. . . and I have nothing to do but relax and enjoy the warmth. I am so very relaxed.

"I am sitting in one of my favorite places in the whole world. I am enjoying the peace, warmth and relaxation. I am getting very drowsy, just relaxing and enjoying the warmth that fills my body.

"I enjoy the feel of the sun warming me. The sun's gentle rays bathe my body in warmth. I am wearing exactly the right amount of sun lotion to protect my kind of skin, so I can relax and enjoy the sun's energy. My skin is protected against burning.

"I feel the sunlight warming my chest and stomach. It is so soothing and tranquilizing. The sunlight warms my back and shoulders. My arms and hands are getting warmer and warmer. I feel it especially in my hands. They have begun to perspire from the heat. . . and it feels so good. . . this soothing warmth and relaxation."

Keep repeating thoughts like these to yourself, feeling the warmth of the sunlight in your body, especially your hands, for about 20 minutes. At the end of the 20 minutes, open your eyes and look at the thermometer again.

VERY GOOD! If you are about average, by the time you've done this exercise three times, you will have increased your hand temperature by as much as 10 degrees! In the next chapter, we will add affirmations that empower and speed your adventure.

Chapter 4

Reconnecting With The Spirit

A young girl came home from her Sunday School class looking very troubled. When her mother asked her why, she responded, "Mrs. Harrington covered Genesis today, but it never explained when God created malls."

ANONYMOUS

A Common Experience

Have you had times in your life when you felt everything you were doing was going so well that you knew you had to be getting help from somewhere? Have there been other times when everything seemed to be going so badly that you were ready to throw in the towel? Have you also experienced feeling alone, even in a crowd? How about occasions when you sensed a presence with you when you were by yourself?

Most of us laugh at the anecdote at the beginning of this chapter when we first read it. But when we take the time to stop and think about it, modern life has reduced spirituality in most people's lives to a non-existent point. We call this *"spiritual malnutrition"*. It usually manifests as a void in one's life. A sense that something is missing, or that there must be something more to life or, as the song says, "Is that all there is?"

Spirituality Not Religion

When we say spiritual malnutrition, we are not speaking about organized religion. We are speaking specifically about spirituality. Spirituality is included in all religions to be sure, but religions go far beyond spirituality. Each religion has its own set of rules; you can do this on even-numbered days, you must do that on odd-numbered days and you can never do thus and so. Spirituality is not cluttered with written rules.

The major religions today lament the fact that attendance is down; that people are not attending services as they used to. If we are suffering from spiritual malnutrition, why don't we just go to the various houses of worship to cure it?

A New Age

Historically, people flocked to their religions to get the spirituality that lay within. But times have changed. Many of us have examined religions and decided that the rules were not necessarily for us. We often sense that all the extras that come packaged with the spirituality somehow lessen or negate the spiritual experience itself. So we stopped going. But this is usually a case of throwing the baby out with the bath water. In turning our backs on religion, we have often left spirituality behind also.

Interestingly, we don't generally seem to notice its absence for many years. It appears we can get along just fine without religion... because we can! But, we cannot get along as well without spirituality. This is the quiet part that sneaks up on us when we least expect it. Its loss is felt in subtle, but ever-growing ways. Eventually, we notice an emptiness that is hard to describe or explain, that "Is that all there is?" feeling.

A Unique Experience

Spirituality itself is difficult to describe or discuss because it is so very personal. It has no written rules of conduct or behavior. There is no one else to tell us how to believe, feel or act. To each of us, it is something unique. When discussed, our individual experience of spirituality often appears a little bit different from what others describe as their experiences.

One of the reasons the major organized religions have declined in attendance is that religions make no allowances for our individuality and our individual experience of the spiritual. Instead, we are told what spiritual is or should be. When this handed-down description doesn't fit, we turn to another religion to check it out, or turn away from religion(s) completely.

None-the-less, we shall present our definition for you to consider. Spirituality deals with that part of us we call spirit. There are two essential aspects of spirit.

First, spirit transcends the physical world. It is not bound by our everyday knowledge of time and space. It is infinite and timeless, unbounded and eternal.

Second, it somehow unites, connects, ties or binds us with everyone and everything in the universe. You may experience this sense of connection in many ways and times. Remember the feeling you had, while walking through a warm woods on a beautiful day, when you came to a place that overlooked the surrounding countryside. Or perhaps it was gazing up at the night sky filled with so many stars that it took your breath away. Maybe it was holding a new-born baby kitten.

Maybe it was a feeling of deep empathy for strangers on the other side of the world when their plight was shown on the evening news, which described the famine and showed the little children literally starving to death. Or perhaps any of countless other experiences in which you could actually feel that connection, nothing physical, but still a connection to someone, something, everyone or everything else.

But while spirituality connects us to everything else in the universe, so, too, does the mind. How then do we distinguish between mind and spirit?

Six Billion Points of Light

Imagine, for a moment, a star. Its bright light emerges from the center as individual points of light. It is as though each of us was a different point of this star. We are thus unique from one another, just as one point of the star may be longer or may shine brighter than another. Yet, as you travel back down any point toward the body of the star, the points all merge into a common star body. Here we are united. Our own physical bodies are the points of the star, our spirit begins deep in the center of the star (and is part of it) and continues right out into our individual points. From within an individual point, the connection to the body of the star is less obvious, especially if you are near the tip of the point.

In fact, from many viewpoints, any star's point may seem to be entirely distinct and separate from the center of the star. Here, then, is where the mind fits into our analogy. The mind is the means by which we can communicate between the physical body and the spirit. The mind links the physical body (the point of the star) with the part of the spirit that extends into the point.

And, because the part of the spirit that extends into the point of the star is connected to the body of the star, the mind and the body are also linked back into the very body of the star itself through that connection. We feel or sense a connection to everything and everyone else because, at this level, we *are* connected to them. And as you examine the body of the star, you discover we are *more* than connected to them. *We are them.*

A More Theoretical View

If you find it more palatable and easier to grasp, you might also consider that what we referred to above as the body of the star is a universal consciousness. Universal consciousness has abundance, health, peace, truth, knowledge, happiness, and all else within it. The part of that consciousness which extends up into your individual point (i.e., the aspects of that universal consciousness you personally experience as *you*) already contains everything that is within the universal consciousness.

However, we experience consciousness (internally) through the mind. That experience becomes our personal consciousness. Unfortunately, each individual mind can be, and almost without exception has been, conditioned by extensive negative, limiting programming. (We discuss this in more detail in the next chapter when we examine your inner terrain.) The individual mind therefore only admits (recognizes) those parts of the universal consciousness which it has been conditioned to believe are available to it. This limited experience is what we believe to be consciousness. It is what we *think* we are.

We express our personal consciousness (our limited experience of universal consciousness) internally and externally through the brain and its subservient organs. Our unconscious minds strive to make our expressed reality consistent with our internal (believed) reality. We then express, within and without, only a portion of the abundance available to us. The conditioning we had received limited our ability to experience what is rightfully ours.

Our limited experience of the universal consciousness restricts our ability to express it in our lives to only that which we have experienced and, therefore, believe. What we do express is often manifested in ways other than those we would consciously like it expressed: unhappiness, illness, poverty, and so on.

A Rose By Any Other Name

One place where a discussion of spirituality always heats up and agreement breaks down is when we try to decide what to call the star itself. It really doesn't matter what we call it. If your own background and beliefs are most comfortable with names like "God", "Allah", "Jehovah" and so on, that's fine.

If you are better served by considering the star to be "Universal Intelligence", "a Higher Power", "Higher Self", "Inner Wisdom", Universal Consciousness" or "The Universe", that's fine too. If you feel most comfortable with "Fred", that too is perfectly acceptable. You see, no matter what we call it, the star is still the star. The name we apply to it is only for our own comfort. It doesn't make the slightest bit of difference. . .to the star itself or to our personal and unique experience of it. This is certainly a departure from organized religion.

For many years, mankind has been arguing about, even fighting wars over, what name *they* attach to the base star. In the course of history, more wars have been fought for "religious" reasons than for all others combined. You might want to take a moment to think about the logic in that as you travel down your individual point back into the body of the star and reunite with those who had been labeled "infidels". Another wonderful way to look at this is the adage that *"God has no religion."*

The Vital Link

Notice that it is only through our mind connecting with the spirit that we are able to reach the interior of the star. This will immediately explain the sense of "aloneness" that results from losing our contact with our spiritual side. It also explains the sense of help and support we feel when we are in touch with our spiritual aspects. How, then, do we reignite our spiritual fire?

It is important to realize that we never lose our spirituality, we only lose contact with it. But it is there and waiting for us to reunite with it. It is as if we tried to deny the existence of the star while accepting the point. We can focus on the point and ignore the body of the star, but it is still there when we are ready to see it. All that is needed is the desire and the willingness to allow it to happen. It also helps if you invite it to happen, and that is what the following exercise does for you.

Reconnecting with the Spirit Exercise

First, enter your Quantum Focused state. Then proceed with the exercise that follows.

> Imagine yourself sitting or lying in a comfortable and safe place. Feel yourself relaxing even more deeply than you usually do, perhaps imagine you are lying on a cloud. It supports you firmly yet softly.
>
> From above you appears a ray of brilliant white light. It comes from the center of the universe, wherever you imagine that to be. The light seems to

encompass your entire body, wrapping it in a blanket of love. Somewhere near the base of your spine, the brilliant white light enters your body. Here, it begins the process of recharging and tuning all your body's own energy centers. It opens all these centers to enable you to achieve inner peace and comfort.

Imagine a spiral of red light within your own body at the base of your spine. Watch as the white light unites with the red spiral, making the spiral brighter and larger. When this red spiral is sufficiently charged, the white light moves further up your body.

It merges with an orange spiral in your lower abdomen. As the orange spiral absorbs this energy, it too grows larger and becomes brighter. When this energy center is empowered, the white light rises again.

At around the level of your naval, it combines with a spiral of yellow energy. The yellow spiral grows and becomes more vibrant, more vivid. When it too has become empowered, the white light moves on to the level of your heart.

Here, the pure white light joins a spiral of green swirling energy. The green spiral grows brighter and larger, stronger and more vibrant. When it approaches its ever-increasing potential, the white light proceeds.

As it reaches the level of your throat, it joins a blue spiral of pure energy. As the white light enters the blue spiral, the blue color becomes even bluer. The white light intensifies the blue color and increases the power within the spiral. The swirling blue spiral grows larger and more intense. And the white light moves on.

As the white light reaches the level of your forehead, it meets a deep red-blue colored spiral of energy. It has the very deep reddish-blue color that appears at the conclusion of spectacular sunsets. This indigo spiral responds to the white light by growing more vibrant and stronger. It is empowered by the pure white light. And the white light moves up to the top of your head.

Here, the pure white light merges with a violet spiral of energy. The white light opens this energy center and unites with it. The spiral becomes instantly brighter and larger. This spiritual energy center grows rapidly more vibrant. Watch as the white light fully empowers this center, this connection to spirituality.

Now project yourself outside of your body and look at the masterpiece you really are — a rainbow of colors, all harmoniously blending into each other, and surrounded everywhere by brilliant white light. Notice also that you are connected, through the light, to the center of the universe. Spend a moment now just appreciating that. And when you are ready, allow your consciousness to come back to the present.

If you are like the vast majority of those with whom we have shared this exercise, you found it very rewarding. It will be very easy for you to practice it regularly. As you do, watch for signs around you in your everyday world. With regular practice, you will discover that your feelings and reactions to events continuously, though subtly, change.

We suggest that you complement this process with several others in this book that go "hand in glove" with it. These are in chapters 7 through 9, which deal with finding your purpose for being here and your sense of worthiness.

Science Studies Prayer...

You may find it very interesting to learn that science has undertaken some very serious studies on the power of prayer. These scientific researchers use the word prayer in a special way, probably quite unlike what convention religious training would dictate. For them, prayer is simply a quiet moment of reflection, often directed inwardly rather than outwardly. In essence, it is that quiet communion with whatever it is you commune with that you experience when you enter a Quantum Focused state.

Imagine your consciousness reaching down into the body of the star described, connecting with the universal consciousness, and then enhancing and reinforcing that which flows into another point. (Remember that this and/or similar states can be induced through other methods besides Quantum Focus, such well-practiced methods as meditation, hypnosis, etc. Two major Quantum Focus advantages, though, are the speed and the ease with which you can master it.) Many times, exactly what is meant by prayer has not been specified to those doing the praying. They are simply told to pray, whatever that means to them.

... And Surprises Itself

Nevertheless, some interesting results have been obtained. Seeds have been planted in several identical pots and cared for in exactly the same way, under the same conditions of light, water, nutrients, and so forth. However, some of these seeds were prayed for. Scientists at Spindrift in Oregon have consistently found that the seeds which were prayed for produced greater growth! The amount of increased growth has even been correlated with the amount of prayer; more prayer equals more growth. And when they stressed the seeds, simulating "sick" subjects, the results showed even greater growth.

Of course, this makes one wonder about praying for people, especially ill people. One study by cardiologist Randolph Byrd, M.D., looked at patients arriving in a coronary care unit at San Francisco General Hospital. Without their knowledge, they were arbitrarily assigned to one of two essentially equal groups. One group, again without their knowledge, was then prayed for by prayer groups which were specifically asked to do this for the study. The other group was not prayed for, at least by the prayer groups used in the study. It is reasonable, of course, to expect that their loved ones prayed for all the patients.

What happened? When the results of the study were tallied, there were significant differences between the two groups, even though the doctors involved didn't know who was in which group, and neither did the patients who didn't even know there *was* an experiment going on.

Overall, the group which was prayed for fared much better than the other group. They needed less pain medication, and had fewer cardiac arrests and deaths.

A Modern Wishing Well?

Is there a reason to connect with that higher power? Can we benefit from tying in to the abundance of all things good that it offers? We leave the answers to you.

Chapter 5

Emotional Stability

"By starving emotions we become humorless, rigid and stereotyped; by repressing them we become literal, reformatory and holier-than-thou; encouraged, they perfume life; discouraged, they poison it."
JOSEPH COLLINS

Why is it that most people, even when life is kind and everything is going well, find so little joy in their lives? In our opinion, it is because most people live in a series of cultural trances, compounded by millions of suggestions, that cause them to continuously postpone their lives. Most people put themselves last on the list of things to do, behind their jobs, family, mundane chores like shopping, and their social responsibilities. After all these comes self. These people survive but they never thrive. This is because, below their level of awareness, they are living in the shadows of their beliefs, feelings and emotions. Everything they experience is dulled by these shadows.

The sages told us (usually credited to Heraclitus) we cannot step into the same river twice. Yet most people live a joyless "been there, done that" kind of existence. Even if they don't think so, most people can cope with the big crises; it's the small stuff that breaks them down. So why do folks sweat the small stuff? Do you?

Poisoned Emotions

Postcard visionary Ashleigh Brilliant tells us, "Life offers its greatest challenge at the point when nothing seems challenging." It seems to us the greatest challenge in life is to get out of living in our minds and to actually start living dynamically in the moment. Reliving our resentments or worrying about our futures is not living in the moment. In fact, anytime we are not passionately involved with life, it is a major sign we are out of the moment and cut off from the very quantum energies that enliven and repair us.

Do you ever have experiences in which you find yourself reacting with feelings which are far more intense than the situations actually warrant? We are all familiar with the notion of the straw that breaks the camel's back. Life can easily collect these little straws for us, placing each one essentially unnoticed on our backs . . . until!

The Antidote

The Quantum Focus antidote to this subconscious addiction of avoiding being in the moment is the Basic Exercise. It automatically leads to centering yourself in your being and opening your attention to the moment. Mastering the moment, that is participating in life by putting your undivided attention into whatever you are doing, is the Tao of the Quantum Focuser. We are confident that, if you put your heart into this practice, in a short time you will personally experience states of enhanced consciousness in which your imagination will spontaneously build the bridge between where you are and where you want to be.

Once mastered, the Basic Exercise is your passport to a new life. It is the foundation of Quantum Focus, and the key to this very loving self-mastery is practice, practice, practice. As you rediscover and re-experience the awesome quantum powers available to you in the moment, you will also discover that you always had the ability to consciously re-create yourself anytime you so desired. Somehow this information is very healing in and of itself. By utilizing the quantum powers of the moment and the awesome powers of your imagination, in time you also will rekindle within yourself a deeply felt sense of confidence and esteem.

We are also certain that, as you begin to detoxify your own emotions, you will find improved health, and you will find you are able to be at peace within yourself in any situation. (We deal more extensively with the repercussions of "toxic emotions" in the chapters entitled *Increasing Self-Esteem* and *Staying Healthy*.)

Are You Seeing The Flowers Or The Weeds?

The imagery used in this book will help you recognize and eliminate the very toxic habitual thoughts, feelings and beliefs that promote unhappiness and disease in all who are addicted to them. Once free of these psychospiritual viruses, you will notice more energy and enthusiasm flowing from you into your life. Many people report that as soon as they recognized their very own patterns of toxic thinking, feelings and beliefs, they also recognize the relationships that contribute to those addictions.

What Happened?

Studies of people with serious illnesses point out the tremendous impact our emotions have on our health. People with cancer, who did not know they had cancer but who were not feeling well, are consistently found to deteriorate at a much accelerated rate from the moment they are given the diagnosis. Somehow, the emotional reaction to hearing that they have cancer changes the body's response to it.

Could it be that most people harbor some deeply held beliefs regarding cancer? You bet we do! Could it also be that the doctor who informs the individual about the cancer contributes to this accelerated decline? Absolutely. It is very important to find a doctor who fits with you and is to your liking. You may have cancer either way, but you will fare better with the right physician.

For example, firing a doctor and finding a new health care professional is often a turning point for people with chronic health problems and survivors of life-threatening diseases. They suddenly realize that the reason they dreaded going to their doctor was because the highly charged overt and covert suggestions their nice doctor was giving them actually increased their anxiety and diminished their sense of well-being. At the moment they understood that their attitude played a major role in their health, they also understood that the attitudes of their health care providers and the people around them can and do help or hurt their efforts. Are your health care providers and the people around you on your side?

Finding Hope

We are not suggesting that you keep changing doctors until you find one who will tell you whatever you want to hear — you need a honest partner in your healing journey — we are just suggesting that some may have more useful (to you, not them) ways of telling you what you need to know.

The following reports of two oncologists using the same combination of chemotherapy drugs illustrate this dramatically. The first referred to the protocol as "EPHO", which were the initials of the drugs used. He had about a 25 percent rate of favorable response with them.

The other physician treated people who were just as sick with the same kind of cancer, and he used the same protocol. However, the second physician got about *three times* the rate of favorable response to the drugs as the first.

Oh yes, they were not called "EPHO"; they were called "HOPE" instead. Can our emotions be toxic? Hmmmm!

If You Want A Choice

When a person is out of the moment, they have no choice but to react to whatever is going on rather than act on whatever is going on. The difference is this. When we *react*, we subconsciously add a lifetime of emotional loads to the experience. All our opinions, beliefs, hurts, insecurities, fears and resentments that our subconscious mind associates with the current situation are added to the current experience. When we are *in the moment*, however, all the baggage is automatically put aside and we respond to what is actually happening. These Quantum moments are also called religious, or peak, experiences. It is in these moments that we are at our best.

Keeping in mind, however, that almost everyone carries around a lot of emotional baggage, if we go through our lives reacting rather than being alive, you can well imagine how this can lead to disastrous ends.

Underlying Principle

When we appreciate our true selves, we can avoid the baggage reactions. The very basis of Quantum Focus is to provide Quantum Focusers with a practical technology for self-enrichment, as well as a meaningful theoretical basis for that practice. One of the most basic benefits you experience as a Quantum Focuser living in the moment is the awareness of what we can call your "inner terrain". This is a measure of your true free-from-baggage self, that special part of each of us which supports health, wealth and happiness, or negatively, ill-health, poverty and unhappiness. Let's explore this inner terrain for a moment.

Your Inner Landscape

Everyone's inner terrain comes equipped at birth with the potential for all things, both good and bad. However, its natural inclination is towards all positive and desirable things. . .like health, wealth and inner peace. You will become aware, as you go through this book, of how often we unconsciously subvert this natural tendency (as we discussed above).

We regularly can and do overpower our inner terrain's natural drive for the good with programs directed toward the other side. Once a negative or non-useful belief has been accepted, we then move heaven and earth to make our lives consistent with that belief. Even if it wasn't a true statement when we accepted it and began using it as an internal program, it certainly will be by the time we're through working toward it. We manage to use these programs — which we "inherit" from others who are often well meaning — so very effectively that we often wind up unhappy, discouraged, depressed, uncentered, unhealthy (both physically and mentally) and in poverty to boot.

Tending Your Garden

The good news is that many, if not most, of our deeply held beliefs were constructed from ideas which were untrue when they were instilled in us. This is good news because it means we can again regain our inner terrain and its natural propensity for all things good. Specifically, this chapter offers you the means to achieve a state of emotional well-being. Actually, it helps you *to recover this state*, not create a new one.

As with all other positive things, the seeds for emotional stability already exist deep within your psyche. When a person makes a conscious effort to unlock the power of these inner seeds and let them take root, we are sure from our own life experiences that the seeds of emotional stability will take root. They quickly grow and bear fruit. To borrow from Abraham Lincoln, "A man is just about as happy as he makes up his mind to be." Quantum Focus will help you regain control over that part of your mind that you are making up so you can consciously decide what programs you want to run rather than letting the Auto-Pilot decide for you.

"May The Force Be With You"

The concept of a higher power is central to the most effective use of Quantum Focus. As we discussed earlier, the name applied to this higher power is irrelevant. To help people to stay outside of old religious training or beliefs and hence not be distracted by them while they are mastering Quantum Focus, we often like to use "Star Wars" imagery. Let yourself think in terms of being one with "The Force". When a person goes into Quantum Focused states and thinks of being one with "The Force", he or she creates — deep within their psyche — the perfect terrain for the inner seeds of emotional stability to take root. The following imagery, to be used after you enter a Quantum Focused state, can help you do just that.

Emotional Stability Exercise

As you enter your Quantum Focused state, think about being ready for a spiritual adventure . . . in your mind quietly shout, "I am ready for a spiritual adventure". Now move more deeply into that special experience of profound peace and ease. Allow yourself to drift and relax so that from head to toes you are completely at rest in your bodymindspirit. You can feel it . . . nothing distracts you. You are at peace with yourself and aware of the wonderful sense of inner security you are now beginning to experience.

Now, moving from this "here and now" experience, imagine yourself beginning to float right out of your body, as if you were a mist of steam gently rising from a tea kettle. Floating up, up, up and away into a universe of harmonious energies filled with brightly colored lights. Imagine your very own energies are being drawn into this glorious mix and, without even thinking about it in terms of actual events or experiences, you are able to reconnect to the energy associated with the painful experiences or hurtful feelings that interfere with your total emotional well-being.

As your individual energies are mixed into the greater energies of the universe, the energy associated with negative beliefs and emotions are, in a manner of speaking, "steam cleaned". Your inner terrain is now perfectly prepared for the seeds of emotional health, already deep inside you, to respond to the inner light now showering them with the special energies needed for them to take root and grow.

Imagine now your seeds of emotional stability getting the sun and rain they need to continue growing every time you enter Quantum Focus states... and that each time you practice the different Quantum Focus exercises you are tending your inner garden with self-love and the powers of enhanced consciousness.

A Sigh A Day

We like to think of this exercise as Groaning For Health, or, for the pun enthusiast, A Sigh A Day Keeps The Doctor Away. This simple exercise is unbeatable for unloading negative emotions. And within 30 nights of practice you will discover for yourself that a sigh a day truly keeps the doctor away, and is a gateway to a healing restful sleep.

Clearing The Way

This exercise is designed to utilize the natural healing powers of groaning and moaning. While we reject the notion that emotions cause particular diseases, we fully recognize that, in many cases, your emotions are a significant co-factor in the development of any stress-related disease you might be suffering from (see chapters 6, 8 and 29). Very few things can wear a person down more efficiently than their own negative emotions. What if you could detoxify those emotions before they harden and compromise your inner physician?

The good news is that, not only can you dump your toxic emotions — and toxic feelings about those emotions — in a very calming, relaxing and fun way in just five or six minutes before going to bed, but you can also initiate the deeper and more profound emotional healing which seems to occur with regular use of this exercise.

The Cleansing Sleep Exercise

Prepare for a restful, healing night's (or day's — if you're on the night shift) sleep. Get as physically comfortable as you are able, close your eyes and just be with all the emotions and feelings that you had during the day. You could think about the different events that occurred, or you could just feel the sum total of the day's emotional load. We recommend you try both ways, see which way works better for you and stick with it for the rest of the month.

Now take a deep breath and start groaning out loud. Just let those big deep groans flow from your diaphragm . . . and continue to groan until you feel a shift and notice that you are beginning to feel at ease.

Very good, now just start to moan (which is a far gentler type of groaning) and moan away any long-held emotional wounds which added to the day's stress. In other words, just moan away the hurts and resentments that toxify you simply by intending to do so, without any need to identify or deal with the underlying experiences. Just moan away the lingering emotional toxins until you feel another shift from being at ease to feeling completely relaxed, at which time gently shift your attention to what you need to do tomorrow.

Think about everything planned, allow some room for the unplanned, and tell yourself that, as you sleep on it, you will clean out the old and prepare yourself for anything and everything that comes up. Now give yourself a long sigh of relief knowing that tomorrow will creatively take care of itself. So go to sleep . . . that's right . . . it will all take care of itself while you enjoy . . . a good . . . restful . . . cleansing . . . sleep.

Chapter 6

Relieving Dis✦stress

"Never trouble trouble till trouble troubles you."
ANONYMOUS

It's All Around Us

Pick any day and look around at the news media. Headlines somewhere warn us about the danger of stress to our health and well-being — often, to our very lives. You'll see the warning in magazines, on newscasts and in our daily papers. But for all their hype and visibility, they never really tell us what stress is or how we can combat it effectively. They suggest we all know what stress is and that we eliminate (in 20th century living!), avoid (we can't) or manage it (we don't know how). Most of these articles and news reports merely leave us with a sense of impending doom if we do not do something about our stress, whatever stress is. We are even left with confusion about just what stress is.

This is a disservice. Because we do not know what, when, why or how to do whatever it is that can help us protect our health and well-being, we generally do nothing. This is also a disservice because there are some relatively simple and easy things we can do on a daily basis. These are not necessarily things that eliminate, reduce or avoid stress; they are ways of reducing the *effects* of stress!

The Truth About Stress

A very popular misconception about stress is that stress is the factor that causes wear and tear on our overall health. In fact, *stress is neutral*. It is our reactions to the potential stress-causing aspects of our lives which determine whether or not each particular stress is either good for us or bad.

What Is Stress?

Some of the confusion in the mind of the general public stems from the way researchers use the word stress. It is often used in two different ways. First, stress is the term applied to an outside force or event (e.g., getting fired, a death in the family, a change in a relationship). I will use the term 'stressor' for an external event.

We are using the term stress in its other meaning; that is, the reaction within the body to these outside events (e.g., heartbeat speeding up, adrenaline pumping, depression of the immune system).

Which is the "right" interpretation? Actually both are correct. A better question is, which is more useful? The answer is obvious when we are looking at ways to "manage" (whatever that means) stress. We cannot do much, if anything, about the outside events. In today's economy, people are being fired every day for no fault of their own. It is usually called downsizing. Children are born. People die. Relationships begin and end. But, on the other side of the coin, we can do something about our internal reaction to these events.

Once We Know They Are There

Can we control our internal reactions? You bet we can . . . once we are aware of what is happening. One of the amazing things about a person's stress load is that, by and large, most people are completely unaware of most of their stressors and their reaction to them in their moment-to-moment lives. Most people use their imaginations to fret over the past or worry about their futures. They respond to the current situation or problem automatically, usually based on deeply-held beliefs or preconditioned responses learned in childhood.

But when we learn to observe what is automatically happening within us when we encounter each stressor, we can begin to make conscious choices about how to respond rather than just react from habit. We can see what mental associations we unconsciously make when we are not present in the moment. We can then learn to make better mental connections between a potential stressor and the outcome it leads to.

This, in turn, activates different mechanisms and systems within the body. Ever wonder why two people who are faced with the same situation react so differently? One may fall apart under the "stress" of it while the other is spurred on to greater achievement and is invigorated by the challenge it presents. The difference lies in the internal connections. Useful connections turn potential life-challenging stressors into positive factors in our lives.

Instead of feeling pressured, we can sense an excitement. Instead of being anxious or afraid, we can feel peace and serenity. Once these connections (i.e., our internal representations of what each stressor means to us) are in place and operating automatically, we feel challenged instead of threatened.

It's Only Our Reactions That Count!

Studies on stress, from the 1960's to today, find several key points. First, no matter how carefully we plan our lives, things will go wrong. Second, when they do, we will react to them. Third, these reactions can produce devastating effects within our bodies, effects that make us more vulnerable to health problems ranging from asthma to zoonosis (literally from A to Z), and many in between.

Correlations between stress and heart disease, cancer, diabetes, infections, allergies, bronchitis, autoimmune conditions, thyroid disorders, assorted endocrine disorders, ulcers, hypertension, insomnia, lethargy and many other conditions have been discovered.

And this doesn't even consider the effects of stress on our feelings of peace and happiness. The insidious aspect of all this is, these illnesses and conditions occur before we even reach burnout, the most obvious symptom of too much stress.

Many studies (such as those of the Glaser's at Ohio State discussed below) confirm a decrease in immune function when we are under stress. Our immune system normally keeps us healthy by protecting us against foreign invaders (bacteria, viruses, yeast, and so on) and internal errors and accidents (cancer cells). What happens when it dips, falls asleep at the switch as it were? Nothing good! The point is, stress can induce reactions within our bodies that can seriously impair our lives, mentally and physically.

Is there any hope? Yes, there is a great deal of hope. (If there wasn't, there would be no point in including this chapter unless we wanted to depress you.) That hope lies, not in avoiding stress, as we can avoid only a small amount of our daily stressors, it lies in learning ways to *neutralize the harmful effects that this stress can otherwise cause in our bodies.*

Stress Is Not Always Negative

One of the easiest ways to identify stressors (those external events which induce the stress reactions in the body) is to look for change. This is how most standardized tests determine stress levels. You are presented with a list of events and asked to check off those events which you experienced during the last year (or some other specified period). Different point values are associated with each event. You add up the points for all those you checked to determine your total.

Interestingly, although the events on the list include negative occurrences, such as the death of a spouse, they also include events you would rate as positive, like getting married, being promoted, the birth of a child, going on vacation, etc. In most instances, there are fewer points associated with the more positive events than with the horrific ones, but they still add to your stress. The change itself is a stressor and can cause stress reactions in your body.

Two Types of People?

Research in the 1970's, as reported in *American Scientist* by Meyer Friedman, M.D. and Ray Rosenman, M.D., suggested that there were two types of people, type A's and type B's, whose body chemistry reacted differently to stressors. A's demonstrated the negative biochemical effects of being stressed while B's did not. Outwardly, type A's were characterized as competitive, hard-driving, always in a hurry, overachieving perfectionists. B's appeared to be laid-back and easygoing. Everything seemed to upset A's, nothing seemed to upset B's. But it wasn't this simple. Some apparent type A's did react strongly to stressors, but others did not. Conversely, some apparent B's demonstrated A type internal reactions to stressors. We are still sorting this out today.

Everyone Benefits

So who really needs to learn to control their stress responses? Because we can all benefit, the safest assumption to make, until science fully understands stress, is that *everyone* can be healthier (and happier) than they are today, or will stay healthier longer by learning how to control their body's stress responses. Benson's breakthrough book, *The Relaxation Response*, first documented the benefits to the system. Since then, numerous studies have reinforced the conclusion that less stress means better health.

What About Getting Well Again?

While the final verdict isn't in yet, mounting evidence says that the simple step of learning to handle stress can help sick people recover their health. Consider the following research results.

It is commonly believed that immune function declines as we age. (Immune function decline with age may be true ... or it may just be another example of how we get culturally hypnotized, readily accept the idea and then unconsciously bring it about.) This phenomenon ostensibly explains why older people are more prone to diseases like cancer. Janice Kieclot-Glaser and Ronald Glaser, Ph.D.'s at Ohio State University's College of

Medicine, have extensively studied the impact of stress and "destressing" on the immune system. They have found significant reproducible increases in immune system functioning with destressing. The examples below are typical of the effect they have seen.

Base line values for natural killer (NK) cells (a component of the immune system important for protection against cancer cells) were determined in a nursing home population. The population was then divided into two groups. One group was taught meditation (a great stress dissipater); the other was left alone as a control. Six weeks later, new measurements were made. The group that meditated had DOUBLED its natural killer cell counts! Seems this would be a very valuable response if you were already fighting cancer, doesn't it?

Now that may impress you, or you may say, "So what? It worked with older people just to bring them back to my usual level of functioning? How does this benefit me?"

The second study (reproduced many times since the original) measured the natural killer cell activity of a normal population. They were induced into a meditative state for 20 minutes, either through training or with the help of an external guide, and then blood samples were taken for comparison. The NK cell activity had increased, even though these were "normal" people to begin with.

But I'm Already Healthy

On the other side of the coin, numerous studies have followed people under stress. They have repeatedly found that these people have higher incidences of disease. By following normal people during times of higher stress (e.g., medical students at examination time) and comparing what happened to them then versus what happened to them when they were not under higher stress, variations that might have been attributed to the sample population have been eliminated. Under stress, the same people get sick more than they do when they are not stressed.

Despite all the accumulating evidence that stress can depress the immune system, and that eliminating or reducing stress can enhance it, not everyone agrees that controlling stress responses within the body will lead to healthier living. Even though there may still be a few votes to be cast, the evidence to date strongly suggests that taking control over your stress is vital to living both long and well.

How To Make It Work For You

Quantum Focus helps the individual change his or her basic responses to stressors and therefore change the stress in his or her life. Quantum Focus helps you turn on the seeds of tranquility deep inside you, much like you did with the seeds of emotional stability you learned about in the preceding chapter. These seeds of tranquility allow you to respond to life's stress from that base of inner security and deep-seated (or, in this case, deep- "seeded") confidence in your inner terrain.

When you master Quantum Focus, nothing in your life seems out of control any longer. You are able to quickly move into Quantum Focused enhanced states of consciousness in the here and now of the situation, and you are acting instead of *re*acting. You are in control of yourself and dis✪stress is replaced by healthy stress (sometimes called eu✪stress).

In the following Quantum Focus exercise, the practitioner is free to mentally review or preview past or future events in a way that promotes healing outcomes of the imagined event. This automatically removes the negative stress reactions that might otherwise occur. In addition, previewing helps prepare you to choose your course of action when the future event arrives.

The End-of-Dis✪stress Exercise

Enter a Quantum Focus state and be aware of the here and now reality of this experience. You are sitting or lying down, allowing yourself to become at one with yourself . . . that is, at this moment you sense your "self" at total peace . . . bodymind and spirit in this precise moment in time. You are aware of yourself being in total peace in the moment.

Now let your imagination take you to a past or future situation or event; one that you might be thinking of in your ordinary consciousness, one that is worrisome or bothersome. Watch yourself handle, deal, or cope with this mental play with ease and confidence. See-hear-feel yourself acting with confidence and self-assurance as you act out the new improved or future outcome with a tranquil heart and mind.

Invest as much time and energy in this as you feel comfortable with. You will know you have accomplished your objective when you notice the serenity that replaced your original feelings of pressure, anxiety or dread. Now there is just this sense of peace and control. When you feel this peace and confidence, then permit yourself to return to your normal waking state, knowing you will automatically re-enter this state of control and confidence whenever you need or desire it.

The basic practice of moving into the alert Quantum Focused states during real action-packed experiences is the key to unlocking the great powers within you. The reviewing and previewing of events described above is also very useful for re-creating your inner environment of tranquility. This automatically converts most stress we experience into eu✪stress (healthy stress) rather than dis✪stress (unhealthy stress). And the nicest part is that, with regular Quantum Focus practice, this conversion occurs at the time it is needed without any conscious effort on your part.

The lesson in this chapter is, be prepared to enter a Quantum Focus state before and during your real life experiences, and trust that deep inside you is everything you could possibly need in the encounter. The tranquility and power of your enhanced state of consciousness — that is, of being in the here and now of your life — insures that you are not wasting your time or energy and that you are bringing your best to whatever you are doing.

Your Power Image

After you feel you have mastered this exercise you can start incorporating the finished product into your Power Image. You remember from chapter 2 that this is your overall ideal self-image which reflects all the progress you have made and allows for continued improvement as you Focus on where you want to go. We will continuously point out that these updated Power Images can intensify your results dramatically in multiple areas of your life by just viewing your ongoing progress. Again, we recommend you spend about 15 to 30 seconds recreating your Power Image every time you shift into a Quantum Focus State.

Here's How It Worked

For example, Elena is a multimedia artist who was referred by her nutritional counselor. She had been determined to take charge of her life and overcome her health-related challenges, which included mood swings, depression, allergies and a host of self-limiting fears and doubts. She was quite disʘstressed when we began working because all the hard work she had done up to now on improving herself appeared to be blowing up in her face. The only time she felt in control lately was when she was creating and/or working on her different art-related projects.

She was particularly concerned about an upcoming family reunion because many feelings and thoughts she had been relatively free from for the last several months were coming back. More than just coming back, they were coming back with a vengeance. Lack of energy was a major problem at the moment and she hoped Quantum Focus could help her create a new inner reality which would support the changes she wanted to make in her life.

Elena was taken through the basic End of Disʘstress exercise. Following that, it was suggested to her that we take a Power

Image approach; incorporate all the changes she desired to make into this moving image of herself. Let it start where she was and then switch to where she wanted to be . . . seeing herself feeling loose and calm, brimming with energy, free of allergies and filled with confidence. She was told to use the same technique of seeing herself as if all the above improvements were in place, view her relationship with her family at the family reunion, and move the image until the new and improved Elena was able to view her family situation as she would like it to be. The key was that she was to concentrate on her Power Image whenever she practiced the basic exercise (which was about six to ten times a day for about three or four minutes at a time).

It was explained to her that this work would give her the confidence she needed to shift into the moment and be at one with herself and her family. She recently breezed through the reunion, having a blast and never feeling those feelings that always diminished these events for her in the past. She has made great strides and has learned how to use this technique in the other areas of her life she wishes to improve. In her words:

> "By using this technique I was able to modify patterns of thought, recreate my belief system, change habits and implement desired behavior. It's been an easy, painless and timeless process. In these sessions, which are always a calming experience, I was able to overcome lifetime disturbances such as fears of all sorts and undesired reactions in stressed situations. I have enhanced my learning abilities, created a buffer zone of quiet in a highly active working environment, removed depressive feelings, and increased my energy level dramatically. It's an emotional, intellectual, fascinating and educational experience. And the pleasure of the outcomes are so remarkably rewarding. It has been working like magic for me."

We really enjoy hearing from Elena and seeing all the different ways she continues to grow and improve by simply modifying her Power Image.

A Final Thought On The Subject

Consistent with the concept that stress comes only from worrying about the future or the past, never the moment, here's a technique to help decrease worry about the future. Learn to prioritize your daily tasks and events according to their importance to your life's purpose. This means first doing those things which will have the greatest impact on your life, not those which are easiest nor those which may cry out the loudest. The squeaky wheel gets the grease. But when the squeaky wheel isn't attached to the right chariot, why bother?

If you build a daily "to do" list, be careful about getting lured into the simple stuff. Your list might have a project for work, the study of a subject at home which really interests you and will help you grow (How about Quantum Focus practice?), get milk and call Sally about tennis. You look at your list that morning and say to yourself something like, "Work Project . . . that'll take a couple of hours, so no sense beginning now. Reading the next chapter . . . too long for now. Milk? I can't do that until later. Sally! That's easy. Let's see, 555-1234. OK, Sally. Let's play. . . ."

Next, allow enough time to do these important things without putting yourself under a time pressure. This means begin them early. Learn to differentiate important items from urgent ones. Most urgent items are not important. Many can simply be forgotten about with no serious consequences. Don't let them get in the way of the important ones.

Obviously, determining your life's purpose is essential to this approach. The next chapter will help you do this.

Some Other Tools

There are many other things you can do to help overcome stress before it overcomes you. Nutrition can play an important role in protecting you against the ravages of stress. While we are not endeavoring to be a nutritional manual, there have been very favorable arguments made for the use of extra vitamin C, magnesium and several B complex vitamins (notably thiamin, niacin, pyridoxine, folate, pantothenate and B^{12}. You may also find some of the remedies for conquering anxiety useful in dealing with a particularly stressful day. Check out chapter 11. We think you'll enjoy the music, bath and sex ideas. It might take you a little longer to get into the exercise routine. Regular exercise is a great stress reduction technique though, so we encourage you to give it a try. Here's an easy start to exercising.

Putting It All Into Motion

More than just stress relief, exercise is also one remarkable way to beat the blahs and the blues. And one excellent and highly enjoyable way to inspire your life and energize your inner healer is to take a Quantum Focus Hike. The Quantum Focus Hiker begins by centering themselves in their being and focusing their enhanced state of consciousness outward as they begin to walk briskly. They bring their attention to the act of walking, noticing their breathing and movement. They mentally scan their bodies, re-center and open their attention to their environment. Any time, and as soon as, they notice their attention wandering, they get right back into their center and pay close attention to the actual walking again. Then they quickly re-scan their bodies and choose a Power Image to concentrate on while they continue their brisk walking, consciously shifting this activity to their auto-pilot while they program themselves for improvement and joy.

Getting Stoned

In this healing ritual, you will learn how to incorporate the power of aromatherapy into empowerment rituals. These rituals will greatly enhance your mastery of any situation which makes you feel ill at ease.

The power of certain scents to influence healing and emotional connections has been appreciated for thousands of years and proven scientifically in the present. The incredible relaxing power of rubbing and handling polished stones is also well-established. What we do in Quantum Focus is teach people to scent their stones with the scents that have long been associated with promoting relaxation, inspiration, sensuality, sexuality and clarity, and incorporate them with imagery that complements their self-treatment.

Imaginary Ups And Downs

For example: Imagine you suffered from fear of elevators. Just the thought of getting stuck in an elevator makes your skin crawl. By simply doing the following exercise you can often quickly overcome your fear.

Put a few drops of the essential oil chamomile on your healing stone. Now pick up your stone and hold your hands together in a prayer-like manner. Gently begin to roll the stone around between your hands. Move the stone in such a way that it comes in contact with your fingers and roll them down into the palms of your hands. Put down the stone and gently cover your nose and mouth with your hands, cupped around the nose and mouth so you can smell your scented hands.

Now picture yourself riding the elevator with a sense of ease and confidence. Believe or not, if you actually have a problem using elevators, you've been desensitized and are free to enjoy riding up and down elevators. All you have to do to initiate your newfound power to overcome any fear relating to elevators is to rub your stone, sniff your hands and ride, baby, ride.

(Try this also with the techniques in chapters 15 to 25.)

Choosing Your Stones:

Pick a stone . . . any stone. The first consideration should be the feel of the stone. Your stone must feel good in your hands. Now ask yourself what color would best suit your needs? Red could be very well-suited for inspiring passion. Green could be very well-suited to inspiring calm or better finances. Blue could be very-well suited to inspiring confidence. A violet stone is probably best for inspiring healing. Size your stone to fit your needs: for travel you might want a stone small enough to put in your pocket or purse, whereas a larger stone might be more suitable for home or office use.

And Your Aromas

Here is a partial list of some essential oils and how they might utilized:

Stimulant:	lemon, peppermint
Sedative:	lavender, orange blossom
Calming:	frankincense, chamomile
Sensual/euphoric:	jasmine, clary sage
Arousing/aphrodisiac:	jasmine, ylang-ylang

A Quick Boost

Let's say you've had a hard day at the office. You have lots to do at home, and find yourself feeling tired both mentally and physically. You could use a stone scented with a drop of lemon and peppermint, get into a Quantum Focus state of mind, put your attention on the stone, and begin to roll it around in your hands for about three or four minutes. Now imagine yourself getting a second wind as you cup your hands over your nose and mouth and then imagine that you are filling up with mental and physical energy. Take two deep breaths and return your attention to what needs to be done. We like to think of this as the Quantum Focus pick-me-up.

Peaceful Sleep

Before going to sleep, put a drop of lavender and a drop of orange blossom on your stone. You might also try a drop of each on your pillow to encourage sweet dreams. Now slip into a Quantum Focus state and put all the day's troubles and cares aside, agreeing to sleep on them. Now gently rub your stone, imagining a peaceful and restful night's sleep. Now cup your hands over your nose and mouth and take three deep breaths. Good night! (And take a look at chapter 13 too.)

Great Sex Keeps Getting Better

By putting a drop of jasmine, clary sage and ylang-ylang on your stone you can really psyche yourself into experiencing more pleasure and excitement. All you have to do is shift into a Quantum Focus state, zoom in on your favorite sexual fantasy, rub your hands together, cover your nose and mouth and take three deep breaths. Keep your stone handy and before having sex take a deep breath, rub your hands, see yourself having a rewarding sexual experience with your partner and put your attention into the moment. Now be with your experience. (But later read chapter 34.)

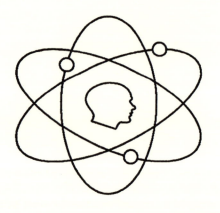

Chapter 7

Finding Your Life's Purpose

*"Don't mistake pleasure for happiness.
They are a different breed of dog."*
JOSH BILLINGS

A Bane of Modern Life

Do you have a job that takes up more of your time than you want it to? Does it interfere with other things you would like to do, like spending time with the family, pursuing a hobby, developing your own inner potential? Does housework so fill your day that you are exhausted each evening? Has your life become nothing more than dragging yourself out of bed in the morning, filling the day with a series of seemingly important but unfulfilling chores and tasks, and then dragging yourself back to bed at night? Does is seem like something important is missing in your life?

What's Missing?

In today's hurry-up world, we seldom take the time to follow that old advice, "Stop and smell the roses." We get so caught up in doing what we believe we have to do to survive that we cannot do the things we really want to do. We get totally immersed in such activities as making a living, raising a family, caring for the house, and so forth. And even if we are very good at all of this 'busywork', we can't help but feel that something is still missing. One well-worn example is the person who successfully climbs the ladder of success only to find out that the ladder was leaning against the wrong building. We've accomplished everything we felt we had to do. Yet, we wind up asking ourselves, "Is that all there is?" Where is the aroma of the roses?

Well, there is a way to solve this dilemma. We can combine all our activities into one that more than permits us to smell the roses. By following this road, we usually wind up growing roses for a living.

Choosing Your Path

Recognize that what we call "your" path is just that. The road to happiness is different for each of us. And that bliss, that inner peace you seek, lies at the end of your road, not at the end of anyone else's. Follow your path and it all unfolds before you. Follow a path that leads someone else to happiness and you may wind up a long way from where you want to be. Your bliss may lie in creating landscapes with your pen, teaching others how to cook, traveling for profit or just about anywhere else. Even if you are allergic to roses, you can be blissful. (And if you are allergic to roses or anything else, see chapter 32 to learn how you may overcome the annoying symptoms.)

The Crux of the Matter

What are we really talking about here? We're talking about the fact that each one of us on this earth has some special purpose. There is something that needs to be done to make this world a better place for everyone. With six billion inhabitants, if each one made the world just the tiniest bit better, made just the slightest bit of a difference, the total impact would be staggering.

Each of us comes into this world with the talents and abilities to do something, whatever that something is, in a way no other person could do it. We have both a mission and a special set of tools with which to accomplish it. And once on line with achieving that mission, everything flows for us.

It is like swimming in a river with a strong current. When we are not on our mission, it is like trying to swim upstream against the current. We work hard and long, swimming furiously but getting nowhere. When we recognize this is not working, we pick out some goal on the opposite shore and swim toward that. Still swimming furiously, we find that the current keeps taking us downstream away from our target.

But when we get on our life's purpose, when we discover our mission and begin to fulfill it, it is as though we are swimming with the current. Everything goes easier. Things are brought to us as we need them to carry out this mission and we feel great about what we are doing. We pop out of bed in the morning, put in more time and effort than ever before, yet end the day with more energy than we had when we began it.[1]

How Do I Know What's for Me?

Aha! This is the question people have pondered as long as there have been people. It may be phrased a little differently, like "What is the meaning of life?", or, "Why am I here?", but we're asking the same question. Now you are asking it specifically for you.

There are many "gurus" of all kinds who claim to know the answer. In a general way, maybe they actually do. But they can-

---

1. When we use the metaphor "go with the flow", it is important to point out that, in life, before you go with the flow, make sure you know where it's headed. You don't want to flow over the waterfalls or into unhealthy situations, do you? In our experience, finding one's purpose in life opens many doors and creates many opportunities. However, in some special situations your higher purpose may be a path that, in certain instances, requires you happily swim against the flow. Think, for example, of Mother Teresa's life. We could not describe this as "easy".

not know the specifics that apply to your life. Only you can ever know these, and only you can discover them. The good news is that it is far easier to do this than you suspect. You need only the positive intent to find your path, some perseverance and the intestinal fortitude to trust the answers you find, even if they seem too simple to be true. In our experience, one good test of having found a purpose is that it is just that. . . simple and easy to understand.

Keep in mind that your purpose in life may change over time. As you learn and grow, you may move on to another segment of your development. Therefore, you are well advised to continue using the following exercise even after you've gotten your initial answers. It is a useful thing to perform it once or twice monthly, just to sort of check in to see if you are still following the river's current or if the river made a turn while you were not watching. Of course, it is very useful whenever things seem to be getting a little out of hand also.

Discovering Your Life's Purpose Exercise

Begin by entering your Quantum Focused state. Then imagine yourself deep in a lovely, friendly forest. Take some time to enjoy the aroma of the forest, the feel of the air where the sunlight has filtered down to the path on which you are walking, the alternating shades of light and dark as you pass under the trees. Listen to the sounds of the forest around you. Take a moment to enjoy all of these things. It will feel, perhaps for the first time, that you are taking a moment for yourself, and it feels absolutely marvelous.

As you walk along, you will come to a stream of clear running water. There is a path crossing yours that follows the stream. Take that special path that diverges from the one you usually walk on. Enjoy the changing forest around you as you proceed.

After a minute or two, you will come to a small waterfall. It is just high enough for you to stand in the crystal clear, cleansing water that cascades down. Step into that waterfall and feel the magical powers of the water as it cleanses you of all your prejudices and preconceived notions. Feel the special energy it fills you with in their place. Note that the temperature is exactly the way you like it. Note also that the water leaves you completely dry rather than wet. It simply cleanses you of any obstacles to getting where you want to go.

When you feel refreshed and invigorated, step out of the waterfall and begin again to follow your path. Shortly, it comes to a small glen at the base of a mountain. In this glen are several paths. They lead to various places. Some lead up the mountain. Others lead into the forest. Still others seem to follow the stream.

Also in this glen, in the side of the mountain, there is a small cave. This is the cave of wisdom. Inside lie the answers to questions for which we search. When you are ready to discover which path is for you, enter the cave with the desire to find your answer.

There are many parts to the cave. You may find many different symbols or messages. You may even meet the wise old sage who lives here. Take the torch that burns near the mouth of the cave with you so you may see as well as hear or sense whatever messages await you within. Just take your time and explore the recesses of the cave with the expectation that you will discover which path to follow.

When you have your answer, exit from the cave and take your path. Be observant as you follow it for there are many messages you will find along the way. There will be special people sent to help you, maybe even one or two sent to test your resolve. There will be symbols, tools and signs for you. Some will be obvious as you go along. Others may appear to be coincidences or accidents. You are very aware of their presence.

Walk this path for four or five minutes. Gather what you need. Take more time if you need it, and when you are ready, return to your customary waking state. Be alert as you continue through life, for your messages and symbols will abound around you.

Chapter 8

Increasing Self-Esteem

"Oftentimes nothing profits more than self-esteem, grounded on what is just and right."
JOHN MILTON

The 90's Great Malaise

This is a good news/bad news chapter. The bad news is that, in working with literally thousands of people, we can candidly state that there is no more common affliction than the lack of self-esteem.

Low self-esteem is the great malaise of our era. It is the result of all the misinformation we utilized in forming our opinion of ourselves. And how we really feel about ourselves is often our best-kept secret, sometimes even from ourselves. All the things we blame ourselves for, all the things we regret doing or not doing, all the frustrations and resentments we rehash over and over again . . . all these can take a toll on our zest for life and our general health.

Almost everyone in our culture is subject to this kind of mental self-abuse. Left unchecked, these psychological pathogens go deeper and deeper inside us, becoming more and more toxic every time we beat ourselves up.

What's more, these toxic feelings, emotions and thought patterns are the hidden stressors that diminish our ability to enjoy the simple pleasures in our lives. We believe they are the underlying reasons why so many people feel helpless and hopeless in all the uncertainties they must cope with. To make matters worse, quite often buried feelings and emotions such as grief, hate, anger, guilt and shame corrode our sense of well-being without our having the slightest idea why we feel so burnt-out all the time. A lack of interest in one's life, and general feelings of "being stuck" can be viewed as precursors to a wide range of physical and/or psychological problems.

There are many correlations between "stress-related" diseases and a person's attitude. Some of the more commonly-suffered physical complaints, and the emotions, thoughts and feelings that have been linked to them are:

Condition	Thoughts, Feelings and/or Emotions
Allergies	Fear; Lack of confidence; Perpetual "rundown" feeling
Arthritis	Anger; Unresolved tensions; Low self-esteem; Feeling helpless and unloved
Cancer	Loneliness; Depressive feelings; Anger; Hopelessness; Helplessness; Feeling that things can't get any worse
Heart Disease	Hostility; Anger; Grief; Feeling there is never enough time
Hyper-tension	Anxiety; Insecurity; Fear of doctors; Feeling something bad is just about to happen

This is just a short list of the many diseases and conditions that people develop when their emotions, feelings and thoughts become chemically toxic. (Note that you cannot reliably tell what condition will develop from any of these toxic emotions. For example, what would you predict would result from anger? Arthritis? Cancer? Heart Disease? All we can reliably say is that whatever develops from toxic feelings or emotions will not be anything positive.)

Take this simple test. During the last 24 hours did you have any of these thoughts? — I am not good enough, I am not tall enough, I am not old enough, I am not young enough, I am not thin enough, I am not smart enough, and so on. Or how about the flip side? — I am too good, too tall, too old, too young, too thin, too smart, etc.

All are complaints we come into contact with every day. In fact, we have seen no one, for whatever purpose they sought our help, who could not have benefited from an enhanced sense of self-worth.

Therefore, no matter who you are, what you have accomplished, what you think you think of yourself now, or even how you answered the above questions, do the exercises in this chapter regularly. Trust us, they will help you, perhaps in ways you might not yet recognize.

Could This Really Apply To Me?

The reason for the universality of this statement is that it is universally true. The trick in recognizing this is being able to see under the persona we show to others. Your authors have worked with some very powerful, together, in-charge people who have sought our help for a variety of reasons. None of them came to us because they felt their self-esteem was in need of development. Some even appeared outwardly as though they might be a little too sure of themselves. But they had esteem wounds at the unconscious level, just like all the rest of us.

While they were unaware of them — in fact, they would have bet big money against their existence — clearing them out resulted in new heights of achievement. The proof of the "theory" is in its application. It works. We've all been "infected" with some esteem-robbing beliefs. So, even if you doubt that your self-esteem could be greater, do the exercises!

Is It A Virus?

We start our journey through this world as perfect human beings. Then we are born. From this point on we are then subjected to all kinds of criticism and comment from many, many sources. These include parents, family, friends, teachers, religious figures, and so on. For some of us, it seems as though they were lining up, just waiting for their turn at us. (And for some of us, this may even start during the prenatal period.)

Once we become infected with the "I am not good enough" beliefs, we often unknowingly self-poison every life experience we have. These unrecognized, deep-seated beliefs often show up as the blahs, the blues, and feelings that life is not worth living. They can also show up as unrecognized saboteurs.

Good People Can Make Mistakes

Now, while this criticism is sometimes meant to be cruel and harmful, it is usually meant to be for our own good. Those who are in positions to criticize us do not mean to cause any harm. It is their way of taking care of us. Ironically, their intent is to protect us from the world rather than wound us. But somehow, in some parts of our lives, we get the message that there are some things we simply cannot do.

These somethings can seemingly be as innocuous as being unable to cross streets correctly (how many times do we have to be told to look both ways before we figure out that we are not smart enough to remember that ourselves?), or being unable to make decisions competently ("Be sure to go to the post office *before* you go to the drugstore" — like it really matters one bit!), or being told we are unable "to do anything right". Haven't most of us heard that at least once in our lives? While we know, consciously, this is untrue, that we can do lots of things right, at the unconscious level it stays with us. And it weighs us down in some fashion.

Anyone You Know?

Think about the number of people you know who have started a career or a relationship or anything else and it has gone very well for them . . . for a while. Then, just when it seems they are going to be able to coast into a perfect life, they do something to sabotage themselves. They may not recognize it, and it can take various forms, from not having an important report finished on time to carelessly (deliberately?) getting caught in an affair. And there are hundreds of shades of this same self-sabotage.

It's as though some part of ourself sits in judgment and says, "You don't deserve to have this. You are not good enough." And it then introduces us to a variety of ways we can lose whatever it is we "don't deserve", ways that outwardly appear like something just went wrong. But be assured there is a part of us working underneath this that has deliberately sabotaged us. After all, we are always "fair". No reason to give life's good things to an "undeserving" person.

There Is An Antidote

Now for the good news. It has been our personal and professional experience that spiritual nutrition keeps these unconscious beliefs in check. But these doubts can continue to lurk in our subconscious minds waiting, waiting, waiting for an opportunity to strike. It seems that whenever the person is spiritually malnourished, the doubts become reactivated. For some people this develops into a chronic living hell, in which they never feel good enough.

We believe the "I am not good enough" beliefs are only able to function when a person is spiritually malnourished, or living in the past or future. When people get spiritually nourished or move into the "now", these doubts seem to automatically fade from our awareness, or else are seen for what they really are. It has been our personal and professional experience that when we and our clients are spiritually nourished or living in the now (meaning "being present in the moment"), the "I am not good enough" beliefs are automatically held in check without any conscious effort required.

A Natural Balance

Because it is the very nature of all biological systems to strive to correct and balance themselves, whenever a person's pyscho-spiritual/emotional development is arrested for whatever reason(s), there is an irresistible panconscious impulse to remedy the problem. This is the terrain in which illness or crisis manifests. Very often, the bigger the crisis, the more urgently the change is needed. In some cases, it seems that when the attempt to rebalance is made but frustrated, the problem seems to fade away only to remanifest with an even greater urgency.

When illness and personal crisis are viewed from this perspective, the crisis or problem can be seen as an attempt to bring balance and order into our lives, rather than as an enemy with which to do battle. It is a signal telling us something is wrong, and it is already trying to correct it. Shouldn't we be appreciative, knowing this is happening?

Listen To Your Symptoms

Healing is more likely to occur when a person sees their problems (i.e., symptoms and crises) as allies. By using this model, we have helped many people take charge of their health and/or their lives, often for the first time ever. We are certain that making friends with your challenges (or problems, as they used to be called) and seeing what they might be trying to communicate to you is what is needed to bring your life into balance. And bringing your life into that special balance that is yours alone is an essential part of your healing process.

How Quantum Focus Can Help

The psychodynamics of Quantum Focus allow, and encourage, you to process these buried emotions and feelings without years of analysis or therapy. By simply doing the exercises and guided imagery in the Quantum state, you can off-load these toxins at the same time you are programming yourself to improve your life. Even more importantly, as you learn how to live in the moment, all your inner resources are automatically freed to work for you rather than against you.

Living In The Moment

There is something very special about living in the now. Being in the moment provides instant spiritual renewal and is often described as "peak experience" or "being in the zone". It is the highest level of waking consciousness and the secret of the ancient mystery schools.

And Making It Brighter

There is more good news! Not only can we keep these doubts at bay, we can also selectively erase these unwanted toxins. Of course we can never undo what has happened to us in the past, but *we can undo the effects that these previous events have had on us*. In essence, we can start with a clean slate again as a perfect human being. And, to erase the prior notes on our slate as rapidly as possible, we use our Quantum Focused state.

As pervasive as wounded self-esteem is, it is an easy matter to reverse. So, make the mental decision that you may have one or two of these wounds yourself and you don't deserve them. Decide that you deserve to sense yourself as the perfect human being you are regardless of others' prior impact on you. You can re-become who you already are, but who may have somehow slipped from your own unbiased evaluation into an incorrect picture presented by the remnants of others' poor judgment. It's time to wipe out the biases and take a brand new look.

Self-Esteem Exercise A

Begin by entering your Quantum Focus state. Allow yourself plenty of time and give yourself permission to relax completely. Now take a moment to just enjoy this for a while.

Imagine now that someone is approaching you. You cannot yet tell who this is. You may not even know him or her. But sense the presence as the person comes closer. Notice that they are carrying something in their hands. You cannot yet see what this is for certain, but it looks like a big book or tablet or drawing pad.

As your person comes even closer, he/she stops in front of you and hands you the tablet. You look at it and see that it is the slate of your life. On it are recorded all the things you are and are not. It lists all the positive things on the right side. On the left are all the negative things people have told you that you are or are not. Perhaps the right side shows you are a positive thinker and that you are not prejudiced. Maybe the left side says you are lazy and you are not ambitious. Maybe it says you are too stupid to amount to anything. Perhaps it reads you are incompetent.

As you look at these things, you may even remember being told them by someone earlier in your life. Perhaps you remember telling them to yourself. But as you look at them now, recognize that they are on the left side of the slate. They are not right. And because they are not right, you have the right — even the obligation — to erase all these things that are not right. You have the obligation to clean off the left side of the slate and start over.

Reach down and pick up the magical eraser lying by your feet. Erase everything that is not right from the slate. Erase all of these ideas and concepts and judgments completely. Keep all those that are right. When you finish, look up at the person who brought you the slate. Do you recognize him or her? Do you realize why they brought your life's slate to you to erase all the things that are not right? Notice that this person is smiling at you with unconditional love, and that he/she is very happy to see you starting over as the perfect human being that you are.

As you feel the wonderful sense of a weight being lifted off your shoulders, realize that you don't have to do anything or get anywhere in order to be a perfect human being. You are a perfect human being just for being. And you have the right to immense happiness and riches of body, mind and spirit, and inner peace. For these are infinite in their abundance . . . and we all can claim our fill, with plenty left over for others who come after us. All this just because you are a human being; a gift from the universe to say, "Welcome. I'm glad you're here".

Spend a moment or two to really take this in, and let it be real for you. For it is right and you are right, exactly right. Then allow yourself to return to your usual state of waking consciousness. You will feel the difference immediately.

Self-Esteem Exercise B

Exercise B was designed to help you keep any and all unrecognized beliefs in check by providing you with your daily spiritual nutrition. Please read the instructions for counting from 1 to 10, put the book down, count slowly from 1 to 10, repeating the instructions given below to yourself, and then continue reading when you have reopened your eyes.

Shift into a Quantum Focused state, then begin mentally counting from 1 to 10.

1. At the count of 10, I will open my eyelids and remain Focused.

2. At the count of 10, I will open my eyes and remain deeply relaxed.

3. At the count of 10, I will open my eyes and continue going deeper and deeper.

4. At the count of 10, when I open my eyes, it will be very easy to create constructive images in my mind's eye.

5. At the count of 10, I will be able to function while remaining in a peaceful, calm, and centered state of mind.

6.

7.

8.

9.

9¾, and

10.

Read the following mentally and out loud (you may do it at the same time).

- Worrisome thoughts and doubts fall on deaf inner ears — I can handle them.
- I feel more and more at ease in every situation.
- Love is my birthright. I am able to love and be loved.
- I am at peace with myself now and nothing can convince me otherwise.

Now go to chapter 38 and read the Magic Smile. When you are finished reading the Magic Smile, you will be ready and able to be in the moment.

> This is also a good time to become aware that you reside in a body. Scan your body from the bottom of your feet to the top of your head. Stretch out and as high as you can. Take an extra deep breath and be aware of everything going on around you. Open your attention outward . . . see, hear, taste, smell and feel your immediate environment without any judgement. Just be with what's there.

Excellent! Remember, even during the course of the most hectic day, the most frustrating moment, or the most challenging obstacle, you are perfect . . . just for being you. You may find it very helpful to focus on the phrase "human being . . . not human doing" to reinforce your new beginnings.

Some Other Ideas That Will Help

When you get up each morning, go into your bathroom and look in the mirror on your medicine cabinet. Look directly into your eyes, smile and say aloud, "I like myself", three times. If it feels good, great! If not, keep doing it every day until it does feel good. Just keep doing it. It will feel good.

When this feels right to you, change the sentence to, "I love myself". Again, three times aloud each morning until it too feels good. (If you do not live alone and are concerned with someone else hearing you, close the door and run the water. The only one who needs to hear you is you. Looking right into your own eyes, repeat the phrase three times, until you find it becomes so easy and so comfortable that you can really feel it.

Rate Yourself

When you finish telling yourself that you like/love you, look at the palm of your non-dominant hand. (If you're right-handed, that's your left hand. If you're left-handed, it's your right hand.) Imagine you have a magic marker in your favorite color. But this one is really magic.

Now, choose a number between one and ten (ten being the highest rating and one being the lowest) to grade yourself. (That is, what are you worth?)

If your number is three or below, add six to it. If it is four to six, add three to it. If it is seven or eight, add one to it. Look at your final number.

Now write that number in the palm of your non-dominant hand with your imaginary magic marker. Within two and a half seconds, press your palm against your forehead so you transfer that number to your forehead while the mark is still wet. Don't worry that it will be backwards to anyone else who reads it. No one aside from you can see it, backwards or otherwise. It will, however, be forwards to you whenever you look in a mirror that day. And it will be forwards to you whenever you raise your eyes and look through the back of your forehead. It is there to remind you, all day long, of how much you are worth. Repeat this exercise daily until you have nines on your bad days!

Become A Volunteer

One easy way to feel more worthwhile is to help someone else. Make the time to do some kind of volunteer work. Maybe it is visiting a local hospital and reading to children or spending time with someone who has no family nearby and can use the company. Perhaps it is helping at a homeless shelter, preparing or serving meals. You will find many ways to volunteer your time and services (read that as volunteer your "self") that can help others. There is truly something magic about what this does for your sense of value, image, esteem and worth.

Look Around The Book

You will find ideas and techniques that will help your healing processes, whatever they may be, in chapters 5, 6, 9, 11 and 29. These are effective methods which you can use to both "jump-start" your healing and avoid future problems.

Chapter 9

Achieving Self-Forgiveness

*"The weak can never forgive.
Forgiveness is the attribute of the strong."*
MAHATMA GANDHI

The Greatest Gift

In our work with people living with life-threatening diseases, one key part of the healing process is forgiving one's self for whatever. Interestingly, this is also the key to forgiving others for whatever. Forgiveness of both — one's self and others — is always beneficial to the forgiver, regardless of the impact on the others.

One of most difficult parts of forgiving is that anger and hurt begin to feel like old friends. Most people do not want to give up this old friend the pain has become. The following exercise can be very helpful in your forgiveness process.

Forgiveness Exercise

Enter a state of enhanced consciousness and let the following mantra draw you into the feelings that arise when you repeat these magic words. "I am open to releasing all feelings of shame and guilt about myself and anger at myself. Knowing I can and will do my best from now on, I am now ready to heal all thoughts and beliefs that hurt me. In so doing, I take the pain out of the hurt and allow the healing to begin.

"I now release all conscious and unconscious resistance to the awesome realization that everything in my life is perfect. All my experiences were necessary lessons in my life. I can and will take something positive from each and every experience. I will use these lessons to make my life continue to expand and improve."

Now visualize any events or situations in your life in which forgiveness is desirable or necessary. See yourself surrounded by the bright lights of forgiveness while you quietly shout in your mind . . . "I forgive you. I forgive me. From now on I'll be all I can be".

These simple sentences repeated over and over in the enhanced states of Quantum Focus can open up the doors of forgiveness and let the healing come rushing through you. Practice often.

One Closing Thought

As one moves on this path, it becomes clear that true forgiveness is simply the understanding of releasing all our perceived hurts while in Quantum Focus meditative states. As we continue along this same path, we begin to shed our excess ego. As we overcome our ego — as our perceptions change — we find we no longer feel (or perceive) that these "wrongs" are occurring against us. This, in turn, means that forgiveness becomes unnecessary as there is no longer anything to forgive.

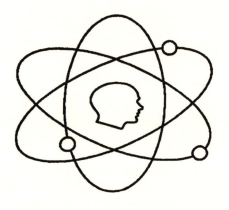

Chapter 10

Healthier Finances

"Money is not required to buy one necessity of the soul."
HENRY DAVID THOREAU

Money Isn't Everything

Having opened this chapter with the essential spiritual truth of the Thoreau quotation above, we now add a counterbalancing thought. Money is required to buy almost everything else! And, while money can't buy happiness, poverty is no guarantee of great joy. It seems to us that being poor and unhappy is a little worse than being comfortable and unhappy.

How does Quantum Focus, a program of mental, physical and spiritual balance, relate to our finances? Because most of us have exactly what we feel we deserve. That is, we are all entitled to share in the abundance of the Universe, but somehow most of us limit ourselves to very small portions. Some aspect of our subconscious mind seems to have decided just how much, or how little, we are entitled to . . . and it is determined to see to it that this is all we get.

Singing Our Own Song . . .

We all have talents. They vary greatly among us. Some of us are musically inclined, others are efficient, still others are academically gifted. It doesn't matter what our gifts are; we all have some special talent that others would like to have. And, very often, someone else will pay us for the "loan" of our talents.

... And Getting Paid For It

In the most common form, this loan of talent occurs in the form of our working for someone else. We loan them our labor and they pay us in the form of wages. But there are many other forms in which we can loan our talents. And there is someone out there who will pay for our talents regardless of what they are.

That statement usually is met with skepticism. But think about some "ridiculous" talents and then look to see who is already getting paid for them. For example, are you a good shopper? Or perhaps you can bake the world's greatest banana nut muffins? Or maybe your talent is simply in being a good bullthrower? Who would pay for these talents?

It is probably easy to see that someone would pay for the world's best banana nut muffins. But imagine what you would have to go through to achieve this. Finding the customers is the first obstacle. Then a place to bake them once your kitchen has grown too small. How about delivering them before dawn to the places that would want them? Stop here for a moment and see how many other problems you would have to overcome. (We can think of at least four more immediately. How about you?) Most people (99.99 percent) give up when they encounter these "problems". But who would pay you to shop? Or to toss the bull?

If you are not already aware that there are professional shoppers, this would be a good time to get acquainted with the profession. People who are too busy with their careers often pay others to go shopping for them. For special items like gifts, or for their wardrobes, even for groceries. Are you also aware that there are people who make a living — often a very good living — as storytellers? Others pay to go and listen to these people tell stories. Not necessarily their own stories, as they are not authors, but stories like myths and legends that were handed down from generation to generation, and stories that the storyteller heard somewhere once upon a time and maybe even changes each time they are told.

Creating A Monopoly

Suppose you identify a talent you have, but you cannot find anyone who is getting paid for doing this (yet)? Recognize that this doesn't have to mean no one will ever pay for it. It may only mean no one has yet realized who will pay for it. This could be an even bigger opportunity for you. Now is the time to think creatively. This is one place Quantum Focus can help you.

The Underlying Foundation

But there is a more important aspect to enjoying a sound financial future. No matter what your talent is, no matter whether you want to loan that talent, in the form of working for wages, or sell it as a service or product to people who want it enough to pay for it, the primary obstacle to our achieving success is our own mind. No, it is not actually our mind. It is the thoughts our mind creates. Mostly, it creates thoughts that tell us why, in undeniable terms, we cannot possibly do whatever it is we do best for money. Even in the case of the world's best banana nut muffins, look at how quickly we identified all the reasons we cannot do this profitably.

But, people like Famous Amos and Mrs. Fields are constantly proving it can be done. And there are a zillion other examples of people who have done it? What is the difference between them and the average person? They learned to overcome their negative thoughts and beliefs. More importantly, they also overcame any limiting beliefs within their subconscious minds. Even if you can only see the positive and charge forward with great enthusiasm, if you do not overcome these unconscious limiting beliefs, you will do things to sabotage your own success. This is the other place Quantum Focus can help you to turn your financial life around.

The Success Formula

Your Quantum Focus practice has two goals for achieving your financial success. One is increasing your awareness of opportunities in which you can become more valuable (we're speaking here strictly of *financially* valuable, as you are already a perfect you in every other way) to those who have the ability to reward you. These could be employers or they could be customers.

The second goal is resetting your internal evaluation of how much you deserve to have, from whatever limit is currently operational to a new and sensationally bigger piece of the pie. You see, the pie is actually unlimited. By helping yourself to a bigger piece, no one else gets less.

Healthier Finances Exercise

Find a comfortable position and enter your Quantum Focused state. Permit yourself to relax completely and just enjoy that for a moment or so. Then, when you are ready, proceed with the rest of the exercise.

Imagine yourself doing something you really enjoy doing. It can be anything that comes to mind that gives you true pleasure. Spend a few minutes enjoying the sense of peace and well-being this creates in you.

Now imagine someone else observing you doing this or observing the result of what you have done. Imagine that person approaching you to ask you how you became so good at it. Listen to your answer and to this person's next comment. Keep up the conversation as long as it is comfortable. Then someone else comes along who appreciates how well you do this. Enjoy further conversation with this person. And another joins in . . . and another . . . and another . . . as many people — all impressed by your ability — as you wish. In the many conversations that ensue, note all the opportunities that keep arising for you to turn this into a moneymaking activity. Perhaps someone offers you employment; perhaps others offer to buy your services or the results stemming from them. Take full advantage of this opportunity to discover how many different ways this can become profitable, as well as enjoyable, to you.

Relax even deeper. Imagine you are now on the way home on the next day. You pass a beautiful park that you never noticed before, even though you may have come this way many times before. There seems to be a gathering of happy people in this park. Go in and look around.

Enjoy the beauty of the park, the colors of nature, the sounds of the happy people, the feeling of peace and well-being. As you stroll around, you overhear others talking. It seems there is a truckfull of riches in the middle of the park and on the side of the truck is a sign that reads, "Take all you want." Then, just ahead of you, you see this enormous truck gleaming in the sun.

Find something to carry your share of the riches in and get on line. The line moves quickly and you will reach the truck within moments. As you approach, you again overhear others coming back from the truck carrying their share of riches and talking about the truck. They say that the truck is always here. They know the truck is always full, no matter how many people take from it or how much they take. In fact, they even mention that the more people who show up, the bigger the truck seems to grow. And now it is your turn. What did you bring with you to get your share? How big a container do you have?

Fill whatever you have. And recognize that you can come back again and again. Maybe now you want to think about bringing your own truck with you next time. You can take as much as you want. Whoever put that ever-full truck in the park wants each of us to have as much as we want.

Now is also the time to recognize that we are unlimited in what we deserve. We deserve to bring the largest container we can find . . . and all the help we need to carry it . . . to claim our limitless share of this limitless treasure. And we can share it with others. The more people who show up to share in the riches, the larger this truck becomes. We can receive even more.

When you really appreciate that you deserve unlimited riches, when you realize that the more you have, the more others will have, when you are ready to take your generous share of life's bounty, let your consciousness return with these realizations to its waking state, ready to serve you with your new-found awareness.

Some Everyday Aids

It is fine to program your share of the universal abundance. However, you may find that several things you do daily can help speed it on its way. Learn the basics of money and budgeting. There are many good books on the subject. You should not need to plan to live under very tight restraints. Still, you should do some things that are just good sense.

For example, don't borrow money by running up credit card bills that you cannot pay off completely when they are due. Many credit cards charge exorbitant interest rates, commonly around 20 percent. It could take the money you would customarily use to repay the loan just to keep up with the interest payments. While preparing for your financial success, don't dig your current hole any deeper. This is financial suicide. You may not be able to reach the rim in order to grab the brass ring when it shows up.

If you find that you are presently living above your means, adjust by eliminating things that are not important to your purpose in life. Maybe you shouldn't be on the Internet so much that you run up $200 per month in bills. Perhaps eating out four nights each week is excessive. Only you can judge which items are important and which are expendable for the time being. You will add them back later as your financial position improves. Putting them on hold temporarily in order to get your financial ship off the rocks and back into smooth water is only prudent.

A good way to see where your money is going now is to pay cash for everything for a few months (as far as you can do so practically). Somehow, checks and credit cards don't have the same impact as watching the tens and twenties pass through your fingers. This often points out places where we can save some money we were not even aware we were spending.

Too Late For Everyday Measures?

If you find yourself already in a very deep hole, you could be wise to consult one of the not-for-profit credit services. (Watch out for the ones that claim to be able to repair your credit, give you new credit cards, etc. Only *you* can repair your credit.) Legitimate services are often available for free. They can help you get yourself back on track. Frequently, they can help consolidate your debts, or arrange reduced payback schedules for you. You will still have to get yourself out of the hole, but they can provide a ladder. Once back on level ground, you will be in a position to reach new heights you never dreamed of before.

Take heart, no matter where you are now financially. You do not need to have money in order to make money. People like Henry Ford went bankrupt several times before they finally made it. But that means they started from zero each time, including the time that worked. Keep the faith and keep on keepin' on!

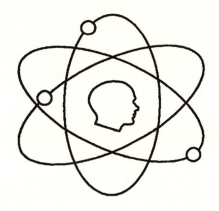

Chapter 11

Conquering Anxiety

"How much have cost us the evils that never happened!"
THOMAS JEFFERSON

What Is Anxiety?

We all tend to have times when we worry. Sometimes it is about something in particular. Other times, it seems we are simply caught up in the sum total of all our worries without any particular one being identifiable. It is this latter condition that we commonly call anxiety.

The most interesting fact about anxiety and its composite worries is that most of the things we worry about never happen. So why then do we worry?

Why We Worry

We worry largely because we are programmed to worry. From the earliest years we are taught about all manner of things we need to plan for. "Save for a rainy day." "Will you have time to get your homework done if you go out now?" "Take an umbrella in case it rains." And so on. All these comments are made with the best of intentions, in the hope that they will teach us to plan. However, notice how each comment suggests an impending disaster! And inherent in each one is the message that we have to control what happens to us.

By the time we have reached puberty, many of us have been conditioned to worry as a part of life. We also learn that we don't have control over many things in life. It seems like most events are beyond our control. Those of us who haven't yet become worriers are subjected to redoubled efforts by our parents (who have become concerned because we do not share their sense of impending disaster). Remember, they are not trying to make us worriers, only planners. Most people, which includes most parents, simply aren't very skillful at this. So we often wind up prone to worrying. When we cannot identify that worried feeling with any one event, we are suffering from anxiety.

The Positive Intent

The insane part of this is, if we were to become really good planners, we would have nothing to worry about. Every eventuality would already have been planned for. But even those of us who tend to be more planner than worrier come to realize that there are too many eventualities to plan for them all. So we begin to worry about what we might have missed in our planning for the future. This too shows up as anxiety.

Trust The Solution

How can we get around this nondescript fear, anxiety? Simply by learning to trust. Remember that most of the things you worried about in your life never happened. And most of the things you might want to worry about happening in the future won't actually happen. Learning to trust that most of your fears will not be realized relieves you of the obligation of worrying about them.

As you continue your Quantum Focus practice, you will probably find that you automatically worry less. If you have suffered from general states of anxiety in the past, they have most likely become less severe already. This is an offshoot of your Quantum Focus practice. As you continue to practice, you will find that you have power over more aspects of your life than you ever realized before. You are developing a greater sense of control over your life. This greater sense of control has in turn given you less need to worry. You are becoming confident that things are going to go your way.

To speed this process, you can use the exercise below. It is designed to do several things at once, all of which leave you relaxed and free from unidentified fears, worries and anxiety. This does not imply that recognized fear is always inappropriate. Should you identify something that requires your attention (e.g. a person driving erratically in front of you), you are intelligent enough to do something constructive about it (e.g. slow down and leave enough room to stop safely in case they do). But, having taken the appropriate precaution, you can then be free of the uneasiness that remains behind for so many people. You can be relaxed, comfortable and confident . . . for you know that things are going to work out just fine for you.

Anti-Anxiety Exercise

Begin by finding a comfortable place and entering a Quantum Focused state. You already know you are deliberately changing your bodymind's reactions and chemistry when you do this. Now you are going to show them the reactions you expect them to have for you in the future. With this intent, relax even deeper.

Imagine yourself in a very special place. This is a natural place, maybe with trees and water and sunshine. A place you feel very, very good to be in. A place where everything is just perfect, exactly the way you like it. The temperature of the air is perfect as it gently caresses your face, hair and arms. The fresh, clean smell of the day — perhaps scented with just a hint of one of your favorite aromas — helps you relax even further. The natural sounds around you — maybe waves or running water, perhaps birds singing, maybe just the silent rustling of the leaves — relax you even more. Everything about this special place makes you feel calm, peaceful, relaxed and at ease.

As you explore your special place, notice there is a closet with a big bolt lock on the front. Open that closet and notice that it is empty. Also notice that it is more than big enough to hold all your cares, concerns and worries. Place all of these in your closet. Simply take them off or set them down one by one and put each into the closet. Take your time and be sure to put everything that keeps you from feeling at peace into the closet.

When you have put all your cares into the closet, close the door and slide the bolt across to lock it. All your cares are now safely stored right here. They will be there if you want them later. Or you can leave them there forever. Or you can pick and choose among them, taking what you want with you and leaving the rest behind. They are safe in this closet. You can be comfortable about that.

Find a special spot here in your perfect place where you can feel even better; a place where you can let go completely. Sit back or lie back and simply enjoy how good that feels. Just enjoy that for a while.

Now, keeping these feelings of peace and serenity and confidence which are being programmed into your bodymind as you do this, imagine yourself free from that closet forever. Imagine that you never have to get anything out of that closet. See how good this feels. Enjoy it and your bodymind learns even more about this being the way you want to respond to your closet and its contents. Relax even further.

Again, keeping these feelings of absolute comfort, imagine going back to your closet, opening the door and removing any one of the cares you put in there. But notice how calm, confident and relaxed you are. Your bodymind just learned that you can carry this care without anxiety. You can deal with this concern in peace and comfort. Relax even more.

By now you are sure you can handle another care or concern. Keeping these peaceful feelings, open the door again and take out a second care. Notice again that you can handle two of these at the same time, both with absolute comfort and confidence. Your bodymind already knows this. In fact, while you are fiddling around with these old concerns one by one, you bodymind has already learned it can carry all of them without any discomfort, worry, concern or anxiety. It knows it can handle all these items with grace, poise, comfort and confidence. You can verify this by taking each item you want out of your closet and feeling that sense of security, comfort and safety remain with you as you pick any of them up.

You now have more choices about how you live your life. You can retrieve all the items you put in the closet and carry them comfortably and confidently. You can retrieve some of them, and carry these with confidence and serenity. You can leave them all in the closet. After all, you could come back for them if you decided to do so. Or you could forget all about them and just enjoy your life, knowing you will automatically deal with the issues you need to deal with from your enhanced state of mind. You can enjoy your Quantum Focused future.

When you decide how best to make your life the most comfortable, leaving anxiety behind, permit your mind to return to your normal waking state . . . and enjoy the peaceful feeling.

Some Additional Aids to Being Calm

Here are several behaviors you can consider and ask yourself, "Do I do this?" If so, you might find that changing these behaviors leads you to a calmer, more peaceful and relaxed state of mind overall.

Do You Procrastinate?

One of the behaviors that seems to increase anxiety is a routine tendency to put off doing things. In the beginning, you may only worry about getting one single thing you have put off done as its deadline grows closer. Soon though, you will find there are several things approaching deadlines that could have been done sooner and you carry mental concerns about them all. Before long, there are so many items on your list that you lose track of the individual items. You have set yourself up for that uneasy state of generalized anxiety.

Now, training yourself to do things promptly may not make all your anxiety go away, but it will reduce it significantly. Conversely, if you already suffer with anxiety, procrastination can make it worse.

Are You Late . . . Again?

A close companion to procrastination is being late. The act of being late is in itself a major source of anxiety. This anxiety is often compounded by its effect on others, if and when you are late.

Resetting your inner and outer clocks is one quick way to resolve this dreaded habit. Now this particular activity works best when it is performed in a hot bubble bath. (Note that just the bath alone can help. See below. Also, some of you guys out there may need to get in touch with your feminine side for this, but *it's worth it*.). Candles and soft music (taking appropriate safety precautions with the fire and electricity) are also required.

Light the candles and turn down the lights. Now start the music. Then glide gently into the tub. Aaaaahhhh! That's it! Just relax and enjoy that wonderful sensation of absolute ease for a moment or two. Then, mentally scan your body and focus on how nice it is when your whole body relaxes in a hot tub. Notice how the bubbles just lift your worries away.

Now we want you to get in touch with any personal experience in which things were happening much faster inside you than they were happening outside of you. Just be with that experience. Feel the freedom. Enjoy the sense of control and imagine that there are two dials in your mind's eye. The red one can adjust your inner experience of time and the green can adjust your outer experience of time. What adjustments do you have to make in order to be on time? Well, as they say, just do it. Then enjoy your relaxing bath a while longer before you begin operating on your new time.

Are You A Caffeine Abuser?

Take a look at your daily intake of caffeine. Be smart now and don't get caught in the "I don't drink coffee" trap. Many other sources of caffeine exist in daily diets. Tea, soda, chocolate, tablets made to overcome drowsiness (if you think these are rare, check out students at midterm and final examination times) and some over-the-counter headache medications all contain appreciable amounts of caffeine. In fact, drinks artificially laced with excess caffeine to deliberately provide a jolt to your system are even available.

If you find yourself consuming any of the above in other than moderate amounts, you will probably find relief in several areas of your life when you cut down. While some people are so sensitive to caffeine they must eliminate it completely, we have seen others who only have to *reduce* consumption in order to benefit.

We have encountered a significant number of people who suffered several days of withdrawal symptoms as they greatly reduced or eliminated caffeine from their diets. The most common symptom was a headache. To get through the few days of discomfort, pain relievers without caffeine can be a great help. However, for those of you who would rather avoid medications when you can, we have found these headaches can also be handled rather easily with the techniques described in chapters 30 and 31.

Are You A Couch Potato?

One of the keys to relieving anxiety is to refocus your mind away from any discomforting thoughts. The trick, of course, is to refocus your mind onto something else instead of on those unwanted thoughts or feelings. The last chapter in this book provides useful methods to accomplish this mentally.

You can also do this by getting really involved in something. Literally, take your mind off your "troubles" by putting it fully on something else instead. Hobbies, intellectual pursuits and physical activities can all help you to accomplish this. It is impossible to feel anxious when you are completely engrossed in a good book, arranging a stamp collection or lifting weights.

While all these distractions can work equally well, there is an advantage to physical exercise. You don't have to consciously refocus your mind as you do between mental activities. In any exercise you really enjoy, or any one that is truly strenuous, this shift happens without your conscious intent to make it happen. Keep the exercise within your current physical limits however.

In addition, the exercise will help to build greater physical health while it improves your mental outlook.

Music Hath Charms

There is something about music that can capture our minds and spirits and carry them off to someplace else. Experiment to find the type of music and the specific pieces that calm you the most. There is a wide selection of New Age and other relaxation-oriented compositions to choose from. You may prefer something in the more classical vein. Selections from the Baroque period seem to be especially well-suited to relaxing and calming the mind. Many people love Mozart. Give Handel, Vivaldi, Bach (Senior or Juniors) and Pachabel a play also to see how they do for you and you do with them. (If you want a sample of the type of piece your authors enjoy, give another listen to the background music on your Quantum Focus practice tape.)

Take a Hot Bath

Here's an easy one, even for coach potatoes. It has been shown that many people respond positively to soaking in a hot bath. (Could this explain the popularity of Hot Tubs?) The water needs to be quite warm, yet comfortable. Usually, the research has used water at about 105 degrees. You need to experiment to find the most comfortable and relaxing temperature for you. The idea is to keep it warm enough to be relaxing, yet not so hot as to be injurious. You want to relax your inner self, not make soup.

As described in the section explaining how to reset your clocks, you can add some candles and music to your experience (of course, keep your stereo far enough away from the tub to avoid any accidents that prove water and electricity are not a relaxing mix). Then, step into your tub, just lean back and enjoy it for 20 to 30 minutes. You'll be a new person when you emerge.

Dare We Suggest It?

There is a great deal of information in this book about how to have fantastic sex . . . which is a major anxiety and stress buster and a great aid to being soooo calm and relaxed. You might begin by inviting your partner to take that hot, candle-lit bubble bath with you!

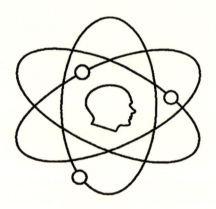

Chapter 12

Setting and Obtaining Goals

"Do not attempt to do a thing unless you are sure of yourself; but do not relinquish it simply because someone else is not sure of you."
STEWART E. WHITE

How To Find Anaheim

If you want to go somewhere, there are two basic pieces of information you must have before you can plan your trip. You need to establish 1) where you are, and 2) where you want to go. As the old saying goes, if you don't know where you are going, any road will get you there. But it is important to know your starting point as well as your destination.

Suppose you decided you wanted to go to Disneyland in Anaheim, California, for a vacation. How would you get there? By plane? Drive? Or maybe take a cab? The answer depends on where you are starting from. If you are in New York City, you'll probably decide to take a plane. If you are in Las Vegas, maybe you'll take a plane or maybe you'll drive. If you are in Orange County, maybe you'll just hop a cab.

It is the same with life and the goals you seek. You need to 1) know where you are, and 2) where you want to go. Once you have established these two reference points, figuring out just how to get to where you want to go becomes infinitely easier. In fact, you can let your unconscious mind plot the pathway . . . once you've clearly instructed it as to the starting point and the destination.

Now there is a contingent of well-meaning people who will point out that your unconscious already knows the starting point. At some level, this is undoubtedly true. However, consciously we often delude ourselves as to where we really are in life. If we have been making a habit of this, it is possible we have introduced other levels of unconscious thought which are confused. Maybe our unconscious mind is already clear on this point, maybe not. But by clearly defining the starting point right up front, we can eliminate any possibility of confusion. This is beneficial if there was any unconscious uncertainty, and it certainly does no harm if there was none. So it is a highly recommended step in your process.

Should Goals Be Written?

This same discussion can go on about whether goals can be in your head or should be written down. Without a doubt, writing them down forces you to crystalize them, make them unambiguous in your own mind. Reread the last paragraph, substituting the words "destination" for "starting point" and "want to go" for "are in life".

Why Set Goals At All?

There is also a large number of individuals who believe goals are a waste of time. They believe that whatever is going to happen will happen anyway. So they say why pick targets that you want to reach? The answer is simple. Life is not so predestined that whatever we do is insignificant. Quite the opposite. Our intentional striving towards certain goals we select decidedly increases the probability of our reaching them.

In 1953, the graduating class of one of the Ivy League schools was interviewed about their plans for their lives. Of particular interest to us is the fact that, while a large number of this class had goals in their heads, fewer than three percent had written them down.

In 1973, the interviewers followed up with the members of this class who were still alive. They found a number of interesting things. Those with goals, either written or unwritten, were enjoying greater success in life than those who had begun their journeys twenty years earlier without goals, and those with written goals were enjoying greater success than those with unwritten goals.

The interviewers judged success by a number of criteria. Some were subjective, such as happiness or good marriages/relationships while others were objective, such as income or net worth. We won't bother you with a lot of statistics, just one that makes the point vividly. When the interviewers added up the total wealth of the class (an objective measure because you can count money), they discovered that the three percent of the class who had written goals upon graduation controlled over ninety percent of the class's total wealth twenty years after graduation. So why have goals and why write them out? Because goals, particularly written goals, *work*.

The Goal Setting Exercise

This exercise is different from many of the others because you will need to do both mental and physical work for it to be the most effective. The mental part will use your Quantum Focus state, which you already know is more fun and enjoyment than work. The physical is limited to picking up a pen or pencil and writing out your goals. And before you ask, yes you can write them out on your computer too. (Now this really isn't "physical work", is it?)

Begin by choosing some aspect of your life that has not been working for you the way you would like it to. With the intent of correcting this aspect of your life in mind, enter your Quantum Focused state. Permit yourself as much time as you feel you need to relax completely without letting go of your intention.

Now, bring your attention to this area of your life. Look at it as it is right now. What is working? What isn't working? Take plenty of time so that both your conscious and unconscious mind get a good grasp of what is what right now.

When you have clearly identified what is and is not working, let your imagination now change these aspects so they are the way you want them to be. You may want to keep the aspects that are working now, or you may decide to change these also. You certainly want to convert all those things that are not working into a more useful outcome. Take your time and see all these areas in detail.

For example, if you are working on a relationship, rather than just seeing yourself happier, imagine the specific changes that made this so. If you are working on finances, rather than just being wealthier, define the things that contribute this wealth to you. Be as specific as you can. You do not need to make conscious decisions about these specifics, just permit your Quantum Focused imagination to provide the answers for you. All your conscious mind needs to do is take mental notes to transcribe later.

Spend as much time as needed to allow this process to continue to a natural conclusion. Then return to your usual state of waking consciousness.

Now Write Them Down

When you have brought yourself back to your usual state of waking consciousness, write out the specific changes, events or activities you imagined yourself doing. Your Quantum Focused imagination has provided you with goals. Your unconscious mind understands both the goals and the starting points. More importantly, it also knows how to get from where you are to where you want to be. You need only encourage it to get you there.

You can provide this encouragement by reading your goals each morning, then entering your Quantum Focused state and reflecting on them, thus reinforcing them. Be advised that your goals will change with time, so don't be surprised if you notice slight variations in them each day as they evolve into more substantial and more powerful forms.

The rest of the encouragement you provide is by doing those things you feel will help you get to the goals. Your unconscious mind will naturally lead you to these actions and activities. But you still need to perform them in order to catalyze the process. While great believers in the power of the mind to create, we also believe in supplying the raw materials whenever we can, to facilitate the job.

A Modern Parable

Remember how Albert (chapter 1) acted when he first learned about mentally programming for the things he wanted. He programmed his goal of winning the lottery and then set about life acting as if it had already manifested in the physical world in which we live. While we won't retell the whole story here, Albert did all the things that make mental programming stronger and more effective . . . except for one crucial one. Go back to chapter 1 if you want to know what that one was.

So always do your part to provide the raw materials for your mental programming. It really makes some difference!

Some More Hints

The starting point of your process can have tremendous influence over the outcome. By beginning with your life's purpose, you are defining an ultimate goal. (Yes, it is the journey that counts. We are not saying that your life's purpose used as a goal is a destination. It may also be defined as a segment of a journey.)

This goal is one that gives direction to your entire life. Subgoals you choose along the way are much more likely to be aligned with your overall goal.

If your life's purpose were to be in service to others, perhaps in some type of ministerial way, you most likely wouldn't program, as a supportive subgoal, to become the CEO of a Fortune 500 company. It would only be a detour on the path you chose to walk. If you were to plan on being a teacher, you probably wouldn't work toward being a locksmith in the short-term (unless you were going to teach locksmithing). It too would be out of your way.

By beginning with your overriding objective, you can more easily choose subgoals that will support your overall mission. They become easier for you to reach because they lie along your path. They are more useful to you when you have reached them because they serve as bridges to where you ultimately want to go.

Chapter 13

Rising And Shining

"It is a delicious moment, certainly, that of being well-nestled in bed and feeling that you shall drop gently to sleep. The good is to come, not past."

LEIGH HUNT

The Secret of a Good Night's Sleep

In this chapter, we will teach Quantum Focusers how to slip into Quantum states and focus their attention to eliminate circumstances that could interfere with getting restful and energizing sleep. This program is specially designed to develop your skills for overcoming the insomnia you may have suffered from for many years. Mastery could come within 30 days if you are using side B of your Quantum Focus tape, or within 60 days if you are just using quiet and peaceful music of your own choosing.

We have developed this program using a blend of ancient self-mastery approaches and the latest sleep research. If you are one of the two out of three Americans who awaken feeling unrested, or if you are the one person in six with a significant sleep disorder, you can benefit greatly from this chapter. (If you are one of the few exceptionally resistant individuals for whom this chapter alone does not give routinely restful nights, see Appendix A for more powerful techniques that can help you overcome your difficulty.) But first, take the Quantum Focus challenge in this chapter by following the instructions given and begin to enhance the quality of your sleep. You may surprise yourself with how easily you can fall into a deep, restful sleep on a regular basis.

A Worthwhile Life

One of the necessities for awakening refreshed, renewed and raring to go is awakening to a life worth living. If life is awful, if we do not want to go do whatever it is we have to do each day and there is no relief in sight, if there is no meaning or challenge in life, then all the techniques in the world for sleeping better cannot assure that you awaken "bright-eyed and bushy-tailed" in the morning. In fact, you may actually wind up sleeping more and more, and feeling only worse for it. If this is a part of your personal challenge, then go back to chapter 7 and practice its exercise to help you discover your passion and purpose in life. If you practice every day, you will soon notice improvements in this area of your life which will spill over into enhanced sleep.

Quantum Focused Sleep

As in all other Quantum Focus technologies, Quantum Sleeping is self-directed. It is about the realization that the power is already with you; you only need to be with the power to use it. During the next 30 days, as you take the Quantum Challenge, you will be reprogramming your mind to expect and achieve energizing rest.

The Quantum Challenge

[TAPE INSTRUCTION: At this point, start either side B of your Quantum Focus tape or a recording of peaceful music or sounds of your own choosing which runs about 15-20 minutes in length. Then, get ready for a peaceful rest as you follow any of the three exercises below.]

Exercise One

Using your Quantum Focus cue (eyes rolled back as previously explained), try to stay awake for as long as the music plays while you visualize or imagine yourself in a very special place. This is a place where you feel as if everything in your life were finally coming together in exactly the right way for you — all your dreams were coming into being. And as you walk around your special place, looking at the beautiful view, you find yourself becoming very sleepy and tired . . . as if the air you are breathing contained small, sleep-inducing molecules which make you feel very drowsy. Very sleepy, very tired, and getting drowsier with every breath you take, you look around and, sure enough, you find the perfect spot, right there in your mind's eye, to lie down, curl up, and slip into a magical nap . . . a nap which energizes and inspires you.

And here's the challenge. Insert yourself into this imagined special place. Enjoy the imagery, make it real in your mind. Look at it, listen to the sounds in your special place, feel the temperature of the air, and try to stay awake until the music ends . . . if you can.

Exercise Two

For the next few minutes, allow yourself to become as quiet and peaceful as you can. Deliberately relax all your muscles and watch all tension drain from your body. Now use your Quantum Focus cue and allow yourself to shift into a Quantum State as you begin slowly counting backwards. Open and close your eyes with each number as follows: "100", close your eyes and mentally say "tired . . . sleepy . . . drowsy"; "99", open your eyes and mentally say "tired . . . sleepy . . . drowsy"; "98", close your eyes and mentally say "tired . . . sleepy . . . drowsy"; "97", open your eyes and mentally say "tired . . . sleepy . . . drowsy". Keep on going like that.

Here's your challenge. Try to stay awake until you get to 50, then 40, then 30. You'll notice that it becomes harder and harder to stay awake . . . if you are able to stay awake at all.

Exercise Three

For the next few minutes, allow yourself to become as quiet and peaceful as you can. Now use your Quantum Focus cue and allow yourself to shift into a Quantum State. Begin to remember or imagine a day in which you were sooo busy and worked sooo hard that you fell asleep the minute you put your head on the pillow. Now relive that day . . . redo all the things you did that day in your mind's eye. See yourself hard at work or play, but coming home fully exhausted. Feel the sensations of your tired body and see yourself just drift into a deep . . . and rewarding . . . sleep.

Here's the challenge. Play this scene in your mind's eye and try to stay awake until the music ends.

What You Can Expect

Experiment by using each of the exercises at least twice to identify which one works best for you. Then, use that one at night regularly . . . and pleasant dreams. And as soon as you find yourself sleeping easily and effortlessly, you will want to begin working on the next chapter, Quantum Dreaming, as another way to enhance your life and creative powers. So begin the Quantum Challenge and tap into your powers for sleeping.

Some Additional Aids

There are some things you can do to help yourself get to sleep that are almost too obvious to mention. First of all, avoid stimulants. We know of one fellow who loved to play poker. It was truly his vice. He wasn't a big gambler, playing mostly for nickels and dimes, he just loved the game.

He managed to get himself into three games each week, with different groups of friends and acquaintances. Normally, they would play from around 8:00 until midnight or so at the weeknight games, and often until 2:00 or 3:00 in the morning at the Friday night game. Refreshments were always on hand. Usually, beer and chips or some other munchie to go with the beer. He didn't drink alcohol, so while they drank beer, he drank coffee. Some evenings, he would consume two full pots all by himself.

Tough Nights

He struggled to get to sleep on his poker nights, a result he attributed to the excitement of the card games. When we first saw him, he was in desperate shape. His not being able to fall asleep on the nights he had been playing cards had spilled over into not being able to fall asleep on other nights. It was becoming a habit.

Quantum Focus helped him somewhat. but not as much as it usually helps people. It wasn't until about the third session that he finally told us about the coffee. We persuaded him to switch to decaffeinated to see what happened. Within a week, he was sleeping like a baby. Case closed? We thought so.

He's Ba-ack!

About three weeks later, he was back. "It was working great!", he said "Then, last week I had all kinds of trouble again." We were very surprised. He had done so well that we found it incredible he would be having trouble again. After a short discussion, we asked the logical question, was he still drinking decaffeinated? He said he didn't like the decaffeinated so he quit drinking coffee altogether. He had switched to a cola, one which he guzzled by the quart bottle. And one, it turned out, which had lots of caffeine, a fact that was a surprise to him. He never knew colas contained caffeine.

The bottom line was he quit the caffeine-loaded cola and Quantum Focused back to sleeping like a baby within two nights. We were waiting for him to come back again, telling us he was taking NoDoze to stay awake through the games, but it didn't happen. Our last contact was several months after the cola incident. He was doing well. So, don't overlook the obvious.

Sleep-Inducing Foods

As we write this, tryptophan is not yet back on the market in the U.S. following its removal by the F.D.A. It was a good supplement for helping to get to, and stay, asleep. So you may wish to add some tryptophan-containing foods to your evenings an hour or two before you go to bed. Stay away from high protein foods, though. Look to high carbohydrate foods, like bananas, figs, dates, bread, whole grains and beans.

Vitamin B supplements often have a stimulating effect. Take yours early in the day when they will be most useful, and keep them away from bedtime.

As Good As Sleeping Pills

We introduced you to the power of aromatherapy back in chapter 6. Here is one British study you will find fascinating. At the University of Leicester, lavender oil was as effective in the treatment of insomnia as prescription sleeping pills. The floral scent helped insomniacs to sleep as long as they did after taking drugs! But there was *no* aftereffect with the lavender scent.

As Clear As Night and Day

Melatonin is a naturally-occurring hormone whose circulating blood level is controlled by the pineal gland, a small light-sensitive organ at the base of the brain. It appears that the pineal gland detects light and dark (or more correctly, the absence of light), manufactures melatonin and releases it into the bloodstream when light is fading into darkness. This assures us a good night's sleep when it is time to sleep.

Dr. Richard Wurtman, a neuroscientist at the Massachusetts Institute of Technology and Dr. Peretz Levi, Dean of Medicine at the Israeli Institute of Technology at Haifa, have independently demonstrated that supplemental melatonin, taken 30-120 minutes before bed, is a very effective sleeping aid for many people. It has been shown to be as effective as prescription sleeping compounds but without the unwanted lingering side effects of the drugs.

Dr. Alex Duarte, author and nutritionist with Ph.D.'s in nutrition and in optometry, describes even newer research studying melatonin's already-established antioxidant properties, and there are more than a few proponents who also claim it has anti-aging properties. Whether or not this last claim proves to be correct, it still seems this hormone may provide more than just a good night's sleep. There are a number of precautions in using melatonin (i.e., conditions in which you should not use it), so read the bottle carefully.

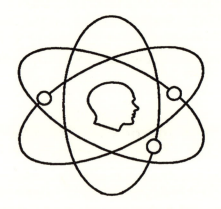

Chapter 14

Programming Your Dreams

"Life is but a dream."
NUMEROUS AUTHORS

We refer to this very powerful technology as "The Supercharger". At the very same time you are sleeping/dreaming, you are reinforcing (or even creating) the many benefits you get by practicing your Quantum Focus when you are awake. Now you can enhance your skills while you sleep like a log and dream your desires into reality.

What *Is* Real?

Many people are unaware of dreaming, and many people dreaming are unaware of even being asleep in the first place. It seemed so real, they say. It reminds us of the old teaching story about the caterpillar who wasn't sure if it was a caterpillar dreaming it was a butterfly, or a butterfly dreaming it was a caterpillar. It never was really certain.

In some respects, we are just like this caterpillar. Are we the dreamer or the dream? We really can't be sure until we begin to develop mastery over both our waking and sleeping dreams. While you practice programming your dreams, you will quickly discover that this technique empowers and enhances the results you are creating for yourself while mindfully "dreaming" in Quantum states.

Do You Want To Make Something Out Of It?

Put into other words, we could say that you are what you breathe, think, eat, drink, and dream . . . whether you are breathing, thinking, eating, drinking, or dreaming, consciously or unconsciously. The more consciously you direct your life, the more dynamic and powerful your ability to do so becomes. The practice of consciously living from moment to moment is the key to enriching one's life and every experience in it.

As you have already learned, Quantum Focus is a series of developmental technologies aimed at helping you move into and experience conscious living. While it seems paradoxical at first to think that dreaming enhances conscious living, you will rapidly see the improved results of your conscious world when you use the dream state productively.

Kissin' Cousins

Dreams are related to the Quantum Focus state, and other enhanced states of consciousness, in that your brainwaves are identical in all these states. Hypnosis, meditation, dreaming and Quantum Focus can all lead you to this arena of mental power. Ormond McGill, the "Dean of American Hypnotists", says of the relationship between hypnosis and meditation, "Hypnosis and meditation are two sides of the same coin. The sides are different but they are both part of the same coin." Many believe that this hypnomeditative "coin" is the cornerstone of all great achievement and is behind all works of both science and art.

Dreams are but one additional tool for your toolbox. Most of the time they are undirected, at least by your conscious mind, and simply unfold as they will. Why not learn to use them positively, rather than simply let them pass by each night merely as a form of amusement?

As you develop your conscious dreamweaving skills in both the waking and sleeping states, your Quantum Focus experiences will automatically lead you to conscious living. Quantum Dreaming will open new doors for you, creating the inner reality to make your dreams come true!

If you are now able to remember your dreams easily, proceed directly to the next section. If you are not currently able to remember your dreams, please read Appendix B and practice the exercise given there. The Appendix is very instructive and helpful in developing your ability to remember dreams with ease.

Programming Your Dreams

There are some people who teach programming dreams through a ritual to be used upon retiring for the night. We have used this technique and found it often helpful. However, the real key to programming dreams is to teach yourself to recognize that you are dreaming in the course of the dream. This is often called "lucid" dreaming and is sort of like waking up inside your dream.

Then, because you are able to do anything in a dream (for example, alter the dream to make changes that enable you to reach goals or face fears in a safe and manageable way while you are dreaming), when you recognize that you are dreaming, you can alter your dreams *while they are occurring*. Obviously, you will alter them in ways that are supportive of the goals and objectives you desire. This is a much more awesomely powerful tool than just preprogramming the night's events when going to bed.

The Exercise

For the next month, while you are preparing to go to sleep each night, think about what we've described above. Then, before you drift off to sleep, enter your Quantum Focus state and tell yourself you are both open to, and desirous of, waking up inside your dreams. Affirm that you are ready, willing and able to become a conscious participant. In fact, you are going to be more than a participant; you are going to become the director, the screenwriter and the major player.

Then go to sleep. When a dream begins, you can decide what its significance is and how you will use it. Dreams are very personal experiences, and there are literally millions of possible dreams. But you will usually be able to recognize the potential value in each dream once you have learned to identify that it is a dream and you are dreaming it now.

For example, let's say the next dream you have finds you in the middle of a crowded shopping center during the Christmas rush. You have always been very uncomfortable in crowds, even to the point of avoiding some events in life in order to avoid being in a crowd. The dream's situation in which you find yourself makes your skin crawl and your head spin. But all of a sudden you realize it's only a dream. Once you realize this, you seize the golden opportunity to change your dream because you are 1) now aware that you are dreaming and 2) because anything is possible in a dream. You could:

a) fly away
b) become bigger than everyone else so no one bugs you
c) imagine them all stepping back out of your way, or
d) make up any other outcome of your own.

Just remember that anything is possible.

An Explanation

What has happened? You have met one of your fears head on and discovered that you can come through it unscathed. You escaped whatever dangers your unconscious mind had imagined were associated with crowds. This begins to condition your unconscious mind to deal with this situation in waking life. Your unconscious mind is learning that you can "escape" whatever dangers it previously felt would inevitably befall you in a crowd.

And your waking life improves because you have overcome what used to be a stumbling block in your life. You can laugh at the roadblocks that block your progress, and smash them into powder while you sleep peacefully.

4/9/00

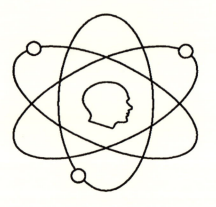

Chapter 15

Overcoming Agoraphobia

"Nothing is so much to be feared as fear."
HENRY DAVID THOREAU

Irrational Fears

Most people who suffer from a phobia feel they are alone in their misery. Yet, it is estimated that one kind of phobia or another affects between five and ten percent of the general population. Once again, you see that having a lot of company does absolutely nothing to resolve the problem.

Phobia is a term used to describe intense and persistent fear. This fear can be of an activity, a situation or an object. Because of its intense reaction, the person with a phobia is often confined to a very restricted life. Even though they have emotional reactions — extreme anxieties — that are way out of proportion to the situation eliciting it, and even though they know these are in response to an admittedly irrational fear, phobias can take a very firm hold.

Phobias in general, and agoraphobia in particular, are not very responsive to conventional treatment. People have spent literally thousands of dollars on conventional psychotherapy, without any measurable improvement. In many cases, antianxiety and antidepressant drugs are given to relieve symptoms, but there is no reliable evidence that these drugs do anything useful for the patient. They certainly do not address the underlying challenge the person faces.

The Panic Button

Phobias and anxiety are distinguished from each other by the fact that a phobia occurs in response to some specific event, object or situation, while anxiety is a generalized uneasiness or fear. Panic attacks with phobias seem common. The panic attack reaction is typically manifested in a pounding heartbeat, sweating, facial flushing, nausea and/or diarrhea, shaking and sometimes fainting. The phobic person often feels like he or she will either go crazy or have a heart attack and die.

Unfortunately, when a panic attack begins, the person detects one or more of the beginning symptoms. Worry about that detected symptom causes an increase in the whole physiological cycle and worsens all the symptoms. Detection of the worsened symptoms causes further escalation of them. And so it goes, in a vicious circle. Increased worry worsens symptoms, worsened symptoms increase worry. Fortunately, the body's physiology cannot maintain this high state of arousal for more than about 20 minutes, so panic attacks are self-limiting. You may feel as if you were going to die or go crazy, but nothing happens other than an inevitable calming down of the system as the chemicals the attack depends on are expended.

Major Classes

Three types of phobias are generally recognized. First is the fear of a specific object or situation, such as the fear of heights ("simple" phobias). Second is agoraphobia which is its own class and which we will discuss below. Third is the group of "social" phobias, fears of looking foolish or stupid in a social setting (e.g., the fear of public speaking). We have provided you with a Quantum Focus approach to all three types in the chapters that follow.

Agoraphobia

Agoraphobia is a diagnosis originally used by psychologists to describe an unreasonable fear of open spaces or going out in public. It literally means fear of markets, which were once the crowded spaces filled with activity and commerce. (The name comes from the Greek word "agora" which was the marketplace of ancient Greece, not unlike our supermalls of today.)

There is no agreement on what initiates phobias in general, or agoraphobia in particular. It has been noted that there is often a history of alcoholism in the families of agoraphobics. It has been further speculated that people who are especially susceptible to issues of separation and loss are also more susceptible to agoraphobia. Again, agreement on this is far from unanimous.

Because of agoraphobia's prevalence and generalized nature, its description today has become broadened by many psychologists to include the fear of fear itself (although there is not general agreement on this). In this case, fear is seen as being brought on by something unidentified in the outside world. If we are fearful of that fear, we avoid the outside world to eliminate the possibility of the fear occurring.

A New Approach

It is important to understand that we are not psychiatrists or psychologists. In this chapter we present tried and true solutions for people who are experiencing fear over leaving their homes and going out into the world. Our solutions are not psychological techniques, nor do they subscribe to the tenets and principles upon which psychology is based. They are simply methods that have worked for many, many people. What follows are two easy exercises to help you create a new inner reality which supports your going out into the world.

Method One Exercise

Put yourself into a Quantum Focus state and just drift deeper and deeper into profound feelings of inner peace. When you feel totally at peace with yourself, take several deep breaths to anchor yourself to this peaceful place.

Now, keeping these safe, peaceful feelings, begin to imagine yourself going out into the world and visiting situations that would usually be disturbing or fearful to you. Begin with situations that would only be mildly threatening or uncomfortable.

See yourself as if you were watching yourself on a movie screen. Watch as you deal with everything going on inside and outside of you with ease and grace. See yourself going about whatever activity you choose in comfort, poise and style.

If you feel even the slightest tinge of discomfort, simply breathe in deeply to reactivate the peaceful feelings of your Quantum Focus state and dispel the discomfort.

As you find you can comfortably begin to expand your mental horizon, gradually increase the difficulty of the situation in which you imagine yourself. This may require a series of days, with each one increasing your ability to handle the situations comfortably, but you will rapidly notice a difference in your reactions.

By the third or fourth session, you will be able to handle situations that, only a day or two earlier, might have been beyond your tolerance. Now, notice how you are able to handle these increasingly difficult situations with comfort. See yourself moving with confidence into places or situations that you wish to address with a deep sense of ability and ease.

Very good. This is the key to programming new inner realities for yourself and it is as powerful as it is simple.

Method Two Exercise

Seeding your dreams is the first step towards programming dreams. Because dreams can enhance other actions you may take, this method is strongly recommended to heighten your ability to change your life. Before retiring tonight, please do the following exercise and sleep deeply and peacefully . . .

> Relax by scanning every part of your body for tension or strain and then releasing it. Actually tense and relax your toes, feet, ankles, calves, shins, knees, and on upwards until your entire body is fully relaxed.
>
> Concentrate on the idea that tonight, as you sleep, you will be having an adventurous and thoroughly enjoyable dream. It will involve going out to a very busy place and just having a ball as you discover how much fun it can be to move about this environment freely and without fear.
>
> Now imagine that all the blood in your brain is flowing downward into your hands and feet.

This exercise can promote a deep, peaceful sleep, and the prior thinking about dreaming helps you become conscious of your dreams as they occur. (Go back and reread the end of Chapter 14 if you want to know how these exercises work.)

Power Image

Just as soon as you can comfortably do so in the exercises above, add your 30 second Power Image solution to your challenge. It may take a few practice sessions until you can readily imagine yourself gently gliding right into a scene that you would like to conquer. Stay with it though. It will happen and you will find yourself simply relaxing further as it does.

First Aid

If you suffer from panic attacks, here is a very simple method to minimize these attacks as you first feel them coming on. Don't fight the impending attack. Instead, gently slip into a Quantum Focus state of relaxation and invite the attack. This very act of invitation in a Quantum state dispels fear, while your Quantum relaxation breaks the physiological cycle the attack needs to intensify and sustain itself.

Some Other Thoughts

Lay off the caffeine. This seems to help a considerable percentage of people who experience a phobia of one type or another.

There are now some clinics that specialize in treating phobias. The more successful use desensitization techniques. They incorporate various techniques of conventional psychotherapy along with the desensitization. The caveat: psychotherapy without desensitization doesn't work very well. But, desensitization without psychotherapy *does* work pretty well. So, why include psychotherapy?

Chapter 16

Overcoming Claustrophobia

"Fear is a kind of bell . . . it is the soul's signal for rallying."
HENRY WARD BEECHER

Claustrophobia, a member of the "simple" phobias group, is defined as the abnormal fear of small, enclosed or confined spaces. It can take a number of forms, extending to elevators and tunnels, or even bridges, which are "confined" by the edges. Most commonly, it is noticed by an uncomfortable feeling when reaching into a closet, or an inability to walk into a walk-in closet, or perhaps a dread of having to squeeze into the attic stairs or even the attic itself.

Where Does It Come From?

As with other "irrational" fears, there is no well-accepted theory to account for the origin of claustrophobia. It is speculated that simple phobias begin in childhood and persist into adulthood. Certainly, for every person suffering from claustrophobia, in whom some traumatic childhood event can be documented (e.g. having been accidentally trapped in an old well or other small space, or having been locked in a closet as punishment), there is an equivalent number or more for whom no such event can be established. This does not seem to be the case when one also considers past lives.

When one adds past-life experiences to the equation, there usually seems to have been some traumatic event to which irrational fears can be traced. It is not our intent to determine here whether or not past lives are real. Whether they are real or only imaginings of the unconscious mind, addressing them, and acting as if they *were* real, has some very real benefits.

How Can I Get Rid Of It?

This gives us two methods of overcoming claustrophobia. The first is simply a desensitization technique, whereby we retrain the mind to learn that there is no inherent danger in these confined spaces. The second deals with recognizing the "past life origin" of the fear, the mere realization of which dispels it in this life.

Desensitization Exercise

Put yourself into a Quantum Focus state and just drift deeper and deeper into the profound feelings of inner peace. When you feel totally at peace with yourself, take several deep breaths to anchor yourself to this peaceful place.

Now, keeping these safe, peaceful feelings, begin to imagine yourself going out in to the world and visiting situations that would usually be disturbing or fearful to you. Begin with situations that would only be mildly threatening or uncomfortable. Perhaps you are stepping into only slightly confined spaces.

See yourself as if you were watching yourself on a movie screen. Watch as you deal with everything going on inside and outside of you with ease and grace. See yourself going in and around these places with comfort, poise and style.

If you feel even the slightest tinge of discomfort, simply breathe in deeply to reactivate the peaceful feelings of your Quantum Focus state and dispel the discomfort. After spending a comfortable time here, return gently to your everyday awareness.

As you find you can comfortably begin to expand your mental horizon, gradually increase the difficulty of the situation in which you imagine yourself. It may require a series of days, with each one increasing your ability to handle the situations comfortably, but you will rapidly notice a difference in your reactions.

By the third or fourth session, you will be able to handle situations that, only a day or two earlier, might have been beyond your tolerance. Now, notice how you are able to handle increasingly difficult situations with comfort. See yourself moving with confidence, ability and ease into places or situations that you wish to address.

When you are feeling really confident with your new ability, simply allow yourself to return to your normal state of waking consciousness, knowing you have retrained your mind to react more usefully to these situations.

Your Power Image

As soon as you can comfortably incorporate your Power Image into your practice, do so. Just see yourself gently and easily gliding into the resolved situation.

Dispelling Past Life Origins

As you remember from the last chapter, seeding your dreams is the first step towards programming dreams. Dreams are messages from the unconscious, so we can use them to discover and reorganize things while we sleep. Before retiring tonight, please do the following exercise and sleep deeply and peacefully.

Relax by scanning every part of your body for tension or strain and then releasing it. Actually tense and relax your toes, feet, ankles, calves, shins, knees, and on upwards until your entire body is fully relaxed.

Concentrate on the idea that tonight, as you sleep, you will be having an adventurous and thoroughly enjoyable dream. In this dream, you will cross a bridge or walk through a door, or in some other way connect with a past life. You will know when you have made this connection for there will be a small waterfall of white light just before you arrive at the connecting link. Stop and bathe yourself in this white light, and know that it confers absolute protection on you.

You will go as an observer, that is, a tourist who can see and hear everything that is going on, but in absolute safety. You are able to move about just by wishing to do so, as in any dream. And you will go to the past life which contains the answer to the question you seek, "Why do I feel this way about confining places?" Relax and discover how much fun it can be to move about this environment freely and without fear.

Now imagine that all the blood in your brain is flowing downward into your hands and feet.

This exercise can promote a deep, peaceful sleep, and the prior thinking about dreaming helps you become conscious of your dreams as they occur. You will probably discover something directly related to a fear of confined places, for example, having been held as a prisoner in a very small cell. But you will meet it in safety and comfort.

And the realization of the prior experience can release any unconscious fears that have lingered and made your life today less pleasant than you want it to be. The best part is that you don't have to do anything at all, just recognize that this event happened. And act as though it were real.

(You might want to reread the end of Chapter 14 again.)

Chapter 17

Overcoming The Fear Of Driving

"Have you noticed? Anybody going slower than you is an idiot, and anyone going faster than you is a moron."
GEORGE CARLIN

You Can Get There From Here

We have met and worked with many people who were always a little uneasy behind the wheel, even some who had driven accident-free for decades. And we've seen others who were so terrified by the thought of driving that they never even learned how. (Remember the story of Alice we recounted in chapter 2. This one had a happy ending because Alice is now taking driving lessons as we write this book.) Still others would drive only on side roads; or only below 25 miles per hour; or only during daylight; or only on sunny days; or only on routes that had no left turns; or some combination of these and other restrictions that kept them from coming and going as they pleased.

There is a surprisingly large number of people who have a fear of driving. For some, it is only a minor discomfort. For others, it is a major impediment to enjoying life. But for all, it represents some degree of inconvenience they do not have to tolerate any longer.

The Road To Mastery

Driving is a skill. It is like any other skill in that, the more we practice, the better we become at it. It is reasonable to expect to start out at a low level of ability and build our skill to higher levels. You can do this very comfortably. So, if you are a beginning driver, along with doing the exercises below, remember to practice driving in safe situations until you have mastered them before you increase the level of difficulty.

You will proceed quickly and easily into the most congested streets and high-speed highways as you increase your level of competence. If you are an experienced driver who already handles these situations but are a little uncomfortable in any of them, just incorporate either or both of the exercises below into your routine and you will find immediate improvement in the comfort you feel behind the wheel.

Desensitization Exercise

Put yourself into a Quantum Focus state and just drift deeper and deeper into profound feelings of inner peace. When you feel totally at peace with yourself, take several deep breaths to anchor yourself to this peaceful place. Now, keeping these safe, peaceful feelings, begin to imagine yourself going out into the world and visiting situations that would usually be disturbing or fearful to you.

Begin with situations that would only be mildly threatening or uncomfortable. Perhaps you are just sitting behind the wheel of a parked car to see what it feels like from the driver's seat. Perhaps you are pull-

Overcoming The Fear Of Driving

ing out into a deserted street without other traffic. Maybe you are driving in light traffic.

See yourself as if you were watching yourself on a movie screen. Watch as you deal with everything going on inside and outside of you with ease and grace. See yourself going in and around these places with comfort, poise and style.

If you feel even the slightest tinge of discomfort, simply breathe in deeply to reactivate the peaceful feelings of your Quantum Focus state and dispel the discomfort. Have a good trip. When you are done, return gently and peacefully to your ordinary state of consciousness.

As you find you can comfortably begin to expand your mental horizon, gradually increase the difficulty of the situation in which you imagine yourself. You might imagine yourself in heavier traffic, or on a super highway, or in rush hour's stop-and-go traffic It may require a series of days, with each one increasing your ability to handle the situations comfortably, but you will rapidly notice a difference in your reactions.

By the third or fourth session, you will be able to handle situations that, only a day or two earlier, might have been beyond your tolerance. Now, notice how you are able to handle increasingly difficult situations with comfort. See yourself moving with confidence into places or situations that you wish to address with a deep sense of ability and ease.

When you are feeling really confident with your new ability, simply allow yourself to return to your normal state of waking consciousness, knowing you have retrained your mind to react in this more useful way to these situations.

Power Image It Away

Use your Power Image as soon as you can incorporate it comfortably. The easiest way to do this is to see yourself arriving at your destination, sliding out from behind the wheel relaxed and at ease. Imagine the convenience driving can bring.

Dream Driving Exercise

As you learned in chapter 14, seeding your dreams is the first step into programming dreams. We can use our dreams to instill new messages into our unconscious mind. Here we will use dreams to painlessly reprogram our feelings toward driving while we sleep. Before retiring tonight please do the following exercise and sleep deeply and peacefully.

Relax by scanning every part of your body for tension or strain and then releasing it. Actually tense and relax your toes, feet, ankles, calves, shins, knees, and on upwards until your entire body is fully relaxed.

Concentrate on the idea that tonight, as you sleep, you will be having an adventurous and thoroughly enjoyable dream. In this dream, you will be driving a brand new sports car (or limousine or off-the-road vehicle or whatever else you would like to drive — take your pick). You will drive in and through all kinds of places and situations. You will be going wherever you want to go, with ease and comfort, always driving expertly and safely.

You will start out as an observer, that is, like watching yourself in a movie . . . until you quickly feel comfortable stepping into that movie and taking the wheel yourself. You then feel the thorough enjoyment in the freedom to go wherever you please without any concern about how you can get there. You can drive anywhere you want to go in absolute comfort. In fact, you even enjoy the very act of driving. Relax and discover how much fun it can be moving about this environment freely and without fear.

Now imagine that all the blood in your brain is flowing downward into your hands and feet.

This exercise can promote a deep, peaceful sleep, and the prior thinking about dreaming helps you become conscious of your dreams as they occur. You may be very pleased to discover how comfortable you are when you get into the driver's seat without any lingering concerns about driving. The best part is that you don't have to do anything at all, just let your dreams do the work.

(If you aren't completely familiar with Chapter 14, we recommend reading it again.)

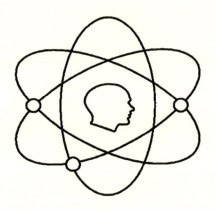

Chapter 18

Overcoming Fear Of Death

"If I die before I wake."
FROM AN OLD CHILDREN'S PRAYER

A Peaceful Vantage Point

Every time we work with a client who is living with a life-threatening disease, the very first step is helping the individual discover that right smack in the middle of their personal terror is an oasis of inner calm. You have been learning to shift into these Quantum Focus meditative states and connect with your inner oasis.

Relearning What We "Know"

The next step is to help them recognize and overcome their fears of progressive illness and death. Our culture's perceptions about illness and death precondition unnecessary fears and concerns that actually hinder healing. We think of this work as "removing the hex" or "breaking the bone". Far too many people die because of their deep-seated belief in the doctor's prognosis and the intense chronic fear this creates, and not the actual disease they were suffering from. And far too many more people never live fully because of their fear of death.

In our experience, breaking the hex appears to be a prerequisite to the healing process. We want to point out that healing and curing are very different. Healing is from the inside out; it is the whole person's attempt to restore balance and health. Curing is healing from the outside in. We don't think much of curing.

We have come to understand that people who present with serious illness have had many longstanding and serious assaults on their health. We have repeatedly witnessed the efficacy of a selective individual program of detoxification when accompanied by physical, mental, emotional and spiritual nourishment.

How Healed Is Healed?

Please understand that healing occurs at many different stages or levels. Some say the end state of the healing process is a cure. Many never reach that stage but still consider their healing as having value in and of itself regardless of the stage reached. In other words a person can heal themselves and not cure the actual health challenge.

In this chapter we share what we have learned from the many remarkable self-healers we have worked with and know of. Many of these people have had full remissions, others made peace with themselves and died with a sense of completion. We will also give you the golden opportunity to see death for what it truly is, a natural part of the ongoing process of life itself.

An Eastern View

It seems that a common thread in mystical teachings is likening death to sleep. In many Eastern teachings, death is thought of as a long sleep between lives. A central theme is that of many lives interwoven between many purifying sleeps. In the sense that we leave our bodies during profound sleep and give the machine a chance to rebalance itself, in death it is believed we remove our spirit and breath forms from our physical body. The body then returns to ashes and dust. Our spirit and breath forms are believed to go through a purification process which leads to rebirth. This process is claimed to be self-evident when people are in profound states of balance and ease. These are the Quantum Focus meditative states you have been rediscovering.

You might imagine yourself moving through a series of lives, each bringing you closer and closer to your real self. Do you see that death is part of the life cycle? We have used the following imagery with our clients and loved ones. It is engineered to inspire a deeply felt inner experience of going beyond the fear of death.

Eternal Source Exercise

Enter a Quantum Focus meditative state and imagine that within your heart is a flame. This flame is radiating a wonderful white light which is spreading inside you and slowly moving through your skin and surrounding you. This light is eternal and has shone from the beginning of time, connecting and animating all living things. Imagine that just becoming aware of this life-giving light illuminates a link between your births and deaths and the grand plan of life.

Every time you enter a Quantum Focus meditative state you are taking an important step in self-development and the practice is bringing you closer and closer to your source. Imagine that within the light is a special vibration that is yours and yours alone. Now imagine what your special vibration sounds like. Listen deep inside yourself and hear the sound within the light. Know that this sound is your cosmic fingerprint and is constant even between lives. This "light-sound" is the only mantra you will ever need. You can easily locate it within your meditative state as your inner ear is sharp and focused.

Do this exercise often. Shift into Quantum Focus meditative states and just listen. Just be with yourself for a few minutes and shift back, mentally sounding your mantra over and over, as if it were a favorite song, and put your full attention into your next activity. Irrational fears, including the fear of death, instantly fade away whenever you tune in to your timeless song and commune with life.

As Clear As A Bell

This work is often linked by myth and ritual and we too find that improvement comes in threes. In your practice, there is much joy, love and deeply felt security to be discovered. Approach the above exercise with a sense of what a sacred work it is! When you hear the sound within the light, begin to work with it as follows:

1) Whenever possible, practice sounding your song verbally.
2) Whenever you have a spare moment, practice mentally sounding your song.
3) Whenever possible, shift into a Quantum Focus meditative state and just listen to your song.

Then bring your attention — calm, centered and energized — back into the moment and stay in the moment. Focus your attention on what is happening in the moment. Stay with it as long as possible.

Overcoming The Fear Of Death

What is the difference between believing and knowing? This question holds the key to unlocking and releasing the fear of death. Think about it at least 3 times a day. What is the difference? How do I know?

It has been our experience that when we, our loved ones and clients unlock and release, old beliefs just become counter-intuitive and lose their power over us. This is very true of irrational fears about death. We are not suggesting you take reckless risks or throw caution to the wind.

We simply want to remind you that you are alive. What the heck, shift into the moment and go for it! Before you know it, you will realize any and all irrational fears about death are non-problems.

Remember Your Power Image

Use your Power Image in any creative way you can. It is often undesirable to imagine somebody close to us dying. So, instead, imagine you are attending the funeral of the parent of a coworker. The parent was 106, had lived well and died well. But see yourself comfortable with being exposed to death.

If you are up to the challenge, imagine yourself being with someone when they die. Again, this is often more appealing if it is someone who is not close to you. Perhaps it is the person in the next bed when you go to visit a friend having some elective surgery in the hospital. Your friend leaves the room to use the bathroom. The very ill person in the other bed kind of moans or sighs . . . and expires. Again, imagine yourself comfortable and at peace.

You will find a Power Image that is just right for you. We find most people do better by avoiding gory accidents, war scenes and the like. Leave *Friday the Thirteenth* for the movies.

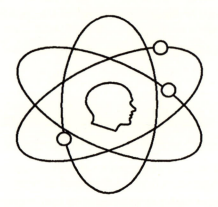

Chapter 19

Overcoming Fear Of Heights

"In the Mountains of Truth, you never climb in vain. Either you already reach a higher point today, or you exercise your strength in order to be able to climb higher tomorrow."

F. NIETZSCHE

What We Learned Watching TV

Television is truly a spiritual wasteland and there is little that can be praised. One program, however — from the mind of the late Bruce Lee — introduced a merger of East(ern) meets West(ern), both culturally and physically. The central character, Caine, is half Asian and half Caucasian. He was raised in harmony with the Tao and is a Master Kung Fu priest traveling through the old American West.

We are introduced to profound Eastern teachings through flashbacks of Caine's amazing education in self-mastery. We mention this because, in one show, the main theme was fear itself, and the sub-theme was the fear of heights. So gather around grasshoppers (an Eastern endearment) and let's flash back to the sacred temple and check into "Overcoming Fear 101".

Setting The Stage

So young Caine is on the temple grounds (based on your author's memories and parametaphoring). Two 2" by 4" boards are placed on the ground and Caine is asked to stand on, and walk on, the boards. Of course this is a very easy thing for Caine to do.

Then the teacher reminds young Caine that "fear is like a magnet" and "we draw to us things that we fear." The master then places the boards across a pool of liquid which he tells young Caine is a pool of acid. The boards are elevated so Caine would have to confront both his fear of heights and his fear of falling into the acid. Now keep in mind, the point has been made that Caine is perfectly able to walk across these boards. Elevating and placing the boards over a pool of acid, however, has changed reality and the experience is a learning one for both young Caine and us. As he walks across the pool, he is overcome by his fears, and falls into a pool of warm water.

A part of you fully understands this information and you will be reminded of it whenever that part of you feels a reminder of this lesson is necessary. This will be especially true in any situation where height is a factor. Whenever issues of height come up, you experience a passionate desire to enter a Quantum Focus meditative state, center, and return to the moment with a profound sense of projecting your attention into the situation with a deep inner awareness that you have nothing to fear. You will remember young Caine and the lesson that fear is like a magnet that draws what we fear to us . . . or us to what we fear.

Not only is fear unnecessary, but it also is counter-productive. So who needs it? The other lesson of course is that, when young Caine was allowed to concentrate solely on walking across the boards, it was a simple task. It became overwhelming only because he feared falling into the acid.

This new inner knowledge will have a positive impact on future experiences whether you are aware of its operating or not. As you advance in your practice, you will become more and more aware of your inner knowing in operation.

The Magic Is Already Inside You

Once again we remind you, the rewards are in both the practice and the results. The main goal of this work is learning that the experience of profound inner peacefulness, and of having our attention in the moment, will provide their own solutions and answers. We also know that this wondrous self-education process can be enhanced by applied imagery and affirmations.

Unlocking That Magic

In addition to the exercise below, memorize the following affirmations:

"Whenever I feel threatened, I automatically shift into the moment, take a deep centering and calming breath, and remind myself I have nothing to fear.

"I feel less threatened every day.

"I am feeling higher and higher and these new heights suit me well."

Mentally repeat the above affirmations 21 times 3 times a day for 21 days or until you hear your "light-sound" in the background of your mental sounding. At this time, you will mentally associate those affirmations with the light-sounding itself and it will be unnecessary to repeat the actual affirmations.

Overcoming The Fear Of Heights Exercise

Put yourself in young Caine's place and visualize yourself walking the boards spanning across a glorious waterfall. See, hear, taste, smell and feel the excitement as you dance and weave across the boards. See yourself doing it with your eyes closed. Elaborate on this freely and have fun!

Another way to use applied imagery is to decide on a height issue you wish to overcome and imagine yourself dealing with the situation in a thrilling and empowering way. This lends itself very well to a Power Image. We also use our highly personal light-sounds as background for these types of imaging with excellent results. Go back to chapter 18 for more about "light-sounds".

It Can Happen Quickly

Dolores Perri, an internationally renowned nutritional consultant and health activist, is also a first rate athlete who doesn't ordinarily require help in mastering her fears. But there was one fear she seemed unable to master and that was her lifelong fear of heights.

In less than ten minutes, she was guided into a Quantum State and was seeing herself standing at the edge of the highest peak, feeling totally exhilarated by her mastery and accomplishment in overcoming her fear of heights. She was advised to focus on her Power Image whenever she had a moment or two for self-empowerment.

She was then guided back, with the assurance that the seeds for overcoming her fear of heights had been planted and would bear fruit whenever she was ready to test them. Within months of our ten minute session, Dolores and her husband went to Colorado and headed for the mountains. But, let Dolores finish this story with her account of what happened:

> "Our group went to Boulder, Colorado to see the Flatiron Mountains, called such because they look like two old fashioned irons standing side by side. I was determined to climb up these mountains and, as I proceeded up the mountain, I had no problem at first because the trails were very wide. As we proceeded up the mountain trails, they became narrower, but I kept going.
>
> "When I reached a point on the mountain where I had a spectacular view of the University

of Colorado, I stopped and was able to sit down and drink in the beauty of it all. The view was unobstructed as I was higher than the trees. The ledge at this point was about five feet and, as I realized where I was, a twinge of the old fear came back to me.

"At this point I was beginning to form a cold sweat. However, I said to myself, Oh No! that's not going to happen to me anymore. I stood up, swung around and felt a feeling of exhilaration and accomplishment at overcoming a lifelong senseless fear of heights. I have taken pictures of this accomplishment and will gladly show them to one and all."

She added her thanks and the comment, ". . .you have opened up other areas in my life that I thought would be off-limits. What a joy to have no limitations put on you by a false sense of fears".

Enough said!

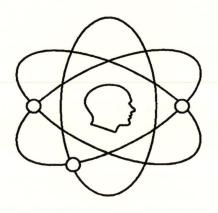

Chapter 20

Overcoming Fear of Water

"The river flows a winding course to the sea. We must be equally flexible if we hope to reach our goals."
N. BOSWELL

Since we were all aquatic during the first nine months of our lives, overcoming the fear of water is very easy to accomplish. We all share memories and images of peacefully and gracefully floating in a pool of liquid much like the water you now fear. In a flash you can reconnect with these images. The safe feelings that bubble up will help you overcome your fear of water and at the same time fine-tune your imagery and affirmation skills. It's a case of now you fear, now you don't. The physical exercises will help you make peace with, and restore, your natural ease in and about water.

Imagery

Let's begin with the imagery. For the next several days, whenever you shift into a Quantum Focus meditative state spend a few moments imaging how cool it was to be floating around in your mother's womb. It's the next best thing to being there. Experience a sense of weightlessness — you are fully supported, and floating around feels wonderful. You feel wonderful. After this, continue on with whatever Quantum Focus exercise you wish to work on.

Affirmations

"I AM AT PEACE WITH WATER. I KNOW HOW TO BE SAFE IN WATER. I LIKE THE FEEL OF WATER. I AM AT ONE WITH WATER." Repeat these affirmations mentally as you wash your face. Hold the cool refreshing water in your cupped hands and dip your face happily into the water. Repeat the mental affirmations as you shower — really get into enjoying the moment and enjoying the water. Repeat the affirmations every time you practice floating in your mind's eye's "womb". Put some joy into your mind's voice . . . mentally repeat the above affirmations in a playful sing-song way.

Water Sports

We highly recommend you do these water exercises as they are both enjoyable and empowering. When one of the authors (M.E.) was in Ft. Lauderdale Florida, he was introduced to a most wonderful flotation device that is perfect for re-establishing your relationship with water. The magical device is an empty plastic ½ gallon water jug (with the top on, naturally). This device, when one is held in each hand, is the perfect floatation tool and helps you experience floating by simply raising your feet off the pool floor. Or you could arch your head, lean into the water, hands spread wide apart and do a live man's float.

Now arch back, raise your hands, put your feet back on the floor and stand up. Notice that you feel at home in the water. Notice that you feel secure in the water. Experience the joy of making friends with the water.

More Imagery & Affirmations

Now let's fine-tune your imagery skills and use water as the old friend who just rolls along as we get back in touch with our Quantum nature.

Shift into a Quantum Focus meditative state and imagine you are a beautiful sunflower in a hot, dry field. The sunlight is suddenly shaded as some needed rain clouds float into view. And now imagine a burst of rain. Feel it, taste it, smell it, listen to it.

And now watch the water turn into a lake — now you are sailing, wind in your hair. Hear the entire environment as if it were a concert created just for you. Gently put your hand and arm into the cool and refreshing water, cup some and splash your face with it. Now take a deep breath and move into another setting.

This time you are at the end of a pool. As soon as you recognize yourself, dive in and effortlessly swim to the other end of the pool. As you swim, play the "Rocky" theme in your head. Hear the crowd roar with appreciation as you gracefully glide though the water and mentally repeat your affirmations. "I am at peace with water. I am one with water. I know how to be safe in water." And, "I do it".

Consider this chapter a comprehensive program in fear management and remember how good it feels to overcome it. Happy sails to you.

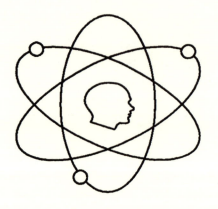

Chapter 21

Overcoming the Fear of Flying

"I must admit I was afraid of sitting next to you on this flight when you said you had a fear of flying. Yet, we've been airborne over two hours, are almost to our destination and you have been totally calm and relaxed," said the businessman to the young man in the next seat.

"I may have used the wrong word," replied the other, becoming visibly more nervous even as he responded. "I have no fear of flying . . . but am I ever terrified of landing!"

ANONYMOUS

Watch That Last Step

While most of you who are reading this chapter probably do not find the above at all amusing, you will probably admit it is very close to the truth. We have helped countless numbers of people overcome their fear of "flying", almost invariably to find that they never had a fear of flying. But they did have great concerns about landing, especially a concern about an unplanned, unpleasant landing into the side of a desolate mountain or a shark-infested ocean.

Some of the discomfort people feel about flying can also be due to a fear of crowds and/or claustrophobia. These additional fears will show themselves in other times than when you board an aircraft. So if your arousal only responds to planes, it is probably a pretty good guess that your fear is more about going down in flames instead of arriving safely than about crowds or close quarters.

A Major Hindrance

There is so much available for us to see and do in today's world. And much of it is most easily accessible or only accessible by airplane. True, we can drive across the United States to visit a distant coast, or sail across an ocean to see Europe, Africa or Asia, but few of us have annual vacations that afford us the luxury of the time required. This means, if we are not willing to fly, or if we can fly only at such great personal discomfort that flying becomes an ordeal, we must of necessity miss out on many of life's pleasures (or suffer so much getting to them that the pain overwhelms and negates that pleasure).

While misery is alleged to enjoy company, it will probably give you very little comfort to discover that some surveys find that as many as 25 million Americans may be facing this problem.

We Already Know Flying Is Safe

Why do we feel this way about flying? We know, intellectually, that air travel is statistically the safest mode of transportation. We know, intellectually, that a thousand times more people are killed in automobile accidents on U. S. highways annually than die in all the airplane accidents which occur throughout the world. (One statistic said there were 1.82 accidents per million takeoffs, and 1.62 per million for the 747.)

We recognize the convenience of flying as regards the tremendous time savings it represents to us. We realize that our fear of flying is irrational, that is, it doesn't make sense. We really have no reason to be afraid to fly. In spite of all this intellectual understanding, we can still be afraid of flying... even terrified of flying. This is simply because fears like this do not come from our intellectual thought processes. They come from our emotional processes.

A Good System...

These emotional processes feed on information that is not necessarily logical. When an airplane does crash, we hear of large numbers of people dying, maybe hundreds. This has a great impact on us, especially at the unconscious mind level.

At the same time, we remind ourselves about the hundreds of thousands of people who survive automobile crashes every year. It seems intuitively obvious there is a much greater chance of surviving a car accident than of surviving an airplane accident. And even as we consider these ideas, our unconscious minds are focusing on these thoughts while imagining our imminent demise.

...Badly Aimed

The lack of logic here is threefold. First, in order to properly evaluate plane safety, we should be considering the 50,000 or so Americans who die in automobile accidents every year, not the numbers that survive them. Second, while we usually imagine that an airplane accident has to be fatal, the history of airplane safety is that most accidents are not the headline-filling disasters that stick in our emotional minds. Third, the odds of getting into an automobile accident are much, much greater than those of being in an airplane crash.

Our risk of dying in any accident is actually calculated from the odds of dying in the accident multiplied by *the odds of getting into that accident*. This is significantly greater for automobiles than for planes. Why, then, can we feel comfortable in our cars but still be afraid of flying? Because our emotional processes don't care a wit about logic or mathematics! They're too busy being stuck on imagining us in one of the newspaper headline type disasters. So what do we do?

Door Number One

We have three choices. First, we can resign ourselves never to fly. It is possible to go through life and never set foot on an airplane. If we look hard enough, we can even find examples that prove this is the right decision. There have been people who were afraid to fly, flew anyway and were killed in a crash. "Aha!", we say, figuring this is evidence that being born without wings means we are not supposed to fly. "No flying for me!" However, this means forfeiting all the benefits air travel offers. It limits life and detracts from our enjoyment of it. For most people, this is not an acceptable option.

And we can find examples of people who were afraid of flying who died in train crashes or automobile accidents, who were maybe even hit by a falling plane while they were on the ground! What your example really proves is only that some people die in accidents, whether they are afraid to fly or not.

Door Number Two

Second, we can decide that we will fly. Some people manage to get from point A to point B through the use of drugs. They pop tranquilizers, take sleeping pills in the hope of actually sleeping through the flight, or drink alcohol excessively, sometimes risking the use of several of these methods at the same time rather than be conscious of being on a plane. Does this work? Only to a minor degree. For the most part, these people still go through the agony of their fears. It is just that they go through them earlier as they preplay the experience in their minds. Then they go through the flight itself in a somewhat reduced mental capacity. Finally, they go through the pain of recovering from their chosen method. Again, for most people, this is not an acceptable solution.

Door Number Three

Which brings us to choice number three. We can resolve to do something about our fear. There are a number of programs available that attempt to combat this particular fear. Some are run by private therapists. Others are run by groups, often at the request, or under the auspices of airlines. Private counseling is also available. And let's not forget the hypnotists of the world.

Of these programs, the ones that are based on rational thought and understanding generally take the longest and have the lowest success rates. (Remember, this fear is not based on rational thought!) Hypnotists, at least competent ones, seem to fare much better. (They are dealing more with the emotional side of the brain.) Or, you can use your Quantum Focus technique which gives you access to the same part of the mind that a competent hypnotist would access. And, you don't need to find a competent hypnotist.

Re-Aiming The System

The exercise is really very easy to do. It is based on replacing the old irrational beliefs with new, less-irrational beliefs. You will use the same powerful part of your mind that has been so effective in producing fear in the past to now produce a level of comfort. Once you set it into operation, it will operate just as automatically as it ever did, but with much more desirable results. You will easily refocus its thoughts (or imaginings) away from the old patterns and onto more useful ones.

Begin by entering your most relaxed Quantum Focus state, whichever one that happens to be for you. When you have comfortably done so, begin the procedure that follows.

I Can Fly Exercise
(or The Peter Pan Principle)

Begin by imagining yourself with a chance to go someplace you've always wanted to go. But it is even better than that. You've won an all-expense-paid trip to this dream destination . . . for two. And, if you haven't a partner you want to go with, the partner of your choosing will be supplied by the contest sponsors. So choose anyone you wish. The only little question in your mind about this trip at all is that it is by air. And you are not quite sure about that.

Now begins the magic. Imagine yourself totally involved in packing your clothes for the trip. You picture yourself doing the things you want to do while you are packing the appropriate clothing. If you pack a bathing suit, maybe you are imagining yourself scuba diving, snorkeling or lazily swimming in blue waters of exactly the right temperature to wash all the stress right out of your body and mind. Maybe, you're just lying on the beach, soaking up the warm soothing rays of the sun. Perhaps you are packing clothes to ski in, and feel the cool wind in your face as you race down the side of a picture-perfect mountain in a picture-perfect run.

You are so involved in the fun and excitement of being there, you simply forget that you are going to fly to get there. It is almost as if there simply isn't room in your thoughts for the actual flight itself.

See yourself, in your mind's eye, en route to the airport. Of course, you are not driving. The contest includes a stretch limousine to take you to, and pick you up from, the airports on both ends of your journey. You can just sit back, relax and focus your thoughts on the romantic evenings during your vacation. You and your ideal partner, in wildly romantic and erotic settings. Wow. Feel what that is like all the way down into the core of your being.

What? At the airport already?

Continue to imagine yourself checking in (at the first class check-in, of course), going through security, totally lost in thought about the great times you are going to experience on this trip. You find a seat in the waiting lounge and sit down to relax. The moment you feel the support beneath you, you relax even deeper . . . and daydream even more peacefully about the upcoming event. Those romantic evenings may have really captured your attention, perhaps even spilling over into romantic mornings and romantic afternoons. Roses, a bottle of wine, candlelight, a tray of fruit and cheeses and your most desired partner.

What? Boarding already?

Imagine yourself boarding the plane, still engrossed in other thoughts. Too busy thinking about the good times to spend even a moment on the flight. Let's get there already!. Buckling yourself into your first class seat. Being served something to drink and nibble on. Damn. Won't they leave me alone? They keep interrupting my plans. Now where was I? Oh yes . . . this is the stuff paperback novels are made of. Only I am a major player herein.

As you occasionally become a little more aware of your surroundings, you are very comfortable. In fact, you are conditioned to relax even more every time you feel your body in your seat. And the more you notice it, the more you relax. Which is fine because it lets you focus your thoughts on the real objective of this trip. Complete and total pleasure . . . physically, mentally, emotionally and even spiritually. Yes, you think to yourself as you realize the truth in it, eroticism can be spiritual as well as mental or physical.

You are always aware enough of your surroundings to follow all the instructions that are given. You know the stuff . . . tray tables up or seat belts fastened, how the oxygen masks work or where the emergency doors are located . . . all that routine. Yet, you are also so deeply engrossed in your mental rehearsal for the main event that you hardly notice them at a conscious level. It's all there at some level where you can retrieve it if you wanted to . . . you just have too much else to think about.

As the plane closes up the doors, pushes away from the jetway and begins to taxi to the runway, your most consuming thought is, "Why aren't we there yet? I have some big plans and you are really slowing me down."

Even as the plane begins its takeoff, your only notice of it is the gentle push it gives you back into your seat. Your perception of the seat triggers that deeper relaxation response you have programmed. You relax completely and almost drift off into a real dream. Just can't wait to get there. You gently relax even more as your imagination now goes into high gear. You think of more ways to enjoy this vacation than you previously thought possible.

Your fertile mind is going to multiply your good time severalfold because you have entered that most resourceful level of mind, the ultimate Quantum State.

Here, you can simultaneously function in both worlds in ultimate ways. You can be conscious of your traveling companion, enjoy the amenities of first class, and still lose yourself in your thoughts of the upcoming holiday. In fact, you are so engrossed in the positive aspects of your trip, you almost miss the actual landing. The somewhat sudden (from your preoccupied perspective) application of the brakes and reversal of the engines alerts you to the fact you have arrived and landed safely.

This is the first time you realize that you have just flown a great distance with complete comfort and ease. That same part of your mind that once caused you difficulty now functions to give you absolute comfort and ease. You know, deep within you, that it will continue to do so for all future flights.

Repeat this exercise until you automatically go through it completely without having to remind yourself of what comes next. Once a day is enough to reprogram your unconscious mind to the state you want it. However, you can do it more frequently if you want to. Just remember there are other things in the world you might want to do with your life too. (Most people get so into this exercise that we have to tell them to stop!)

By beginning this process as little as two or three weeks before you intend to fly, you can program the automatic relaxation response into your unconscious mind so strongly that it takes over for you. You hop on the plane, maybe even still feeling a little uneasy or skeptical, but the rest is automatic. You find yourself relaxing every time you become aware of your body. When you sit down, you relax. When the plane moves, you relax. When it begins the takeoff and pushes you into your seat and you become more aware of your body, you relax more. And once you've successfully programmed it, it will stay with you for as long as it is useful to you.

That is fine if I'm going on vacation, you may say, but what about business travel? The same principle applies. Because it is much easier to become fully absorbed while fantasizing about your ideal lover than about a successful sales meeting, do the above exercise until it flows automatically. Once you have that down, then begin substituting the positive results of your planned business trip wherever you can do that.

Imagine that important client signing on the dotted line, the meeting going better than you'd planned, meeting new contacts, maybe finding a more exciting, challenging and rewarding job. Let your imagination fill in the details that are suited to you. You will still program in that automatic relaxation response, often to the extent that you cannot get yourself upset about flying even if you want to. (Of course, misdirected luggage doesn't count.)

We can almost hear you asking, "Where's the Peter Pan part?" The answer is, you don't have to deliberately insert it. Given enough time, you'll find it occurring in your fantasy all on its own. And it shows up it the darndest places!

Have a great flight.

Some Additional Things To Do

While you are still beginning to overcome your old concern with flying, you may find it helpful to arrive at the airport a short time before your flight. Allow just enough time to get your bags checked (at least 30 minutes before your flight to be reasonably certain they will be on your plane) and enough time to clear security (which varies greatly depending on the political climate). By not arriving too much ahead of time, you will avoid having to spend a lot of extra time sitting and waiting.

This tip has more to do with convenience and comfort than with fear of flying — but if you get bored enough, your mind may want to search for something to occupy it. Until you have completed your Quantum Focus reprogramming, there is always the possibility it may make some light contact with your old pattern. Then again, it may not . . . but why not make it as easy on yourself as possible?

Keep yourself busy during your wait. This can be a good time to practice your Quantum Focus exercise. Try not to smile too much, though, or give audible voice to too many sounds of pleasure while you are practicing. Remember, there are other people around you in the waiting area, some of whom will be getting on your flight. You may spend many hours with them and could find it difficult to explain moaning in the airport. And keep your eye on the time. You want to become unengrossed soon enough to make that flight.

If you find you have only a few minutes, a Power Image is an especially useful tool. Flash on this for 30 seconds and you'll be ready and rarin' to go.

Other Focuses

It is especially useful to keep yourself busy during your flight. Work, read, sleep, Quantum Focus, or do just about anything that occupies your attention fully. This way, you will avoid listening for every sound and noticing the routine changes in the plane's position. These are normal parts of flying. They pay pilots, mechanics and crew lots of money to create them. Let's keep them out of the bag of tricks available to your unconscious mind and keep it busy doing something you want it doing.

It might also be a good idea to avoid stimulants before you plan to fly. This is just one of several times it can be exceptionally beneficial to avoid caffeine, for example. And we know that you would never use any recreational chemicals. You can get a better "high" through Quantum Focusing!

Note: Since this chapter was written, TWA Flight 800 blew up off Long Island, New York, killing 230 people. It dominated the headlines for weeks, which illustrates our point. While the last year was a horrendous one for airline accidents, it doesn't come close to our everyday driving record. While 110 people died in a ValueJet crash in the Everglades, 230 in TWA's crash, and two others in a Delta accident, it took only 2½ days on our highways to kill that many people. Match up one horrendous year for air travel against any 2½ days on our highways. Which is safer? (Also note: Most passengers walked away from the Delta accident and everyone walked away from several other planes which made forced emergency landings due to equipment problems. Most people *do* walk away from airplane mishaps.)

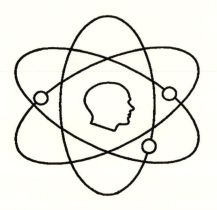

Chapter 22

Overcoming The Fear Of Failure

"Not failure, but low aim, is crime."
JAMES RUSSELL LOWELL

There are two irrational fears which cause our population more trouble than any other person could ever cause. They prevent us from even attempting to do things, thus guaranteeing that we will not do them. Among the things they prevent us from doing are improving our careers, finding better jobs, becoming more successful (financially and otherwise), building better relationships, and having more of every good thing life has to offer. Their names are Fear Of Failure and Fear Of Success. (See chapter 23 for more on the fear of success.)

The fear of failure stems from early lessons we are taught which tell us failure is bad. We never want to fail. Above all else, don't fail. Winning isn't everything — it's the only thing. We are certain you can add dozens of similar comments to which you relate personally. We have all been indoctrinated with this dread of failure.

This conditioning takes a terrible toll. We are trained to avoid failing to such an extent that there are many of us — certainly you know someone, maybe intimately — who avoid taking risks in order to avoid failing. After all, if we don't try to do something, we cannot fail at it! And we can always tell ourselves, "I could of gotten an A in that course, if I wanted to" or "I could have gotten that promotion, if I wanted to" or "I could have gotten that new job, if I wanted to" or "I could have gotten a date with him/her, if I wanted to" or "I could have been elected president of that club, if I wanted to" or "I could have won that contest, if I wanted to".

Think back into your own life. When was the last time you said, "I could have done _____, if I wanted to" to yourself or anyone else? When you remember, you'll know what this fear feels like. Unfortunately, for many people, they don't have to think back very far. Their lives are dominated by the fear of failure. In essence, their happiness has become a prisoner of this fear.

The good news is that, like all our mental programming, the fear of failure can be reprogrammed by us. We can reprogram our minds to view "failure" in a new context. Beginning with reading this chapter, you will never suffer failure again, no matter what you attempt to do or how ambitious your goal. You see, there is no "failure".

No matter what you do, you always produce a result. If you apply for a new job, you produce a result. You may or may not get the job . . . but you produce a result. If you try out for a team, you produce a result. You may or may not get onto the team . . . but you produce a result. If you try to write a novel, you produce a result. That result may be a great novel, it may be a terrible novel, it may or may not get published, it may be nothing but blank pages . . . but you produce a result. So, no matter what you attempt, you cannot fail because you always produce a result.

Now, you have undoubtedly noticed that some of the results listed above are not the desired results. Herein lies the elimination of failure. When we produce a result other than the desired result, we have successfully produced a result . . . just not the result we wanted. So we examine how we went about our attempt, adjust it for the next time, and move ahead with a better idea of how to go about producing the result we want. Results which are not the desired results ARE NOT FAILURES! THEY ARE LEARNING EXPERIENCES FROM WHICH WE GAIN THE KNOWLEDGE TO PRODUCE BETTER RESULTS THE NEXT TIME!!!

The first thought coming into your mind is probably what happens if I produce a second result I don't want? You examine your process and refine it again. You are now in an even better position to produce the desired results because you have more knowledge.

It will help you to appreciate this if you remember the account of Thomas Edison's invention of the incandescent light bulb. Edison tried over 5,000 experiments before he found a filament that would work in his bulb. When he was being interviewed by reporters about his tenacity, they asked him, "How is it you could keep on going after you failed 5,000 times?" To this, Edison replied, "You are mistaken. I did not fail 5,000 times. I SUCCESSFULLY IDENTIFIED 5,000 WAYS THAT DO NOT WORK!"

From now on, whenever you try to do anything, remember that you will successfully produce some result. If it is not the result you want, you have successfully identified a way that did not work. Learn from it and go on.

For those who think this advice is easy to give but doesn't apply to successful people, read the biographies of industrial giants like Henry Ford. Most went broke, usually several times, before they made their fortunes. Could it be that all their "failures" provided them with enough knowledge of what would work to then permit them to use what did work?

The first step in overcoming the fear of failure was simply to realize that the above is so. You cannot fail to produce some result, no matter what you do. Sometimes that result might even be that nothing happens. But that nothing is still a result.

The next step is to realize that you can learn from undesired results. Adjust your method to improve your chance of producing the result you want. Remember, the definition of insanity is taking an action and producing a result, taking the same action again and producing the same result again, taking the same action again and producing the same result again, and then taking the same action but expecting a different result the next time.

So you have already completed half the process of overcoming fear of failure. Step three is to use the exercises below to convey this message into the parts of your mind that haven't yet accepted it. Repeat these as often as you feel the need. Each time you do, they will instill the above ideas into deeper and deeper regions of your unconscious mind from which they will operate with all the force and power that the fear of failure used to.

The No More Failure Exercise

Put yourself into a Quantum Focus state and just drift deeper and deeper into the profound feelings of inner peace. When you feel totally at peace with yourself, take several deep breaths to anchor yourself to this peaceful place.

Now, keeping these safe, peaceful feelings, begin to imagine yourself going out into the world and becoming involved in situations that might have been disturbing or fearful to you in the past. But, now you cannot fail, so let yourself take part in all the fantasies you wish. This is where you start to turn dreams into reality.

Begin with situations that would only be mildly threatening or uncomfortable. Perhaps you are applying for a new job. Maybe you're working on a promotion at your present job. You decide what things you want to do and go do them.

See yourself as if you were watching yourself on a movie screen. Watch as you deal with everything going on inside and outside of you with ease and grace. Notice how often you obtain the result you want and how great that feels. Notice too those times you produce a result other than the one you want. Watch as you learn from these results, modify your approach and attempt your goal again. See yourself going in and around these situations with comfort, poise and style.

If you feel even the slightest tinge of discomfort, simply breathe in deeply to reactivate the peaceful feelings of your Quantum Focus state and dispel the discomfort.

As you find you can comfortably begin to expand your mental horizon, gradually increase the difficulty of the situation in which you imagine yourself. You might imagine yourself getting ready for an interview. Or maybe it's asking that special someone for a date. Maybe it's taking up painting or going into your own business. Whatever you want to do, this is the time to begin it, even if it may require a series of days with each day increasing your ability to handle the situations comfortably, but you will rapidly notice a difference in your reactions.

By the third or fourth session, you will be able to handle situations that only a day or two earlier might have been beyond your tolerance. Now, notice how you are able to handle increasingly difficult situations with comfort. See yourself moving with confidence into places or situations that you wish to address with a deep sense of ability and ease.

When you are feeling really confident with your new ability, simply allow yourself to return to your normal state of waking consciousness, knowing you have retrained your mind to react in this more useful way to these situations.

Dream Exercise

As you learned in chapter 14, seeding your dreams is the first step towards programming dreams. We can use our dreams to instill new messages into our unconscious mind. Here we will use dreams to painlessly reprogram our feelings towards failure while we sleep. Before retiring tonight, please do the following exercise and sleep deeply and peacefully.

Relax by scanning every part of your body for tension or strain and then releasing it. Actually tense and relax your toes, feet, ankles, calves, shins, knees, and on upwards until your entire body is fully relaxed.

Concentrate on the idea that tonight, as you sleep, you will be having an adventurous and thoroughly enjoyable dream. In this dream, you will be doing something you have always dreamed of doing but haven't attempted before because you were afraid it could never be. Let your imagination go and do whatever you would like to do. All kinds of places and situations are fair game now. You will be doing whatever you want to, with ease and comfort.

You will start out as an observer, that is, like watching yourself in a movie . . . until you quickly feel comfortable stepping into that movie and taking over the lead role yourself. You then feel the thorough enjoyment of your new ability, the freedom to do whatever you please without any concern about how it will turn out. You know that you will benefit from any result you produce, and you will always produce a result. You even enjoy the very thought of trying new things. Relax and discover how much fun your life can really be.

Now imagine that all the blood in your brain is flowing downward into your hands and feet.

This exercise can promote a deep peaceful sleep and the prior thinking about dreaming helps you become conscious of your dreams as they occur. You may be very pleased to discover how comfortable you are when you face a challenge in the everyday world from now on. And that is step four, the last step to overcoming fear of failure . . . get out there and attempt the things you want to do. Use your new skill to make your life more like you want it to be. Your exercise and dreams have paved the way. Take advantage of them today.

(If you aren't completely familiar with Chapter 14, we recommend reading it again.)

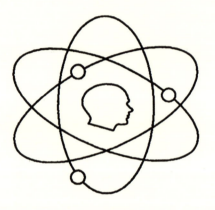

Chapter 23

Overcoming The Fear Of Success

"We must walk consciously only partway toward our goal, and then leap in the dark to our success."
HENRY DAVID THOREAU

Afraid To Succeed . . .

It is difficult for most of us to accept that anyone could actually be afraid of succeeding, particularly if we have suffered from the fear of failure. But this fear occurs much more commonly than is usually recognized. And the irony of it is that both the fear of failure and the fear of success can be operating on us at the same time.

Imagine how quickly that will freeze you in your tracks. Afraid to succeed and afraid to fail. You have to stand still and do nothing in order to avoid this trap. Otherwise, you have to be a little successful, but not too successful. Or, you have to fail a little bit, but not too much. Neither of these options makes sense.

. . . And Don't Even Know It

The reason the fear of success seems to be an unlikely problem is that it operates completely below the level of our awareness. We could feel the fear of failure pulling at us, until we used the exercises in chapter 22 to eliminate it. But we are unaware of the fear of success consciously. We can recognize its presence, however, by the actions it prompts and the results they bring.

Unmistakable Sign

The fear of success creates a telltale pattern, just like an animal leaves its tracks for us to see after it has passed. And the tracks of the fear of success always look the same. It is the beginning to do something, and doing it very well until, always, something "happens" to derail us and the project falls apart. It always appears that what "happens" is something outside of our control. A closer look will prove this is not so. The something that "happens" is always something we have invited into our lives specifically to derail our success. It is something we invite unconsciously in order to satisfy our fear of success. In essence, we sabotage ourselves with invisible booby-traps and hidden internal minefields that keep us from getting what we want.

The forms this might take are numerous. Examples include the bright young businessperson who has begun to climb the corporate ladder, but somehow has a personality clash with the one person above her who can stop her progress; the person whose relationships always get *almost* to where they want them, but then fall apart for some reason (not uncommonly because the person gets involved with an outside affair . . . and gets caught); and the person who demonstrates talent at anything but finds him/herself embroiled in a legal confrontation over something stupid. The story is the same. The person with the fear of success starts a venture usually demonstrating ability well ahead of the average person's ability . . . but then derails for whatever reason.

This happens because something inside has monitored our early success and, because it had already decided we were not to be successful, causes us to do something that will put and end to our successful streak. Technically, it is not a fear. It is a judgment that we are not worthy of that success. For many reasons, all of them irrational, our unconscious mind simply decides we are worthy of only so much success. As long as we do not exceed that level of success, everything is fine. But when we threaten to be more successful, it then kicks in to stop us before we gain more success than it has decided we deserve.

These arbitrary limits as to how successful we are allowed to be come from many sources. Just to give you an idea how this works, consider the following two examples.

Jane's Story

Right out of college, Jane takes a job selling real estate. She is a whiz. Jane sells houses at three times the rate of the rest of the beginners. By the end of her third month, she is earning about $5,000 per month in commissions while her "peers" are only bringing in about $1,700. And she is poised to continue her meteoric climb. But in month four, "funny" things begin to happen to her. She starts to take more time off to do things that she simply "must" do; she forgets appointments with clients, she doesn't get her paperwork in promptly, she misplaces a contract she was to get the buyer's signature on, and so forth. In a nutshell, her sales slow down to a plateau at that level . . . maybe even decline a little.

Investigation reveals that Jane admires her father very much. She believes him to be a good person, hard-working with lots of intelligence, and successful. It turns out that her father is a vice president with an office furniture supplier. He has several stores reporting to him and is responsible for about 100 people and millions of dollars of sales. It also turns out that he is earning $62,500 per year . . . or just about $5,000 per month! Something inside Jane has decided that she is certainly not worth more than her father — that it would be disrespectful or disloyal to him to earn more money than he earns. So this something goes into action to be certain she is not disloyal.

A Superstar

Ted was a natural athlete. He excelled all through high school and college at baseball, football and basketball. He couldn't play all three because of the time required. He came from a rather poor family and, despite offers of several athletic scholarships to colleges, still felt a moral obligation to work part-time to help his family. Ted was most interested in basketball. So he took the basketball scholarship, focused on his ballplaying during the time he had and improved even more. He was good enough to get an offer from the pros at the end of his junior year in college. It was for a lot of money. He took the offer rather than finish school.

Ted had always been a very well-behaved kid. He came from a family that was poor only in financial terms. They were rich in many other ways. He had deep religious convictions about what was right and wrong, he was loved and well-treated by his parents and siblings, he loved them and treated them well in return. But during his first year in pro ball, he started getting into fights with his teammates. Then he was arrested for illegal drugs. He wasn't *that* good a player. The team dropped him, and no other one wanted him.

When he went into therapy, one of the things that revealed itself was his sense of getting more from life than he deserved. At a deep level, he felt he was not worth all that he was getting. His unconscious fear of success took over the job of correcting his perceived imbalance.

It Can Be Overcome

While we would like to report that both of the above people are doing well now, we cannot. Ted just disappeared as soon as his court-ordered therapy was complete. Jane, on the other hand, did overcome her fear of success. As of last contact, she was a very successful real estate broker and was earning over $200,000 a year.

So if you notice a tendency in your own life to sabotage anything just when it looks like you are going to be really successful with it, you may have identified a fear of success. You can overcome it and grant yourself room to reach for the stars with the following exercises.

Overcoming the Fear of Success Exercise

Put yourself into a Quantum Focus state and just drift deeper and deeper into the profound feelings of inner peace. When you feel totally at peace with yourself, take several deep breaths to anchor yourself to this peaceful place.

Now, keeping these safe, peaceful feelings, begin to imagine yourself going out in to the world and becoming involved in situations that might have caused you difficulty in the past, things that might have started well but then gone awry. But, now you cannot fail, so let yourself take part in all the fantasies you wish. This is where you start to turn dreams into reality.

Begin with any situations you remember that might be only minor disappointments and only slightly uncomfortable. You know what these situations are better than we do, so you supply them. You decide what things you want to do and go do them.

See yourself as if you were watching yourself on a movie screen. Watch as you deal with everything going on inside and outside of you with ease and grace. Notice how often you now obtain the result you want and how great that feels. See yourself going in and around these situations with comfort, poise and style.

If you feel even the slightest tinge of discomfort, simply breathe in deeply to reactivate the peaceful feelings of your Quantum Focus state and dispel the discomfort.

As you find you can comfortably begin to expand your mental horizon, gradually increase the difficulty of the situation in which you imagine yourself. As you get to the more difficult tasks or the larger gains, imagine that a messenger arrives with a telegram just as you are beginning to be successful. You open it and discover that it comes from Universal Intelligence (or God, if you are more comfortable with that name). It says you are being granted your success because YOU DESERVE IT. You read it again. Something much greater than you is telling you that **you deserve to be successful**.

Now, feel how good it is to know that you DO deserve to be successful. Notice too how you are able to handle your increasing success with comfort. See yourself moving into places or situations you wish to address with a deep sense of confidence, ability and ease.

When you are feeling really confident with your new ability, simply allow yourself to return to your normal state of waking consciousness, knowing you have retrained your mind to react in this more useful way to these situations.

Dream Exercise

As you learned in chapter 14, seeding your dreams is the first step towards programming dreams for success in your waking life. We can use our dreams to instill new messages into our unconscious mind. Here we will use dreams to painlessly reprogram our feelings towards success while we sleep. Before retiring tonight please do the following exercise and sleep deeply and peacefully.

Relax by scanning every part of your body for tension or strain and then releasing it. Actually tense and relax your toes, feet, ankles, calves, shins, knees, and on upwards until your entire body is fully relaxed.

Concentrate on the idea that tonight, as you sleep, you will be having an adventurous and thoroughly enjoyable dream. In this dream, you will be doing many things, all of them very successfully. Let your imagination go and do whatever you would like to do, all kinds of places and situations are fair game now. You will be doing whatever you want to do, with ease and comfort.

You will start out as an observer, that is, like watching yourself in a movie . . . until you quickly feel comfortable stepping into that movie and taking over the lead role yourself. When you do, notice as you step into your own body that there is a little box, wrapped in old newspaper, lying somewhere around the darker reaches of your mind. You might not have even noticed this old package, except you almost trip over it as you step into your body.

Pick it up, unwrap it and open the box. In it are all sorts of old, invalid judgments about how much you are worth. You recognize that they are useless, so you don't even read them all. Simply crumple them up, throw them out and continue stepping into your body.

Now that you are free of any old estimates of your self worth, feel the thorough enjoyment of your new ability to be successful; the freedom to do whatever you please without any concern about how it will turn out. You know that you deserve all the positive results you achieve, and you will always be able to enjoy success. Relax and take your place at the center of the richly rewarding life you've always envisioned for yourself. You will discover how much fun your life can really be.

Now imagine that all the blood in your brain is flowing downward into your hands and feet.

This exercise can promote a deep, peaceful sleep, and the prior thinking about dreaming helps you become conscious of your dreams as they occur. You may be very pleased to discover how much more easily you can achieve things. It is almost as though your ability to sabotage yourself was thrown out along with that old box. Use your new ability to accept your well-deserved success to make your life more like you want it to be.

(If you still haven't read Chapter 14, shame on you.)

Chapter 24

Overcoming The Fear Of Public Speaking

"Speech is power: speech is to persuade, to convert, to compel."
RALPH WALDO EMERSON

Taming The King Of The Beasts

A Christian who had displeased the Emperor was thrown to the lions for the Emperor's entertainment. As he was tossed into the arena, the half-dozen hungry lions saw the poor fellow and charged up to him in order to devour him. But as the first lion reached him, the man leaned over and whispered something into the lion's ear. The lion came to a screeching halt. The other lions, seeing the first stop, paused to confer with their leader. Then they all turned and walked away from this lucky Christian.

The Emperor was both annoyed and amazed by what he had witnessed. He sent his Centurions to fetch the man. When they brought him to the Emperor, the Emperor asked him what he had said to the lion. "My Lord," replied the man, "I merely told him that right after dinner, he was going to have to say a few words."

You're Not Alone

Now we don't know for a fact that the fear of public speaking goes back this far into history, but we wouldn't be surprised. And as for the current feeling about "saying a few words", a recent survey found public speaking ranked as the most common fear in the United States. The fear of death was ranked second. And fifty percent more people listed public speaking as their number one fear than listed the fear of death as their greatest fear.

While there may be some comfort in knowing there are so many people who are afraid of getting up at a dinner or a party and addressing the crowd, there is sadness too. Misery may love company, but who wants to be miserable? You see, the fear of public speaking is one of the *easiest* fears to overcome.

An Equal Opportunity Fear

We've worked with executives, college students, athletes, homemakers and many, many other people who have had this challenge. There seems to be absolutely no discrimination as to who suffers from this problem. The good news is that they were all able to conquer their fear quickly and easily. In only two to three weeks, even the shiest were able to speak in public in an acceptable way.

You Already Have The Key

There is one sure way to overcome the fear of public speaking! The way is, of course, speaking publicly. It only requires the skills and abilities you have been developing and fine-tuning in your daily practice of Quantum Focus meditation. You already have everything needed for mastery of public speaking. You are able to jump right into public speaking, because your daily practice of meditation and imagery has set, and is setting the stage for you to do so with ease and great success!

Remember that the key to Quantum Focus is self-discovery and empowerment. When you discover the Quantum Forces dwelling within you — when you begin to understand that the practice itself is simply a device for putting you in touch with the awesome power within you — you will automatically shed your fears. Meanwhile you can accelerate the natural process by cultivating your Quantum Mind with profound peacefulness and ease.

Beyond The Intellect

The beauty of Quantum Focus is that, as you practice and develop your creative skills and abilities, you learn by doing. The key to mastering public speaking is the obvious enjoyment of doing so. So let's get mellow, and mentally review the keys of public speaking.

Pause for a moment, and shift into a Quantum Focus meditative state. Scan your body from the bottom of your feet to the top of you head. Mentally become aware of your body becoming loose and at ease. Then bring yourself back to the moment and resume reading, staying aware that you are in the moment reading this chapter about overcoming the fear of public speaking, with every intention of doing so.

Remember that the key to Quantum Focus inner mastery is getting beyond intellect and being totally in the moment. When we are in the moment we have our peak learning and doing experiences. It is also in the moment that it possible to connect to the group you are communicating with and share passion. It is passion and enthusiasm that "em-powers", or lack of passion and enthusiasm that "dis-powers" communications, and separates the great speakers from the mundane. Whether you are reciting the "Bill of Rights" or "Jack and Jill", the energy you project into the communication, and share with the group, determines the impact of your effort.

Let's review. The keys to overcoming the fear of public speaking are to:

1) Be centered
2) Be in the moment
3) Be attentive

You will also notice that these are the 3 B's of Quantum Focus and universal in all paths to enlightenment and spiritual growth.

Are You An Orator?

Now, this chapter is not designed to make you a fabulous speaker with your audience hanging on your every word. You are already this good. Reconnecting with your inner orator may take some additional training and practice, however. But with the tools in this chapter, you can easily get up in front of a group of people, friends or strangers, and make an acceptable presentation without your knees knocking, your voice cracking or your stomach or tongue getting tied into knots.

You may surprise yourself with how quickly you can become accomplished. One young athlete with whom we worked did so well that, after delivering a short speech at a sports banquet, he received several offers to speak at other events. He had originally tried to find a way to avoid this dinner altogether so he would not have to speak. When he found this was going to be impossible, he came for help in a state of near panic. We showed him how to center himself in the Quantum moment and bask in the glow of an explosive round of applause. While he declined the additional opportunities, he is now very comfortable in front of an audience.

Another young woman who was climbing the corporate ladder had an indescribable fear of speaking in public. She had managed so far to avoid being put in the position of having to give a presentation to senior managers. She had been convinced that, when the time came, she would just force her way through it. Well, the day came that she would be part of a team presenting a proposed project to about two dozen senior managers. She was so scared (not nervous, scared!) while awaiting her turn to speak that her face had turned a ghastly, ghostly white color. She trembled as she arose from her seat on the stage to approach the lectern. Her legs wobbled on the first few steps. That's all she remembers. She fainted.

Her pallor on stage was useful to her in covering up what really happened. She claimed she had had the flu and was still a little weak and lightheaded. It appeared that everyone bought her story. But she still had to get through whatever happened to come along next.

The exercise below, coupled to her Power Image, gave her the strength to persevere. She wasn't certain she was ready when the next occasion came up. The setting was similar to the first one, but there would be several more people attending. And most of those who saw her fall over before would again be in the audience.

She was uneasy while waiting, but not panicky. She Power-Imaged her way right up to the lectern, drew a deep breath in her Quantum state, and did a pretty good job of her presentation. She wasn't yet as good as she wanted to be. However, she was better than she expected to be, and improved (both in style and in comfort) with every minute she was in front of the audience. Her comments after it was all over were:

> "It's really hard to explain. I used the Power Image even while I was going on. It almost seemed like it wasn't me talking. It was like someone else was talking and I was only observing, but I was keenly aware of everything going on all around me. I told that other person what to say, and how and when to say it. The more I did that, the more we merged into one. It was almost fun by the time I finished."

It is important to notice her mentioning her total awareness, even if it seemed somewhat dissociated at first. She was in complete control. How's that for being in the moment?

Public Speaking 101

When you incorporate the 3 B's of Quantum Focus into public speaking, (or into any activity) — that is, you are centered, in the moment and paying attention — something mystical happens. The gap between the people you are speaking to and yourself closes and the opportunity to connect opens.

The great speakers knowingly, and more often than not unknowingly, are centered, in the moment and paying attention when they speak publicly. It's natural and second nature for them to move into this space when they are speaking to the public. Often in the Arts, the artists are aware of this shift and aware that their best work is channeled through this clear bodymind-spirit mindset we call the 3 B's in Quantum Focus.

To quote Lowell Fillmore, "When you realize the presence of this indwelling power nothing in the world can offend or frighten you". Become centered, leap into the moment and pay attention, and the fear of public speaking becomes a non-problem.

Overcoming the Fear of Public Speaking Exercise

Put yourself into a Quantum Focus state and just drift deeper and deeper into the profound feelings of inner peace. When you feel totally at peace with yourself, take several deep breaths to anchor yourself to this peaceful place.

Now, keeping these safe, peaceful feelings, begin to imagine yourself going out into the world and becoming involved in situations that might have caused you difficulty in the past; situations where you are called upon to stand up in front of an audience and address them. But now you can only excel, so let yourself take part in all the fantasies you wish. This is where you start to turn dreams into reality.

Begin with any situations you remember that might be only slightly threatening and only slightly uncomfortable. You know what these situations are better than we do, so you supply them. Decide what situations are the most relevant to you and use these.

See yourself as if you were watching yourself on a movie screen. Watch as you deal with everything going on inside and outside of you with ease and grace. Notice how easy it is for you to be comfortable and coherent at the same time. Watch yourself be suave, informed, entertaining and witty. Notice how great that feels. Notice how easily this ability comes to you. See yourself going in and around these situations with comfort, poise and style.

If you feel even the slightest twinge of discomfort, simply breathe in deeply to reactivate the peaceful feelings of your Quantum Focus state and dispel the discomfort.

As you find you can comfortably begin to expand your mental horizon, gradually increase the difficulty of the situation in which you imagine yourself. As you get to the more difficult tasks, imagine a messenger arriving with a telegram just as you are beginning to feel any discomfort. You open it and discover that it comes from Universal Intelligence (or God, if you are more comfortable with that name). It says, "This is just to remind you that you are a terrific speaker." Read it again. You've impressed the creator; you must be good!

Now, step inside that you which you've been watching. Feel how good it feels to know that you are doing a great job. Notice too how you are able to handle increasingly more complex public speaking situations with comfort. See yourself moving with confidence into places or situations with a deep sense of ability and ease.

When you are feeling really confident with your new ability, simply allow yourself to return to your normal state of waking consciousness, knowing you have retrained your mind to react in this more useful way to these situations.

Whenever you have a desire and chance to improve and expand your imagery skills, imagine that you are speaking to a very large group of people. Present are all different kinds of people who just happen to share your smiling face. As you see and hear yourself address this very friendly and receptive group, become aware of how this feels. Whenever you wish to reconnect to these wonderful feelings of rapport, center yourself, think about your special audience bursting into an explosive round of applause, and bring those feelings into the moment. Now pay attention.

Dream Exercise

As you learned in chapter 14, seeding your dreams is the first step towards programming dreams. We can use our dreams to instill new messages into our unconscious mind. Here we will use dreams to painlessly reprogram our feelings towards public speaking while we sleep. Before retiring tonight please do the following exercise and sleep deeply and peacefully.

> Relax by scanning every part of your body for tension or strain and then releasing it. Actually tense and relax your toes, feet, ankles, calves, shins, knees, and on upwards until your entire body is fully relaxed.

> Concentrate on the idea that tonight, as you sleep, you will be having an adventurous and thoroughly enjoyable dream. In this dream, you will be speaking to several audiences. Perhaps one is your Academy Award acceptance speech. Another is upon receiving your Noble Prize. Let your imagination go and do whatever you would like to do, all kinds of places and situations are fair game now. You will be doing whatever you want to do, with ease and comfort.

Overcoming The Fear Of Public Speaking 213

You will start out as an observer, that is, like watching yourself in a movie . . . until you quickly feel comfortable stepping into that movie and taking over the lead role yourself. When you do, notice as you step into your own body that there is a little box, wrapped in old newspaper, lying somewhere around the darker reaches of your mind. You might not have even noticed this old package, except you almost trip over it as you step into your body.

Pick it up, unwrap it and open the box. In it are all sorts of old, invalid judgments about what you cannot do. You recognize that they are useless, so you don't even read them all. Simply throw them out and continue stepping into your body.

Now that you are free of any old ideas of your limitations, feel the thorough enjoyment of your new ability; the freedom to do whatever you please without any concern about how it will turn out. You know that you deserve all the positive results you achieve, and you will always be able to enjoy talking in public. Relax and discover how much fun your life can really be.

Now imagine that all the blood in your brain is flowing downward into your hands and feet.

This exercise can promote a deep, peaceful sleep, and the prior thinking about dreaming helps you become conscious of your dreams as they occur. You may be very pleased to discover how much more easily you can achieve things. It is almost as though your ability to sabotage yourself was thrown out along with that old box. Use your new ability to accept your well-deserved success to make your life more like you want it to be.

(If you still haven't read Chapter 14, it's time you talked to someone about it.)

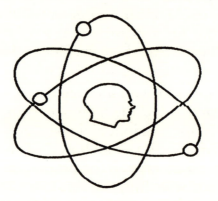

Chapter 25

Overcoming the Fear of Change

"Everyone thinks of changing the world, but no one thinks of changing himself."
LEO TOLSTOI

What Are You Afraid Of?

Change is uncomfortable! Not just for some of us; not just some of the time; not just some changes. For most of us, most changes are uncomfortable most of the time. For many of us, change is downright scary. If you don't agree with this right away, stop for a moment and think back to the changes that have occurred in your life.

What feelings did you have when you:

- Went to school for the very first time?
- Went out on your first date? (Or asked or were asked for that first date?)
- Went to interview for your first job?
- Started your first job?
- Heard through the grapevine on the job that there were "going to be some changes made at work"?

- Learned that you were going to have to park somewhere new instead of where you had been parking your car for years?
- Went for an interview for a new job, even if you'd already done this dozens of times before?
- Discovered that a favorite luncheonette or pizza place or health spa had been sold to new management?
- Moved to a new city? (Or even to a new apartment down the street from where you used to live?)
- Moved into, or out of, your own place?
- Went on a diet?
- Had to take a detour to work through a neighborhood you didn't know?
- First began driving?
- Had your first sexual encounter? (And this isn't supposed to be scary!)
- Encountered death in your circle of family or friends?
- Got married or moved in with someone else? (Or got divorced?)

    I'm sure you can think of lots more. The point is, we all have a tendency to be uncomfortable about change. This is not something we are born with but, just like so many other irrational feelings we experience, a result of the conditioning we undergo as we grow up. Remember that you are born with only two fears: the fear of loud noises and the fear of falling. All the rest are learned as we grow and develop. Just think about how eagerly children go about exploring new things. And for those of you with children, remember how unhappy you were about some of the new things they explored!
    Some of the fears we learn are useful. For example, in New York City, we learn not to step onto the tracks before the subway train pulls into the station and we learn to look both ways — several times — before crossing the street. But the fear of change is

not a useful fear. It prevents us from reaching our potential simply by keeping us away from anything new.

Fear of the Unknown

In all things, change is the agent of progress. In human beings, it is the key to growth. We each have the space we ordinarily function in which we call the "comfort zone". This is not a very good name for it because it only means that we are doing the same things we always did in the same ways we always did them and getting the same results we always got before. The notion of comfort refers only to the fact that we already know what is going to happen. There is no uncertainty.

But it is not necessarily comfortable. We all do things that get us results we do not want. Yet we continue to do these same things and get these same results. Is this "comfortable"? No, it is "familiar", that is, *unchanging*. We, as a society, dislike change so much that we have made the lack of change equivalent to comfort!

So the first thing to change is the name *comfort zone*. We'll call it the *familiar zone* for our purposes so that you begin to think of it in these terms. What happens when you attempt anything new? You have to leave your familiar zone. Just the act of doing something new, or doing something differently than you've done it before opens up the possibility of getting results you've never gotten before. Is this good or bad? Ah, here's where many of us get into trouble. We've been so conditioned to living in our familiar zone that we don't do new or different things because we're actually afraid to leave our familiar zone. Here's where the old name, comfort zone, is applicable. When we leave it, we are uncomfortable.

Enjoying the Unfamiliar

But, beginning right now, you can begin to change this by changing the name and being aware of when you do something new or different that it is unfamiliar. We will separate unfamiliar from uncomfortable in your mind. You will then separate them in your everyday feelings and actions. You will become that kid again . . . exploring new things with an anticipation and joy that will serve you, instead of a fear that makes you its servant.

One of the first things you might like to know is that you only grow when you are outside your familiar zone. If you stay within it, you cannot experience anything new. You cannot incorporate experiences you do not have into your being. So, if you need a little something extra to hang on to when you operate outside your familiar zone, just remind yourself that you are stretching and growing.

Desensitization Exercise

Put yourself into a Quantum Focus state and just drift deeper and deeper into the profound feelings of inner peace. When you feel totally at peace with yourself, take several deep breaths to anchor yourself to this peaceful place.

Now, keeping these safe, peaceful feelings, begin to imagine yourself going out into the everyday world. But the world is different today. You take a new path through it, see new people, do different things and visit situations you would usually avoid.

Perhaps you've always wanted to do something, but just never got around to it. You now know that procrastination is often just a mechanism we use to avoid doing new or different things. Maybe you've always wanted to paint, or go mountain climbing, or just redecorate you home. Choose something you think you might like to do, and then mentally do it.

Begin with situations that would be only mildly threatening or uncomfortable. Perhaps you are just taking a different route to work or shopping. Perhaps you are beginning to look for a new job; reading the want ads, calling about openings, maybe even arranging interviews.

See yourself as if you were watching yourself on a movie screen. Watch as you deal with everything going on inside and outside of you with ease and grace. See yourself going in and around these places with comfort, poise and style.

If you feel even the slightest tinge of discomfort, simply breathe in deeply to reactivate the peaceful feelings of your Quantum Focus state and dispel the discomfort.

Now, notice how you are able to handle increasingly difficult situations with comfort. See yourself moving with confidence into places or situations that you wish to address with a deep sense of ability and ease. When you are feeling really confident with your new ability, simply allow yourself to return to your normal state of waking consciousness, knowing you have retrained your mind to react in this more useful way to these situations.

As you find you can comfortably begin to expand your mental horizon, gradually increase the difficulty of the situation in which you imagine yourself. You might imagine yourself in an interview, or now considering changing careers instead of just jobs, or exploring some new area of life that used to be unfamiliar to you . . . except that you now feel a sense of anticipation and adventure as you proceed with an eagerness you might not yet understand.

As before, in other exercises, it may require a series of days with each one increasing your ability to handle the situations comfortably, but you will rapidly notice a difference in your reactions. By the third or fourth session, you will be able to handle situations that only a day or two earlier might have been beyond your tolerance.

Dream Exercise

As you undoubtedly know by now, seeding your dreams is the first step towards programming dreams, and we can use our programmed dreams to instill new messages into our unconscious mind. Here we will use dreams to painlessly reprogram our feelings towards change and the familiar zone while we sleep. Before retiring tonight, please do the following exercise and sleep deeply and peacefully.

Relax by scanning every part of your body for tension or strain and releasing it. Actually tense and relax your toes, feet, ankles, calves, shins, knees, and on upwards until your entire body is fully relaxed.

Concentrate on the idea that tonight, as you sleep, you will be having an adventurous and thoroughly enjoyable dream. In this dream, you will be doing all kinds of things (or you may even choose one specific thing you would like to change your feelings about) you may never have even considered as possible for you before. You will be in all kinds of new places and situations. You will be going wherever you want to go, with ease and comfort, always enjoying the adventure, always feeling that anticipation of discovering all kinds of wonderful things.

You will start out as an observer, that is, like watching yourself in a movie . . . until you quickly feel comfortable stepping into that movie and eagerly taking the charge of the adventure yourself. You then feel the thorough enjoyment of the freedom to go wherever you please and do whatever you want to do without any concern about how it will turn out.

Naturally, you think through everything first, and only do things which can result in positive benefits for you . . . but you expect these positive results will occur. You have not the slightest reluctance based on being out of your familiar zone. You know that your careful analysis will keep you out of any serious trouble. You can go anywhere you want to go and do anything you want to do (that you deem useful and not dangerous) in absolute comfort. In fact, you now enjoy the very act of exploring new areas. Relax and discover how much fun it can be moving about this environment freely and without fear.

Now imagine that all the blood in your brain is flowing downward into your hands and feet.

This exercise can promote a deep, peaceful sleep, and the prior thinking about dreaming helps you become conscious of your dreams as they occur. You may be very pleased to discover how comfortable you are about all kinds of changes now that you equate them with adventure, new possibilities and personal growth. The best part is that you don't have to do anything at all, just let your dreams do the work.

(If you haven't read Chapter 14 yet, this is the time to CHANGE that.)

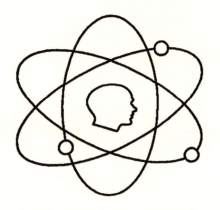

Chapter 26

Stop Smoking Comfortably

*"I know can quit smoking anytime I want to
and I can prove it. I've already quit seven times in the past."*
ANONYMOUS, AND HEARD FREQUENTLY.

Why Should I Quit?

Are you a smoker? If you are, chances are you already know what smoking can do to your health, your pocketbook, your furniture, and the smell of your breath and body. And you know numerous other reasons to stop smoking now.

Would you like to reduce your chances of cancer, heart disease, or stroke and generally strengthen your immune system? Would you like to stop burning holes in your clothing, furniture, carpeting, maybe even other people? Would you like to reduce the risk of fire? How about the thought of smelling better? Wouldn't it be nice not to be a slave to tobacco any longer? To be able to get onto an airplane, or go to the theater or movies, or perhaps a favorite restaurant without having to consider when you can sneak a smoke? Or perhaps you work in a place that has gone smoke-free and you need to stand outside in all kinds of weather just to cop a drag or two? If you feel a little foolish standing in a doorway, during a rainstorm, to smoke, you should only know how you look to others! Or maybe you shop in a mall that has gone smoke-free. Wouldn't it be wonderful not to ever have to bother with going out for a smoke?

Why Haven't I?

The answer to all of these is a resounding *yes* for almost every smoker. But still you smoke. Why? Simply because smoking is addictive. Once most people start, they find it is very difficult to stop smoking by sheer willpower alone. Even though we recognize the benefits of quitting, we hear these addicted smokers say, "I can't quit", or "I've already smoked for 20 (or 30 or 40) years. What hope is there for me (or what good would it do me) now?"

Any thought along the lines of "it's too late for me" is only a rationalization. The moment you quit smoking, your body begins to rebuild itself. Very quickly, you improve your chances for a longer and healthier life. (And if you are one of those whose rationalization goes, "Well, we all have to die of something," you are absolutely right. We all do have to die of something. But we suggest you look into just how horrible a death can be caused by lung cancer, emphysema or heart failure. When you do, you will choose to die of something else. Why not old age, with all our faculties, and in perfect health?)

What Do I Need To Finally Stop Smoking?

Aside from your ability to select your own mental programming with Quantum Focus, the two main ingredients needed to successfully stop smoking are simply the desire to stop and the belief you can. Quantum Focusers who are not yet ready and willing to stop smoking will not stop. Quantum Focusers who are ready and willing to stop will find they are *easily* able to accomplish this goal when they use their focused state and unconscious mind rather than try to stop by willpower alone.

What To Do First

(While we specifically discuss cigarettes here, the same method applies to cigars and pipes. Simply substitute the appropriate poison in the text.)

A good way to begin your nicotine-free program is to gather up everything connected to this unwanted habit, ashtrays, lighters, matches, and any cigarettes lying about, and put them in a bag or box to be tossed in the trash. You don't need them anymore, and this sends a powerful message to your subconscious mind that you are committed to being nicotine free. Remember you do want to be nicotine free, don't you?

Setting The Stage

As you are well aware, the key to Quantum Focus is shifting into Quantum states and then using both imagery and affirmations to rewrite the inner scripts you live with. So let's set the stage and shift into a quantum state.

An Old/New Way

Although this very powerful technique is based on the ancient methods of reading and practicing visualization out loud, it is new to you in the context of your Quantum Focus practices to date. We are certain, if you are ready and willing, you will be able to liberate yourself from nicotine by using this special technique.

Stop Smoking Exercise 1

Shifting into your Quantum Focused state, read out loud . . .

I am, I can, I do. I can be nicotine free, because I am and I do. I can be cigarette free, because I am and I do.

Now I see myself surrounded by the people I love and care about and the people who love and care about me. I look radiantly healthy and sound happy as I tell my loved ones how good I feel about being nicotine free. I feel terrific as I listen to my loved ones cheering loudly and telling me how proud and happy they are that I am no longer smoking. I feel like a million dollars, I am so thrilled to be nicotine free.

Repeat this until you can recite it from memory. Then, close your eyes, enter more deeply into your Quantum Focus state, and just soak up all the good feelings the above imagery creates.

In addition to the above, let's empower the desired results by doing one more visualization which will take you from where you are to where you want to be.

Stop Smoking Exercise 2

Shift into your Quantum Focused state and read out loud . . .

I see myself surrounded by a thick, dark cloud of smoke, gasping for breath. I feel trapped and unhappy and I want to break free. I can hear the voices of the people I love and care about saying how much they hate this dirty, smelly, sickening habit and how much they want me to break free . . .

Now I say, "I am a transformer, I can and I do use all my Quantum powers, my focus is true. I watch the smoke fade around me as I set myself nicotine free. I breathe in deeply and appreciate how good that feels as a non-smoker. I notice my senses becoming keener and sharper as my body begins its return to better health and functioning. I experience the wonderful feelings of power and accomplishment that are mine now. I feel my own self-worth and self-esteem growing. I rejoice and my loved ones cheer loudly for me."

Just as before, continue doing this until you can essentially recite it from memory. Then, slip deeper into your empowering Quantum Focus state and repeat it several times with all the images, sounds and feelings associated with your success.

Congratulations! You are on your way to being nicotine free and to discovering you are quite happy to be.

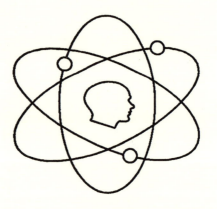

Chapter 27

Taking Absolute Control Over Your Weight

*"There are three things which, if a man does not know,
he cannot live long in this world:
what is too much for him,
what is too little for him,
and what is just right for him."*

SWAHILI PROVERB

If you are reading this chapter, chances are your weight is greater than you want it to be. Here are two good reasons to cheer up. First, you are not alone. In fact, 60 percent of Americans are overweight. Second, and more importantly, *you can do something about it more easily than you ever imagined possible.*

First A Note To The Thin

Before we continue, let us address those people with the opposite problem. Can you eat anything and not gain weight, even when you are trying to put on a few pounds? If you have spent the greater part of your life feeling that you want to be heavier, we would like you to know that most readers of this chapter would give just about anything to trade places with you.

This is not to suggest you don't have every right to be just as concerned as those who are too heavy. It is merely to point out that there are a lot fewer of you. If you are trying to gain weight, only parts of this chapter are applicable to you, but we won't leave you without a solution. Read the chapter, understanding that your situation is the reverse of that described for overweight people. Skip the first exercise and begin again on page 238 with "So you want to gain a few pounds".

On To The "Big" Problem

Now, on to the problem that plagues most people. Do you fit into any of these categories? If so, this chapter can change your life . . . for life. Do you:

- Crave candies (especially chocolate)?
- Crave other sweets like cakes and cookies?
- Simply eat too much?
- Eat "all the time"?
- Diet, lose weight, and then put it right back on again?
- Lack the "willpower" to diet?
- Lack the desire to diet?
- Eat "absent-mindedly"?
- Find your motivation decreasing a few days into a diet?
- Not know which foods are right for you?
- Forget to pick up the healthy foods when shopping?
- Eat when you are depressed?
- Eat when you are angry?
- Eat when you are anxious?
- Eat when you are bored?
- Eat when you are happy?
- Feel you need a "pick-me-up" mid-morning or mid-afternoon?
- Love greasy, fatty foods (like fried anything)?

Taking Absolute Control Over Your Weight

If you answered *yes* to one or more of the above, then follow the exercise in this chapter and you can eliminate these obstacles to having the kind of figure you want to have.

Diet Math

There are really very few tricks to managing weight. The basic relationships that apply are:

1) If you consume more calories than you burn up (technically, "metabolize"), you gain weight;
2) If you burn up more calories than you consume, you lose weight; and
3) If your consumption equals your rate of burning your body's fuel, you maintain a constant weight.

This can be summarized as

[Calories in] minus [Calories burned] = [Weight change]

Making Math Work For You

What does this mean in regard to excess weight? The equation illustrates that there are two important factors in weight management, the calories consumed and the calories burned. These two factors lead to three approaches to managing weight:

1) We can control *the number of calories we consume*.
2) We can control *the number of calories we burn up*.
3) We can control *both factors* (our personal preference).

(A personal note may be useful here. One of your authors got rid of forty excess pounds like this ten years ago. They have never reappeared.)

Stoking The Fire

You might compare your body to a wood-burning fireplace. Imagine you had a small fireplace and a stream of logs coming into your home faster than the fireplace could burn them. Also imagine that there is no way to get these logs out of your house again except to burn them. Since you can't burn them fast enough to keep up with the pace of their arrival, you have to store these logs someplace around the house. This is what the body does with its excess "logs" of calories. It stores them around its "house" in the form of fat.

You could get rid of these stored-up logs by slowing down the rate at which they arrive, until you can burn up the excess, or by building a bigger fireplace, or by both. Please appreciate that calories are not bad. Quite the contrary, calories are the body's fuel and are necessary to live. Without them, there could be no fire at all. Also recognize that *all* food groups contain calories, not just carbohydrates. Proteins and fats also contain calories. In fact, fats contain *lots* of calories!

So, knowing that we need to consume some calories, let's first consider how we burn up (metabolize) the fuel (calories) we do consume. Different people burn calories at different rates. This is unfortunate for those people at the lower end of the range, it's almost as though they had smaller fireplaces. They are still within the range of normal fireplaces, but they may have only three-foot openings instead of four or five-foot openings. If you only have a three-foot fireplace, the same number of logs that would be burned up by a four-foot fireplace will begin to pile up around your house.[2]

---

2. There are also a few people who have fireplaces which lie outside this normal range. In this condition, called hypothyroidism, someone might have the equivalent of only a one or two-foot fireplace. There are tests to determine if your metabolism is within the normal range. If it is outside this range, it can be corrected. But over 99 percent of us are in the normal range, and the exercise in this chapter is designed for this 99 percent. In other words, it works very well with three, four and five-foot fireplaces.

Help For Slower Metabolism

What can we do if we have a three-foot fireplace? We can stretch the opening to three and one-half or four feet and burn more logs in it. How? By incorporating regular exercise into your day. It is beyond the scope of this book to describe the many types of exercise that are available to you, but it is easy to find someone who can help you in this regard. Have your physical condition checked before you begin, and then select an exercise program that is appropriate for the condition you are in now. You may intensify it as you progress.

Why does exercise increase the rate at which we burn fuel? When your body is exercising, it requires more energy from the fuel you've consumed. It is like fanning the flames of your fireplace to get the fire burning faster so as to supply this energy.

Exercising also builds muscle tissue, and muscle is the part of your body that burns up the vast majority of the calories you burn. In effect, adding additional muscle tissue "stretches" your fireplace opening to a larger size.

Continuing Effects

Your rate of metabolism will slow down again after you finish exercising. But it takes some time to do this. By exercising early in the day, you will benefit from this increased metabolism longer, and burn more calories than by exercising in the evening when you are getting ready to turn down the fires for the night. And the increased muscle will continue to burn more calories at all times. (Review chapter 6 and follow the instructions there to motivate yourself to exercise regularly. This should be enormously helpful to you.)

You are ready now to reduce the number of incoming logs; that is, to control what and how much you eat. The following exercise will enable you to do this comfortably, so comfortably you may not have to give it any conscious thought at all.

Getting Rid of Unwanted Weight Exercise

Begin each time by reading through the exercise below to refresh your conscious memory. Then, enter your Quantum Focus state. When you are comfortably focused, repeat the exercise to yourself in your Quantum Focus state, as closely as you can remember it.

Do not be concerned about getting it all right the first time you do this exercise. Weight management is more complex than many other issues because so many other issues can be tied into it. Hence, the exercise is longer than most.

You will get better at it and find it easier each time you do it. Your mind will obey your instructions and bring about the changes you desire in your body and its habits. You will be able to vaporize unwanted weight whenever you choose.

(Note: when you reach the paragraph about imagining yourself in the near future, choose an image and a time frame that you feel is possible; that you can believe. If you are on route to shedding 150 pounds and don't yet feel comfortable imagining yourself at your ideal weight, modify your image to see yourself 25 or 50 pounds lighter. Choose any appropriate time frame, perhaps several months into the future. If you are getting rid of your last two pounds, this may be only a couple of days away. Once you achieve your ideal weight, it might be only a split second into the future. Choose an image you can believe, given where you are.)

> "As I gain greater control over my mind, my body also obeys my deepest desires. I now have the ability to instruct my body and my mind and they will both follow my instructions. My mind and my body follow my instructions without hesitation. My mind and my body fulfill my desires with speed and comfort. I am a new person.
>
> Even as I present these thoughts to myself, I feel my appetite changing. I can feel a shift occurring in my desires. I sense a lessening of desire for foods that

no longer support the new me. I feel an increase in desire for foods that do support the new me. Any desires for rich, sweet, greasy, heavy, fatty or fattening foods are fading away. They are being replaced by an increased desire for fresh, tasty, healthy, life-supporting foods; foods like fruits and vegetables, whole grains, low fat delicacies; foods that are appropriate to my new body.

I can see myself sitting down to a nutritious meal. I eat slowly because I enjoy the tastes and flavors, the aromas, the textures of my wholesome foods. I enjoy moderate meals because they fill me up and keep me content between meals. They carry me from one meal to the next comfortably, without any need to snack, without any hunger.

My moderate, tasty, filling, healthy meals satisfy both my mental appetite and my physical hunger. I am comfortable in-between meals. I feel totally satisfied in-between meals. In fact, I am so well satisfied that it is difficult or impossible to snack in-between meals. I like this feeling.

I enjoy my life-supporting meals so much that I cannot understand why I eat less than I ever did before. I enjoy my meals more. I eat less. I am comfortable all through the day with far less food than I used to think I wanted. I am full sooner and I am comfortable.

My stomach always feels healthier without some of the choices I used to make. My new choices make me feel healthier. My new healthier choices make me feel more energetic. My feelings of greater energy make me feel better than ever before in my life. I can do more than I used to do. I can do this easily.

I feel better about myself too. I know now that I am a normal person. I know that I have a figure and an ideal weight that I can reach and maintain. I can get rid of all the unwanted pounds I choose to get rid of. I reduce my weight easily and with comfort. I reduce my weight steadily and healthily. I discard all the excess pounds I want to discard in a steady, progressive, healthy manner. I create the body I want with ease, without conscious effort as my mind automatically programs my success.

When I am at my ideal weight and figure, my mind automatically adjusts my appetite and my metabolism so I maintain that weight and figure with ease. I automatically adjust my mental appetite, my metabolism and my physical hunger to exactly maintain my ideal weight.

I now find snacks are unappealing. Excessive portions are distasteful to me. Rich, sugary, sweet, heavy, greasy or fattening foods or drinks are distasteful to me. I consume very little of these foods and drinks. I enjoy my fresh juices, fruits, vegetables, whole grains and other tastier and healthier foods and drinks far more than I ever enjoyed my old, outgrown meals. I can live happier and healthier with my new choices.

I can think of times in the past when I ate and I wasn't even hungry. These times used to have control over me. Now I am aware of these times. I am in complete control over them now. I completely and deliberately control them now. I let them pass without eating. I recognize that they are only emotions. I recognize they are unrelated to hunger.

I see myself in the past, somehow chained or bound to these emotions and eating. But now, I cut those chains and dissolve those bonds with my mind. I can pour acid on the chains, I can use a mental chain saw to cut the bindings. I see the chains and bonds falling away, leaving my emotional states free from hunger. I recognize that emotions and hunger are unrelated; that my eating depends only on true physiological hunger. I eat only when I am truly hungry.

I have learned to control my emotions. I can and do use my Quantum Focusing techniques to control or eliminate any unwanted feelings or emotions. I can do this creatively and in a healthy manner. I am emotionally comfortable and a model of exceptional mental health and well-being. I have inner peace to match my healthy mind and body. I use my exceptional powers to make this world a better place for me and all those I encounter.

I now imagine myself in the near future. I imagine myself looking the way I want to look. My body looks wonderful. I can tell that I feel wonderful. I can hear people who are important to me telling me how wonderful I look. They tell me how proud of me and how impressed with me they are.

I step inside that future me. I feel all those feelings of well-being, of accomplishment, of pride, of health, of energy, of increased self-worth and self-esteem. I love the way I feel. I love the way I look. I love that way my whole life has come together to be what I had always hoped it would be. It is even better than I had hoped. And when I get that image and all those feelings and all the others' comments exactly as I want them to be, I quietly shout 'YES!' in my mind.

I now have the power to bring about all the changes I desire, easily and without conscious effort. My unconscious mind continues to program for my well-being according to my instructions, beyond the time I am actually instructing it. My unconscious mind obeys all the instructions I give to it, modifying them only when necessary to make each the most appropriate for me as it proceeds."

Now bring yourself slowly back to the present. You have implanted strong new "rules" which your unconscious mind will begin to follow immediately.

Repeat this exercise on a daily basis when you first begin your program. After three weeks, continue to use it every other day for two more weeks. Then, do the exercise once or twice a week until you reach your ideal weight.

From then on, practice it from once a week to once each month, depending on what you find works best for you. This continued practice will negate the daily exposure to the television, radio and print commercials that endeavor to switch your programming back to where it started.

So You Want To Gain A Few Pounds

If you are among the relatively few people who eat as much as you want and are still below the weight you would like to be, this section is for you. While most people envy your situation, they don't realize that it is every bit as troublesome as theirs.

If you are slightly underweight but healthy, then you might want to reevaluate adding additional pounds. You might be at just the right weight now to live a lot longer than the average person. Current research into longevity has shown that animals raised on lower-calorie diets and maintained below the "average" weight for their species have lived as much as 40 percent longer than the "normal" animals. Even though this isn't yet proven for humans, significant evidence in this direction is accumulating.

But, if you:

- are significantly underweight,
- are unhappy with the way your body looks,
- find you cannot ward off colds and flu as well as others can,

you might benefit from a few additional pounds. This is especially true if your condition is associated with poor nutrition so that your body is not getting all the things it needs to be strong and healthy.

First Things First

First get a physical check-up. This will assure you that there is no underlying disease and that your metabolism is not abnormally high. (Although uncommon, there are those who have a six or seven-foot fireplace instead of the three, four and five footers discussed earlier! As in the case of a one or two-foot fireplace, this can also be corrected.)

Assuming all is well, the next step is to consider your own exercise program. Are you overdoing it? Be suspicious if you are exercising more than one hour each day. Check with someone who can evaluate your exercise and its fit for your body.

Next, examine your food intake. Is it nutritionally balanced? Does it provide the vitamins and minerals you need as well as sufficient total calories for your body? Do you actually eat the meals you think you eat? Keep a journal for a week and write down everything you eat or drink, including amounts. Compare this to your impression of how much you eat.

Then To The Good Part

Here we shall assume that you have passed all the above checks and find that you simply don't enjoy eating enough or find food appealing enough to stimulate your appetite. Something in your unconscious mind is denying you the pleasure of enjoying good, healthy, well-balanced meals. You deserve to enjoy this part of your life as much as the next person, so practice the exercise below regularly. Your enjoyment of your meals will increase and you will find one of the following conditions apply.

1) Your food intake amounts and your weight increase.
2) Your food intake selections change and your weight increases.
3) Both your food selections and amounts change and your weight increases.
4) Your selection of foods changes and although your weight remains about the same, you feel better, healthier, more energetic and become content with your current weight.

In any outcome, you will be pleased with the result.

Gaining A Few Pounds Exercise

Begin each time by reading through the following exercise before you perform it. Then, enter your Quantum Focus state and repeat the suggestions below to yourself as well as you remember them. Relax and you will find your ability to remember increases every time you repeat the exercise.

"I am very relaxed and at peace. I am discovering more and more about myself every time I Focus in this way. I am learning more about the real me, the part that is free from time and space, the part that is perfect and knows all the correct answers. Very soon now, I will be totally at peace and in harmony with the universe around me. I am in harmony with the universe. I can access all the knowledge within it.

I sit here relaxed and confident. I know I am a perfect part of a perfect dimension, a dimension beyond that which I experience in my everyday waking state. In this perfect dimension, I realize that I am worthy of all good things. I recognize that I deserve the best life has to offer. I acknowledge that there may be parts of my mind that contain a few old, obsolete beliefs; beliefs which I can discard now.

I imagine these parts of my mind as small, dark rooms that have not been cleaned in a very long time. Perhaps I once had a reason to leave them as they were, but now I can sweep them clean and let in the light. I recognize that they hold only shadows that distort the true light. I recognize that they contain useless and unneeded baggage; baggage I have outgrown and want to discard.

I picture myself cleaning out these rooms now. I see myself throwing out the unneeded baggage, sweeping the rooms clean, opening the shades and allowing in the light of the truth of my perfection.

I imagine myself carrying this perfection over into the everyday world I experience during my normal waking hours. I see me doing the things I would like to do.

I have increased my self-esteem and my feelings of self-worth. I know I am entitled to enjoy life. I have thrown out all the old obstacles to living a healthy mental and physical life. I imagine myself doing anything I want to do, fully entitled to enjoy my activities.

I see myself functioning comfortably at all levels in the world. I picture me with others, enjoying their company as they enjoy mine. I see myself at mealtimes sitting down to a good, nutritious meal. I see me growing stronger every day. I feel me growing healthier every day. I hear others I care about telling me how much better I appear to them.

I enjoy my meals. I choose healthy, well-balanced meals that provide my body with all the essentials it needs. I trust my body to tell me what it needs. My appetite tells me what to eat and when to eat it to provide my body with everything it needs for optimal health. I eat until I am comfortably full. I enjoy the tastes and flavors of my foods.

I enjoy the textures and aromas of my foods. I eat an adequate amount of foods, always choosing the healthiest foods for me. I grow stronger and healthier daily. I look better daily. I feel better every day. I love my life and the way it gets better each day."

When you feel all the feelings you are describing to yourself, bring yourself back to the present, knowing you have imparted new orders into your unconscious mind which will begin to operate immediately. You may be very pleased to discover that your meals taste better and you eat more, starting right after the first time you do this exercise. Repeat the exercise daily for two to three weeks, then as often as you feel the need or desire.

Use Your Power Image

No matter what your weight, your Power Image can help you adjust it to a healthier level. You already know what you want to eat in order to be your healthiest. When you incorporate those eating habits into your Power Image and use that Power Image regularly, you will find they become just that . . . habits.

Chapter 28

Losing the Nail-Biting Habit

"Cultivate only the habits that you are willing should master you."
ELBERT HUBBARD

You would be amazed by how many people have come to us with their lives seemingly all together but very unhappy about what they generally call "one nasty habit that I just can't seem to break", referring to nail-biting.

These people come from all walks of life. They range from actors and actresses, waiters and waitresses, musicians and even a *model* — people whose careers could make their hands a point of attention to others — to people whose hands are not the center of focus but who are very concerned about the everyday appearance and impression their hands create.

These have included several executives who would hide their hands beneath the table during business meetings, a teacher who had mastered holding a piece of chalk in a fist-like fashion to keep his nails from showing, a top-notch consultant who would always send her written proposals to her clients by courier on the day of her presentations so she wouldn't have to hand them over herself, a cab driver who wore driving gloves even in the hottest weather when there was a passenger in the cab and several housewives who had invented numerous ingenious ways of keeping their hands out of sight. They all shared one desire: to stop biting their nails and gain the freedom of forgetting about all the tricks they had to use in order to hide their hands.

If you have been a nail-biter, you know the anguish it can cause in so many situations. Well, take heart! No matter how many times you've tried to stop before, no matter what or how many ways you tried, what follows here is a powerful method to STOP BITING YOUR NAILS . . . FOREVER!!!

Why is this such an effective method? Because, unlike the bad-tasting solutions you've painted on your nails, unlike putting on gloves to interfere physically with biting your nails, unlike trying to "willpower" it, unlike traditional talk-therapy, all of which address either the desire *or* the physical habit, the Quantum Focus technique modifies both the physical habit *and* the underlying desire (that is, the emotional stress that creates the sense of need to bite your nails in the first place). By removing the underlying desire to bite your nails while you simultaneously interrupt the purely physical habit, you can become permanently free of this embarrassing habit with speed, ease and comfort.

To be successful, you must do some preparation before you actually begin the exercise. For several days, write down the times you find your fingers in your mouth. They may just wind up there automatically. That's OK. As you continue to record the times, you will become more and more aware of the desire to bite your nails. Put down the time, what you were doing and how you were feeling. Because these notes are just for you, be as completely honest as you can! Your list could look something like this chart on the following page.

7:30 am	Getting kids ready for school	Hassled about all I have to do today
8:25 am	Driving to work	Daydreaming
9:50 am	Project meeting	Bored; daydreaming again
⇩	⇩	⇩
8:15 pm	Listening to spouse complain	Unhappy (maybe "wishing I had a different spouse", "frustrated" or any of a number of feelings)

We stress the importance of recording your feelings honestly, even if you don't ever want anyone else to know them. This is not a report card for your boss, your family, your clergyman or anyone other than you. (Depending upon what is on your list, it could be a good idea to keep it in a safe place, away from the eyes you don't want to see it.)

When you have two, three or more days cataloged, create a two column chart from your daily notes. In the first column, write down each of the feelings you have recorded while you made your daily notes. In the second, write the number of times that feeling occurred. For example, using the example above:

Feeling	*Occurrences*
hassled	1
daydreaming	2
bored	1
unhappy	1

Your chart gives you a map of the emotions, conflicts, problems and challenges that you are dealing with through nail-biting. Using the exercise below, you can break both the connection to these emotional triggers and the physical pattern you previously developed. While this exercise can solve your immediate nail-biting problem, we strongly recommend that you also read and use the Quantum Focus exercises in the chapters relating to your most common issues, to eliminate them from your life altogether.

Freedom From Nail-Biting Exercise

You are now training yourself to relax automatically without your conscious effort. Find a comfortable place and enter your Quantum Focused state. Take plenty of time and let yourself settle in deeply.

Repeat to yourself several times mentally, while you are letting all the stress, strain, worries and problems of this day, and days gone by or yet to come, drain away, "I am learning the secret of complete relaxation. I can be completely relaxed. My mind relaxes completely. My body relaxes thoroughly." Relax even deeper with each repetition. Actually *feel* the relief occurring in your body and mind as you imagine yourself relaxing in your mind.

When you have reached a comfortable, deep Quantum state, affirm to yourself, "I am deeply relaxed. This is how I am meant to be. My body and my mind appreciate being relaxed. They help me relax whenever I wish to. They want to relax. They relax automatically whenever my inner wisdom recognizes that it is useful to me. I am deeply relaxed which gives me greater control over my worlds, both inner and outer."

Now, keeping these feelings of inner peace and deep relaxation, look back to the time before you began to bite your nails. Your unconscious mind remembers it vividly regardless of how well your conscious mind recalls that time. When you were younger, perhaps you really did have a good reason to bite your nails. But, just like so many other things you've outgrown, you have outgrown that reason. Just like all the clothes you've outgrown, all the toys and games you've outgrown and all the old habits you've replaced with actions which are more appropriate to you now.

Now imagine yourself in the very near future, in any situation where any of the nail-biting triggers occur. Keeping your deeply peaceful feeling, see, hear and sense yourself successfully handling that situation, dealing with whatever you need to deal with, all in a very relaxed, peaceful, effective, efficient and comfortable manner.

Notice that your imagined self handles the situation with poise and grace, with the proper assertiveness and tact, in short, with perfection. Notice also that you are very comfortable during the entire experience. Now notice where your imagined self has placed your hands. Perhaps folded comfortably in your lap, maybe at your sides, perhaps using them and your arms in subtle, dramatic gestures to help communicate your points. Maybe they are just resting on a table or shaking hands with someone you have just impressed.

Notice too how good your hands and nails look, particularly your nails. Just the right length, neatly manicured, clean and attractive. Isn't it remarkable how you can do all these things and have beautiful nails at the same time? Feel how good that feels.

Spend a few minutes running this perfect scene in your mind. Make any changes you wish to make as you rerun any parts you want to change. When you have it exactly the way you want it, step inside that future you. Make it you now. Listen to all the good thoughts inside your own mind. How easy this was to accomplish. How good and proud you feel. How happy and powerful you feel.

Look back to the present, to the you here in your Quantum State. And, with the inner voice of that future you, tell the present you how surprisingly easy this is. Remind the present you that anytime you even begin to place your hands or your fingers near your mouth, you always remember these feelings of peace, happiness and success . . . and they momentarily take your breath away. They cause you to take a deep breath, and eliminate any desire to place your hands near your mouth. It is almost as though you forget to bite your nails and simply relax instead.

When you are ready, allow your mind and body to return to the outside world, bringing with you all your new-found power and renewed ability. And go on about your new way of living.

You will begin to see results after your first session. Repetition increases the power you generate, so repeat this exercise on a daily basis. As you repeat it, vary the situation you imagine yourself handling so comfortably. Eventually, you want to include all the triggers you identified. Very soon, you will find you simply no longer have any desire to bite your nails.

Chapter 29

Staying Healthy

"Some people think that doctors and nurses can put scrambled eggs back into the shell."
DOROTHY CANFIELD FISHER

One of the harshest facts of life is that too many of us don't consider, or give proper care to, our health . . . until it is too late. Too often, we simply figure that our health is beyond our control, so why bother? We assume that we'll get those two or three colds every year, that our immune system has to decline as we get older, that flu and other infectious diseases "going around" have to "get" us too, and that, sooner or later, heart disease, cancer or some other dread disease will probably get us also . . . unless we die of some other cause before then. Anyway, when we get sick, we'll go to the doctor and he/she will give us something to make us better, or at least comfortable while we decline. Besides, who wants to get old and feeble, and lose all our faculties?

Well, we've got good news and we've got bad news. The good news is that, given the right attitudes, we really don't have to think about our health a whole lot in order to live long, hale lives. The bad news is that very few individuals have the right attitudes. Rather, we have attitudes and beliefs we've been given without our conscious awareness of getting them, and they do not serve us well. It has been the authors' experience, based on having worked with literally thousands of people, that the average person believes something similar to the ideas expressed in the opening paragraph. Notice how, when someone has a heart attack at 40 or 50, we say "so young", but if they have it at 60 we "expect" it.

Our possession of these nonsupportive attitudes and beliefs is often called the hypnosis of social conditioning. Society has slipped these detrimental ideas into our mind through many methods, none of which have to come right out and say you are going to get sick and die (although, some actually do). This insidious conditioning is continually reinforced by the world around us which instilled these erroneous beliefs in the first place. Advertisements which expect us to get ill constantly bombard us. For example, remember the television commercial featuring a nurse/receptionist sitting in a room full of people who are coughing, sneezing and blowing their noses. She looks up at you and says something like, "Working in a doctor's office in flu season means I'm bound to catch something". Even seeing other people fall ill, especially those who are beginning to age — maybe 60 or 70-year-olds — tells our unconscious minds, "There. You see! I told you this would happen. It will happen to you too."

There are two dire consequences that stem from holding those beliefs:

1) We set our bodies up for some terrible illnesses; and
2) We tend not to take care of ourselves as well as we otherwise would.

Thus, we are not as healthy as we otherwise would be.

There is no point to living life if we spend all our time being so concerned with our good health that we cannot enjoy having it. To this end, the idea of not paying any attention at all to our health is probably a good one. That is, it *would* be a good one if it were not for the fact that the inattention we pay contains so many negative attitudes and beliefs in it.

When we experience symptoms of disease (or dis☼ease), they are conveniently viewed as an expression of "something wrong." There is, however, a much more productive and efficacious way of viewing what we feel. Sensations of discomfort can be viewed as an expression of nature's active attempt at a cure. The sensation of discomfort, although telling us that there is some imbalance, is actually signaling us that, fundamentally, something is "right". It is telling us that the healing process is very active, working to rebalance the situation.

Although it is possible to have some obstruction which, until addressed, can weaken this process or keep it at a stalemate, these sensations should initially produce a feeling of confidence rather than one of dread. They are signs of the healing system doing what it is supposed to do. You are being told it is active. The question then becomes whether you are going to work for it or against it.

The more traditional view of health and healing is consistent with current "New Age" thinking and what's being called evolutionary medicine (nature knows how to heal). The other choice is continuing to believe that Mother Nature was just waiting and waiting for the advent of modern medicine to evolve to cure the ills of humanity, or not. We offer a much different understanding of wellness and disease (dis☼ease) which, in our direct experience, makes for a healthier you.

Basic Assumptions

There is a creative healing system engineered into every cell of the body and every fiber of our spiritual/mental/physical being. Life operates in such a way that everything we think, breathe, eat, drink, feel, etc. directly translates at some level into what we experience as health and disease. Rather than believe that symptoms are the disease, as in the conventional medical model, we choose to consider that symptoms themselves are not the disease but rather nature's way of resolving and rebalancing the internal and external stresses of our lives. This holistic model allows us to take responsibility for our health. (Now, be aware that essentially 99 out of 100 doctors will be threatened by this line of thinking, but it can only benefit you.)

Consciousness Changing

The basic Quantum Focus exercise feeds your mind/body/spirit every time you slip gracefully into an enhanced state of mind/body/spirit and exercise your Quantum Powers. The Quantum Focus Shake is designed to help you become aware of, and dance with, the flow of universal energies that nourish you mentally, physically and spiritually. Remember that being centered in your being is very different from being self-centered. One promotes health and the other promotes disease. So please slip into a richly relaxing, spiritually enriching Quantum Focus state of mind, and continue reading this chapter.

Look again at the first paragraph. Do you believe, at either a conscious or an unconscious level, that illness is inevitable? Do you believe physical decline is inevitable? Or are you one of the enlightened few who *knows* (not believes) that we can live very long lives without illness and die in perfect health after enjoying every minute of well over 100 years?

Our society expects decay from about the age of 40. And we see many examples of this decay by the time we are 50 or 60. For example, many heart attacks occur in people in their 60's . . . in our society. But in societies where people expect to get sick and die at 110, they have these same examples of decay in their 100's instead of their 60's. By now, you may be asking yourself whether we believe and accept heart attacks as normal at age 60 because we have them then, or if we have them at age 60 because we believe and accept it as normal to have them then.

Remember, from chapter 6, the nursing home population that doubled their natural killer cell function in only six weeks? The truth is, we can live long, productive, fruitful lives with our faculties intact. But believing it can be so is an important part in making it be so. This is truly a case of that old adage, "Whether you think you can or you think you can't, you're right". So it is useful for us to think we can.

As a consequence of believing we can stay healthy, we also tend to take better care of ourselves. At some level, we acknowledge that our own (voluntary) actions affect our well-being. So, we watch what we eat a little more, exercise a little more regularly, control our weight a little better, maybe add some vitamins and minerals to our daily diet, learn to manage our stress a little better, develop our relationships a little more, and thus further improve our chances of attaining this long and healthy life through all these steps also.

The trick here is to adopt this belief at a deep level of the unconscious mind, not just hold it in our conscious thoughts. That is, we want to *know* we can do this rather than just think we can. But almost all of us have been conditioned to believe (at this unconscious level) that the ideas expressed in the opening paragraph of this chapter are the truth. Our deeply held beliefs do not support continual good health.

Watch Out For The Hidden Traps

What do you feel when we say: Mommie dearest, Daddy dear, the teacher from hell, the kids at school, your dumb boss, etc.? What reaction is triggered by the unconscious beliefs and attitudes within you? What does it do physically? And how does that affect your health?

The Mental Makeover

Fear, anxiety, worry and destructive thinking all take a toll on our health. Confidence, peace of mind, positive expectations and constructive thinking all have a very positive effect on our health. And, yes, laughter is the best medicine, so reach into your memory and reconnect with one of your funniest moments. Laugh out loud and continue to read this chapter. Give yourself bonus health points for self-esteem and loving relationships too. On a scale of one to ten, where is your attitude, healthwise?

Healthy Principles

In our menu for better health, please remember you do not have to be sick to improve your health. The recipes provided take a mind/body/spirit approach to a healthier you. Balance is the key to health and happiness. It is therefore time to nourish ourselves in mindbodyspirit.

Health Is Like A River

Health is very much like a river flowing through green fields and pristine forests. That river, if it is healthy — meaning that it is clean and flowing controllably so it can carry nutrients to, and remove wastes from, the creatures that live within it — supports the health and well-being of everything living within it. Our flowing river of health differs only in that it carries its nutrients as a flow of life energies instead of water: a very special mix of mental, physical and spiritual energies.

As long as this river continues to flow freely, these energies nourish us in mind, body and spirit, and are the source of the condition we know as good health. Should the flow of these energies become blocked or dammed, however, these energies fail to flow as before. Instead they stagnate, depriving us of the nutrients we need and allowing wastes to accumulate. Our river now creates the foundation of what we experience as disease. So, just as with nature's forests and fields, our river of health must keep flowing for us to enjoy *good* health in all its aspects.

Another component of our health is the way in which we meet our physical, mental and spiritual needs. Satisfaction of these needs factors into the quality of our lives, and therefore into our health. The more our life is worth living, the better we seem to live it. Deficiencies or toxicities (excesses) of the daily required spiritual, mental/emotional and physical requirements of life can and do have a direct effect on your health. Yes, you can have too much of a good thing . . . only it is no longer a *good* thing.

Keeping The River Sparkling

In a manner of speaking, we are the health of our river, or our health is the health of the river. Let's start by getting a sense of what makes for a healthier river or healthier person. We believe it is a balance between energy flow and meeting our needs. Health problems develop when something interferes with the flow or when we have too little, or too much, of our daily life needs. Pay attention to what you eat, and to your exercise, and enjoy your loving relationships. As parts of our needs, they all have an impact on our health. They are part of our daily nourishment.

In life and health, flow is everything! While it is possible to have too little or too much of something, both these conditions frequently respond to energy flow therapies and systems (like Qi Gong, acupuncture, Reiki and Quantum Focus). The Quantum Focus Shake is one of our most powerful healing tools to help master our body's natural healing system and build our defenses and immunities.

The Quantum Focus Shake Exercise

Find a quiet place where you will not be disturbed for five whole minutes. Yawn deeply and place your feet so they are directly under your shoulders. Allow your body to become deeply relaxed as you balance your weight evenly between your feet . . . arms hanging loosely at your sides.

Yawn deeply three more times and close your eyes. Mentally scan your body . . . looking for the most subtle tingling you can imagine in your fingertips or toes. When you tune in to the tingling, imagine that it now spreads so all of you feels that ever-so-subtle sensation moving across your whole body.

Now imagine a magical river of physical-mental-spiritual energy surrounding you in a flash of colorful light. In your mind, organize all the death energies on the *left* side of your body. Just stack them up one on top of the other — all your fears . . . anxieties . . .

worries . . . and destructive thinking. Now organize all of your life energies on the *right* side of your body. Stack these up too . . . your strengths . . . passions . . . love . . . constructive thinking . . . all the vital forces of the universe channeling through and energizing your mind/body/spirit.

Now put them all into motion. Watch as your life energies and death energies dance around your mind, surround your body and infuse your spirit. Notice how the life energies dispel the death energies, gently but surely overcoming and dispersing those death energies. Watch until all the death energies have been neutralized and the superior life energies bathe you in deeply felt feelings of confidence, peace of mind, positive expectations and constructive thoughts.

Just be with this experience for five minutes, three times per day, for 30 days. You will begin to experience a new higher level of health.

Models Or Idols

Sometimes excellent models get mistaken for fact and the consequences are disastrous. For example, the staging of terminal illness as proposed by Dr. Elisabeth Kubler-Ross is a wonderful model. Sadly, due to no fault of Dr. Kubler-Ross's, the model ceased to a model. Through mindless oversimplification and application to every "terminal" patient as if they were robots, the "stages" evolved into an idol of death which is now used by an army of "experts" as a battering ram with which they club people who have so-called "terminal" disease until they accept their prognosis.

We believe the same holds true for many of the "New Age" models now moving toward idol status. For example: Inner Child Work, Toxic Emotions, Past Lives and Regression therapies are all excellent metaphors/models with a wide range of healing applications. Over the last ten years, however, many of the practitioner/

marketeers of these powerful modalities have evolved into New Age Fundamentalists, and in the long run this can only lead to the exploitation of believers.

Toxic Emotions?

Toxic thoughts, feelings and emotions are a hot item right now and new industries are forming around how marketable it is to link diseases to emotions, etc. Blanket claims are made that if you hold emotion X, you are liable to get disease Y. Or, if you have disease D, it is because you hold emotion E. These claims are dangerous, at best, and can be deadly at worst.

That is not to say there is not a correlation between emotions and disease. It is only to remind everyone that evidence of correlation is not the same as evidence of a causal role. Chronic toxic thoughts, feelings and emotions are as deadly as any poison — and, as with any poison, the dose is the key to the effect. The universal effect of them in America seems to be a life of blahs and blues.

The good news is, your Quantum Focus practice is designed to take you out of the blahs and blues and into the awesome power of the moment. It is also designed to help you detoxify, safely and naturally, the long-held underlying beliefs which feed and nurture our toxic thoughts, feelings and emotions. We clearly recognize a relationship between toxic thinking, toxic feelings and, yes, toxic emotions and the disease process. We just don't want people to confuse taking responsibility for their health with another reason to damn themselves.

Only after considerable thought and discussion did we decide to include in chapter 8 some of the more common emotional links to symptoms and health problems so widely believed in today. More important than any list of emotions and concomitant problems, we want to give you some options about detoxing these emotions. We do this because so many people seem able to identify with this "model" and because it has been our direct experience that people who only detox physically do not seem to do as well as people who also detox their thinking, feelings and emotions. And it really doesn't matter whether (negative) emotion A leads to disease X, condition Y or symptom X. It can lead to something undesirable. So let's detoxify it before it does.

Food For Thought

Ancient oriental wisdom tells us "you are never angry about what you think you are." What could that possibly mean? Hmmmm?

There are three different exercises in this chapter, all designed to begin to change the beliefs you now hold in your unconscious mind into those that support maintaining health throughout your entire life. It doesn't matter which you use, whether you consistently use only one of them, or in what order you practice them if you use more than one. They are all geared to the same end: a long, happy, healthy life. Enjoy your practice of one, or two, or all three of the exercises as often as you wish. You can only get stronger by them.

A word to the wise. Once you decide you *want* to live your full measure of years and live them in a healthy state, you have the tools to help you do it. But, you have to want to live in order a) to use the tools, and b) for them to be really effective. So, you might want to consider all the things going on in your life. Any that make you feel like you don't really care whether or not you live a long time, or worse — make you feel like you would like to get out of this life — are your first priority. These are literally "life-threatening" issues for you. As long as you permit them to drag on your lust for life, they will drag like heavy anchors. Use your Quantum Focus techniques to change these aspects of your life immediately.

Once you have overcome the weight of the issues above, and as long as you're going to stick around for so long, why not make all aspects of your life pleasurable experiences? Take a mental inventory of all the things you would still like to change in your life — even those you would classify as petty annoyances rather than "life-threatening", prioritize them, and use your Quantum Focus techniques to rebuild your life the way you want it to be. This too will increase the probability of continued good health.

And with every change you make, you will find it even easier to make additional ones.

Young "Old Age" Exercise

In this exercise, you take direct advantage of quantum physics' relative time; that time runs more slowly as we approach the speed of light. Time "slows down" as we "speed up". The origin of this concept, since proven over and over, is Albert Einstein. His version is highly mathematical. While scientifically rigorous, it is somewhat boring to read. The concept is easier to grasp using some simplified and more common examples.

Perhaps you remember Superman circling the earth at faster and faster speeds until he was able to reverse time in order to save Lois Lane. (Einstein didn't say reverse it, but who knows?) And you've probably heard the concept that one twin, returning from a space ship journey, is younger than the twin who remained behind on earth. (He did say this, though.) This occurs because the twin traveling at high speed experienced slower time. This is essentially what you are going to program your body, and all its systems, to do for you — reset your internal clock. But you will be traveling at the "speed of mind" which is faster than any rocket ship.

> Begin by entering your Quantum Focused state. Concentrate gently on all your muscles relaxing and your mind becoming one with the universe. Spend a few moments really getting into your most blissful state.
>
> Imagine yourself out among the stars. Drifting, coasting, sailing. All around you is the mystery of the universe. Beautiful stars twinkling. Bright colored planets and comets all in your view. Let yourself feel connected to all of this. Take a few moments appreciating your infinite self.

Now see yourself beginning to speed up. Feel the sense of acceleration as you begin to move faster and faster. Watch as the stars whiz by all around you. They begin as dots of blue-white light, and gradually turn into stripes of light as you go faster and faster. Then the stripes begin to merge into a field of radiant, energizing blue-white light . . . all the awesome power of the universe surrounding you.

When you are traveling this fast, you need no longer accelerate. Just coast and enjoy the energy all around you. Feel the power as it infuses your being with revitalizing energy. Sense the strength and majesty that unites with you.

As you coast, look deeper into the light. See yourself as you were when you began this journey. Watch as you begin to grow younger. Imperceptibly at first, but definitely growing younger.

See the energy pouring into your body. Imagine yourself going about your daily routine, adding back things you used to do when you began this journey, but no longer did. Perhaps it is simply more spring in your step. Perhaps it is more spring in your heart. Perhaps it is more spring in your soul.

Watch yourself for a while. Imagine doing things more easily than you did at the beginning of this journey . . . much the way you used to do them. Enjoy the feelings that arise with the pictures. Revel in the sounds, the aromas and all the emotions that arise.

Then, when you are ready, allow yourself to return slowly to your everyday state of alertness to the outside world, knowing you are now traveling through mind-space at tremendous speed and your internal clock is now set for your lifelong youth.

An Interesting Case In Point

In 1979, a group of seasoned people was divided into two equal groups. Their seasoning was appreciable, most were over 70 years of age. Each group spent five days sequestered in a resort setting. Both were told they were going to revisit 1959, 20 years in the past.

The first group was told to *remember* 1959 during their stay. Televisions were rigged so only shows of that era were available. Magazines were from that year. No newspapers newer than that were available. They were only allowed to display photographs from 1959 or before in their rooms. They spent their five days remembering and reminiscing about "the good old days".

The second group was told to *live as though they were in* 1959. They had the same shows, newspapers and magazines. They had the same old photographs. But they pretended it was 1959. And the more they pretended, the more they got into the game.

Wow!

"So what?" you may ask.

So this.

Following the five day experiment, a series of a dozen or so different measurements connected to aging were made on all the participants. Reaction time, finger length, memory skills and many others were used. Because there is no general agreement on which of these measurements is the most reliable indicator of age, they used them all and still made a remarkable discovery. The group who *pretended* that they were back in 1959 averaged *eight years younger* across this panel of measurements than the group who *remembered and reminisced* about 1959.

Can our emotions keep us young?

Can mentally setting the clock set the clock?

It sure looks that way in both real life and in scientific studies. Isn't it worth a few minutes each day to add "years to your life and life to your years" as they say?

Perpetual Healing Exercise

This exercise uses the power of the universe around us to strengthen your natural healing abilities.

Begin by entering a Quantum Focused state. Take your time and permit yourself to relax completely. Let yourself melt into a natural outdoors setting, maybe in the woods, maybe in a large field, perhaps on a mountaintop.

As you begin to explore this beautiful place, notice that there is a very bright light coming down from above. At first, you think it is the sun, but you quickly realize this light is different from ordinary sunlight. It is much, much brighter, yet it does not hurt your eyes in any way. You can almost look directly into it before you need to squint at all.

Find a place where you can see the sky clearly. As you look up, you see a ball of fire in the sky. It is coming closer and closer to where you are. It is warm, but not hot. It is bright, but not harmful or dangerous. And it is coming closer and closer to a spot right over your head.

The ball of fire stops above you, just a few feet from your head. You stand beneath it and feel its warmth, its glow, its raw power and its gentleness. You allow your body to bathe in the light. Imagine every part of your body absorbing this healing energy. See it filling your body, all your organs, your tissues and cells. Feel it soothing and healing every muscle, every nerve, every fiber of your body. Imagine it now filling your mind with positive, healthy and helpful thoughts . . . and your spirit with renewed vitality.

Take your time and permit every part of your mind, your body and your spirit to be healed. Focus the star's energy and healing into any place that may require any special care and attention. Feel it working!

When you have filled your being with this energy, realize that you didn't receive healing from this star. It was only a messenger which traveled through you reminding you of your own natural healing ability. It carried the reminder to every part of your being. And whenever you remind yourself of your healing ability, that ability turns on and generates healing within you.

Once you have acknowledged your own natural healing ability, bring your healed self back to the ordinary outer world with your ordinary extraordinary power to heal.

Every Day In Every Way Exercise

This exercise catalyzes the previous two in a shorter version for use several times during the day. You can leisurely complete the following in less than two minutes. So, we recommend you use this many times during each and every day to combat the constant barrage of social conditioning which would have you accept and believe concepts other than those which support your continued good health.

As always, begin by entering a Quantum Focus state. You can use just a light state of relaxation for this and still derive its full benefit.

Think about what you will be doing during the next 20 to 30 minutes. Now imagine yourself doing whatever this is. See yourself in the following, and only in the following, way.

See yourself full of health and energy. See yourself youthful and spry. Imagine yourself comfortable and free from any physical aches or pains. And imagine yourself accomplishing whatever it is you set out to do in a manner which is pleasing to you.

As soon as you sense that feeling of confidence, bring yourself back to your outer consciousness and enjoy your day.

Jonathan's Recovery From Cancer

Jonathan knows that just by being alive today he has beaten the odds and expectations for someone diagnosed with a rapidly growing lymphoma. He also knows that in recovering his health to the extent he has, he is even rarer.

We met Jonathan after his heroic battle with cancer. He took a very aggressive medical approach and buffered his chemotherapy treatments with relaxation and imagery. Jonathan not only survived his treatments and the cancer, but he actually recovered his health and was leading a full active life when one of the authors began to work with him. Jonathan came with the intention of neutralizing and detoxifying the lingering fears and doubts that were beginning to take their toll on his peace of mind.

Even though he was still alive, and even more amazing, well, he was haunted by thoughts like, "What if the cancer comes back?" and "I could never do it again!" True he did it once, but he knew this was not a fight he'd ever want to fight again, even if he could do it. The weeks before his aftercare tests and examinations were the worst. But he began to notice that, even though he felt fine generally, his days were filled with fear and dread. Jonathan had heard Michael Ellner speak about the dangers of toxic thinking and decided he needed a detox.

From the very first session Jonathan felt better! He already had relaxation/meditation skills and quickly drifted into a profound Quantum Focus state where he was instructed to imagine himself enjoying the company of his loved ones twenty years in the future. He was told to see himself in vibrant health, brimming with energy for the future. Jonathan was also guided into re-experiencing all of his fears and doubts, and then helped to expose those fears and doubts to the overwhelming inspiration of his Power Image.

Jonathan continues to thrive and continues to face the shrinking demons that come up with the X-rays and blood tests that are part of his medical aftercare. It can be said with confidence that he is mastering his fears and doubts, and beginning to *expect* health at his deepest levels which is enabling him to live much more fully now. For any of you recovering from a life-challenging illness, perhaps you will find help in his words:

> "I believe the most difficult problem one has to encounter with cancer comes, not with the diagnosis or the treatment, but with the lingering doubts that must be faced every day about whether or not you'll remain healthy. Quantum Focus (experienced in this case as hypnotherapy) was the most effective way that I attacked this problem, and I highly recommend it as an essential part of any overall treatment program."

Catherine's Relief

Catherine was kind enough to volunteer for a demonstration HIV debriefing being given to a group of doctors, AIDS experts and people with AIDS in Italy. The many doctors and AIDS experts in the audience were told that, in many ways, their patients are being hurt by the often fostered and reinforced belief that HIV=AIDS=DEATH. They were also told that they could do something about the medical hex and liberate their patients from the deadly programming that comes with every HIV+ diagnosis. What's more, they could do it in less than five minutes.

This is not just "something nice" you can do for those who have tested HIV+; It is something essential for their continued health. Understand the day-to-day hell a basically heathy HIV positive person experiences. Every cough, pimple and slight fever they have is seen as the beginning of the end! Every one of these people comes in contact with others acting as if they are sick and dying even though they feel great. These people are being programmed to get sick and die.

The easy HIV-deprogramming was demonstrated with Catherine for the conference (an international forum questioning the role of HIV in AIDS and protesting the toxic treatments given to healthy people who test positive for HIV antibodies). Although Catherine had plenty of information which challenged the HIV=AIDS=DEATH hypothesis and was aware that testing HIV-antibody positive wasn't even proof she was infected, she still became very frightened every time she experienced any of the little health problems we all have from time to time.

Catherine was unaware she had been guided into a Quantum Focus state during the short demonstration. She doubted she had been debriefed in the few minutes we worked together. She didn't feel different, and forgot all about the experience by the time she got back home. It took her several months to notice that, although encounters with minor health problems still occurred, her reaction to them had significantly improved. Catherine has taken charge of her life and health and her future looks very promising. When she noticed the change, she wrote:

> "I am writing to let you know about the results of our inadvertent session at the Rethinking AIDS Conference. As you recall, I offered to participate in your demonstration of the techniques you use to help alleviate fear about HIV, never imagining that what you did would produce any effects in my life. I had tried hypnotherapy in the past but always felt it did not work for me so I figured a three minute thing in front of all those people was truly pointless.
>
> "After our demonstration I thought that I felt exactly the same as I had before. Being HIV+ bothered me only when I had something that resembled (even slightly) a symptom. This fear has always won out despite all my knowledge about HIV. And it's always bugged me that I

could challenge HIV intellectually but would give in to fears about it on an emotional level.

"I almost hate to admit this, but after our little session, I began to notice that stuff that used to set me off crying and doubting was not having an effect on me. I didn't even associate this change with what you did until I realized that there was nothing else I could attribute it to. I really think you gave me the information I needed to enjoy peace of mind. I've even found myself laughing at those dopey reports on the latest AIDS news that used to upset me.

"The most significant change is that I've quit vacillating between denial and fear, which is a real lousy way to live. I now deal with any problem I'm having as a problem I'm having, instead of wondering if this is the beginning of the end. It's great!

"Thanks for helping to make a difference in my life."

Is It Just Feeling Better?

In early 1987, Stephen was diagnosed with a rather rare and very aggressive cancer. Conventional medicine couldn't offer him anything except treatments they considered experimental. (On some level, all medicine is "experimental". They did not mean it in this sense!) Faced with an almost certain death from this cancer, Stephen decided to let them "experiment".

The first step was several months of radiation therapy, which almost killed Stephen all by itself. While he survived it by only a small margin, the cancer survived it better. But it was reduced enough to permit surgical removal of much-diseased tissue. This brought him to the point of having exhausted radiation and surgery during six months of physical and mental hell, but with enough cancer still left that it was felt it would still inevitably kill him within the year! It was felt that chemotherapy could help only a little, and that it would make him even sicker than he had been with radiation.

Stephen looked for alternatives. He felt he didn't want to spend his last year, if that was what it was going to be, sick. So he began working with his diet. He began working with supplements. He started to exercise. And he began working with his mind, learning to get into a Quantum Focus state for imaging, for reprogramming for health, for inspiration, for healing his relationship with an estranged wife whom he still loved dearly, and for relief. He literally turned his life upside down, living it closer to the way he wanted to live it . . . but had always felt he couldn't.

That's All He Wrote

We last heard from Stephen in 1994, seven years since his diagnosis. He was still going strong. He had moved to the West Coast — a lifelong dream — in 1991. He explained that his doctor there said he still had cancer. However, it was not growing, and all they were doing was "watching" it.

He was sure it was all in the past and wanted now to completely forget about the possibility of dying and focus entirely on living. He further explained that this meant severing all ties which represented to him that he was still the "sick" Stephen. Without further explanation, his note said he "appreciated all we had done to help him, goodbye, and God Bless!"

Some "Look Both Ways" Stuff

Here are several areas where you can enhance or accelerate your desired results, whether they are to stay healthy, live longer, or recover your health. If you are in the process of again becoming healthy, you would be wise to augment or modify the basic information below with the particular adjustments most suited to your needs. We particularly recommend consultation with a complementary physician to determine the best nutritional approach for your needs. Our advice here is meant as general information and should not be construed as medical advice.

Get To Your Best Weight

It has been repeatedly shown that living at the "right" weight has a wonderful effect on general health and longevity. Interestingly, much evidence is accumulating that suggests being a little "too" thin (recognizing that many people say it is impossible to be too thin) is healthier than being at the weight chart's recommendation. Experiments with animals have found those which were just ten percent below the supposed ideal weight lived up to 40 percent longer than those which were at their ideal weight. Makes you question how ideal the presently accepted ideal really is.

Science also demonstrates that there is a correlation between extra pounds and many diseases, including heart disease, hypertension, cancer and diabetes. Now it may just be that this correlation of overweight to disease results from beliefs deeply implanted through cultural hypnosis. But even if this were the case, why not use this existing belief to strengthen your Quantum Focusing to achieve a longer and healthier life? Simply bring down your weight and let the already operating belief that this will keep you healthier actually keep you healthier. You win this way, whether the real determinant of health and longevity is the weight itself or merely the belief in the negative impact of the extra pounds. Besides, you can do this easily now with your Quantum Focus techniques.

Exercise

You will undoubtedly notice that this topic comes up in many places throughout this book. We bring it up here again because it is an important contributor to general health. In addition to providing increased control of body weight, exercise seems to do a myriad of wonderful things for the body, mind and soul. (Remember, being at your best weight doesn't mean you are fit. It only means that you are not fat.)

For example, exercise keeps your blood vessels in better condition, improves immune function, increases "good" cholesterol, lowers "bad" cholesterol, and makes you feel better about yourself (which in turn inspires you to take better care of yourself). As we always caution, when beginning a new exercise program, get a medical checkup and start with something within your reach. As you improve your condition, then step up your exercise accordingly.

We are often asked, "What kind of exercise should I do?" The answer depends on what you want it to do. Some form of aerobics seems good for almost everyone. Weight training is a good way to lower body fat, increase bone strength and muscle mass, and generate a general level of fitness. Cycling, step climbing, rowing, hiking, swimming, many sports (but, alas, not riding around in a golf cart), even walking, might be the best for you. (The most recent research shows the treadmill burns the most calories, if you want to know.)

You need to choose your exercise based on three criteria. First, how fit you are at the start. Second, what you want the exercise to accomplish (increase endurance, build strength, improve aerobic capacity, etc.) Third, and probably most underrated, what you like to do. The fact is, you will stay with your program much longer and much more conscientiously when you like it. Choose something you enjoy and you are much more likely to do it.

A fourth factor to consider is that the number one correlate to successful exercise programs is convenience. If you have to travel several miles to a gym, the more likely you are to skip it in bad weather, when you're tired, you've had a busy day, etc. If you have your own treadmill in the basement (or better yet, the bedroom), the more likely you are to use it.

Diet

To cover this topic in its entirety would require another entire book. So, let's just summarize the basic principles here

Current thinking shows that, for most people, a low fat, high complex carbohydrate diet (which will automatically be high fiber) is the most beneficial from both the health and weight standpoints. There is argument about whether it is only saturated fat or all fats that should be minimized, and whether the percent of fat or the total fat in your daily intake is more important in keeping you fit and healthy. If you are eating a low fat diet and eating reasonable amounts of food, you'll reduce saturated fat while achieving both a low percentage and a low total fat intake. No matter which perspectives turn out to be correct, you win.

There are even arguments that some people have a better response to a high fat and low carbohydrate diet. It appears that all people are not created equal after all. We seem to have differences in nutritional needs and metabolic types. This fact does not seem strange when you consider that different peoples lived and evolved in different situations. For example, one group of Native Americans (formerly referred to as Eskimos) eats diets of maybe 90 percent fat and thrives on it. Other Americans, with genetics molded in other parts of the world, seem to do much better on low fat diets. The moral is, you need to determine which works best for you. In general, most people do best on the low fat version. However, if you find that a low fat diet does not help you to reduce your weight, get better control over your blood lipids (cholesterol and triglycerides) and generally feel better, experiment with the possibility that you are genetically more like the Eskimo group. Give the low carbohydrate version a whirl.

Having sidestepped that issue, permit us to comment on the use of nutritional supplements. We cannot recommend any specific items for your use, but we can discuss the philosophy for our own extensive use of various supplements. You then need to evaluate this with regard to what you want to do yourself.

Begin by considering that commercial food crops are raised with the objective of generating the greatest yields in terms of pounds, bushels, etc. They are not grown for the greatest nutritional value. Given the depleted state of farm soils (which are fertilized with the minimal number of elements needed to maximize a crop — usually only nitrogen, phosphorus and potassium), it is near impossible to get all our nutritional requirements from our foodstuffs. Where will the plant get the selenium, chromium, zinc, molybdenum and copper from? If it doesn't get them, neither will we.

This is true even if we accept the relatively low RDA's (Recommended Daily Allowances) as sufficient amounts of these substances. It appears, however, that the RDA's represent amounts of vitamins and minerals that are necessary for avoiding gross clinical signs of most deficiency diseases. Mounds of evidence points to other, much higher levels of most nutrients to promote optimum health.

We believe organic produce is most desirable. But even organically grown foods cannot guarantee that nutritional content will be up to par. Often it is not. It is not in more complete nutrition that their advantage lies. It is in their ability to minimize the ingestion of chemicals which act to shorten our lifespans. Finding a reliable source of organic products is not always easy. We have seen places which don't have a rapid turnover of stock, so the foods are no longer fresh. Others carry only a few items. Some large grocery chains are beginning to carry organic produce, though. Their large volume helps keep stock fresh, and their prices on some items are sometimes better than those in smaller places — but not always. The bottom line is, it's probably worth the extra effort and extra cost required to find a good source of organically grown foods. You just may save more than that in medical costs later on!

Given all the above, what about supplementation? Our own includes the B-complex group, the antioxidants (including C complex, beta carotene and preformed vitamin A, selenium, and natural vitamin E as mixed tocopherols), zinc, calcium, magnesium, chromium, boron, molybdenum, vanadium, Co-enzyme Q-10, fish oils, lecithin, flaxseed (linseed) oil, some immune-system-stimulating herbs (e.g., echinacea, astragalus), ginseng, ginkgo biloba, and others.

It is important to remember that everyone is different and, therefore, we each have different needs. We don't all wear the same shoe size; why should the same supplements fit us all? You will need to do some research to discover the most useful combinations and concentrations for your own situation. Our recommendation is that this too is worth the effort.

Stress Management

As you saw earlier, stress can be a big part of disease. Conversely, handling stress appropriately can be a big part of staying healthy. Simply staying with your routine Quantum Focus practice will handle most basic stresses. If you have something special to work on, turn back to Chapter 6.

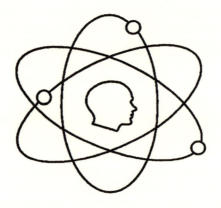

Chapter 30

Eliminating Headaches and Migraines

"In the beginner's mind there are many possibilities, in the expert's mind there are few."
SHUNRYU SUZUKI

The Price We Pay . . .

Headaches are often considered an inescapable part of modern life. They appear to be stress-related, maybe stress-initiated, and many people believe they simply must suffer, at least occasionally, with a common headache. Others seem to experience them on a more frequent schedule, almost to the point of "I get headaches every Friday afternoon," or "Going to the movies always gives me a headache". These are more examples where saying it (or, more importantly, believing it) literally makes it so. You might even be one of these people.

Needlessly

The good news is that headaches are NOT an essential part of life. It is possible to go through life never, or at the very least, seldom experiencing a headache. Plus, should a headache ever threaten to occur, you can abort it at the first sign of onset.

Some of you are now saying, "That may hold true for your average, run-of-the-mill headache, but certainly not for me. I get migraines. You don't even know what a migraine is like!"

Even Migraines

It is true that many people do not even have a clue what a migraine headache is like. Even for those who *have* had migraines, they are difficult to describe so others can understand just what they are like.

There is no understanding yet of just what causes migraines. There is some correlation with the Type A personality, but it is not absolute. And tension may play a role here, just as in simple headaches.

There is not even a standardized migraine. Migraines have several characteristics, not all of which are present in all cases. But, imagine a headache that hurts so bad you cannot see. Everything has halos of bright lights around it. And light increases the pain — not even bright light necessarily, just ordinary room light.

Imagine a headache generating so much intense pain it leads to cold sweats, loss of balance and vomiting. Imagine such a strong headache that aspirin, acetaminophen and ibuprofen are useless. The only relief you can derive is from prescription medications such as barbiturates and going to bed in a dark room for a few hours to a few days! Picture these symptoms. They approach what a migraine headache is like.

If It Walks, Acts and Quacks Like A Duck, Treat It Like A Duck

Well, the even better news is, migraines are as readily controlled as "ordinary" headaches. One of the authors used to suffer with frequent, sometimes weekly, migraines. In the more than eleven years since adopting the techniques described below, he has experienced probably fewer than a dozen headaches, of which no more than one or two were severe. And even these were limited by these techniques in that they were gone within 30-60 minutes.

Be Smart

Pain is a signal intended to warn us something has gone wrong. And, as with all techniques designed to eliminate or decrease pain, you are advised to first be certain there is nothing medically wrong. Migraine sufferers have probably already done this, but people with frequent or chronic headaches are wise to have their headaches checked out also. While the vast majority of times medicine can offer no reason for headaches (that is, there will be no medical reason for the headache or migraine), it is important to be certain before removing the pain.

And use common sense. If you get headaches when you read for an hour or two, have your eyes checked. Sometimes, simple things like this eliminate the source of the headaches.

Other possible sources include dental problems (from TMJ to cavities or abscesses), toxic fumes from the immediate environment, and, the most common reason of all, stress and tension. Reread chapter 6 if you suspect your headaches are coming from stress.

Common Headache Cure/Relief Exercise

Enter your Quantum Focus state and then repeat the following suggestions to yourself while you are Focused.

"I have a headache. I can feel this headache in my head. It is displeasing to me.

I recognize that this headache is a signal. I acknowledge receipt of that signal. I no longer need the signal.

I want to be free of any pain in my head. I have acknowledged the signal and can now let it go.

I am going to count from one to ten. By the time I reach ten, the headache will be gone. I will feel fine. I will be alert and relaxedly energetic. I will be in perfect health.

One . . . two . . . three . . . four . . . five. At the count of ten, I feel fine. I am free of any and all pain. I have left all discomfort behind. My head feels wonderful. I feel wonderful. Six . . . seven . . . eight. Feeling great. Nine . . . ten. Alert and relaxed."

Now bring yourself back to the present and *go on about your business*.

Now go on with whatever it is you wanted to be doing. Do not go looking for the headache. As you devote your time to whatever it is you are doing, you will soon notice, almost accidentally, that the headache is gone. If you go looking to see if it is still there, you are essentially arguing at an unconscious level to keep it. It you ask for it, your unconscious mind will give it back to you. This simple technique works for common headaches in as little as five minutes from the time you begin to go into your Quantum Focus state.

Migraine Headache Control

For most people, migraines can also be controlled using the same simple technique. The only difference lies in how frequently the technique is used.

About half the time, the above will eliminate the migraine just as though it were only an ordinary headache. And about half the time, it will only lessen the pain. In this case, repeat the exercise again five minutes after you have completed it for the first time. Most migraines will give up on the second pass, but there are some migraines that require a third time through the exercise before they go away. If you have one of these really stubborn cases, do the exercise a third time five minutes after completing the second.

The third "session" will eliminate about 85 percent of all migraine headaches. The best aspect of this technique is that it takes so very little time and can be performed just about anywhere you happen to be. For example, it has been successfully applied on the New York City Subway. (Closing your eyes and entering your Quantum Focused state while on the subway may entail some risk, so we do not recommend this. The example is included just to show the versatility and portability of the method.)

Now For The Really Stubborn Ones

Suppose you are among the remaining 15 percent whose migraines are not routinely controlled by this technique. We still have good news for you. Move on to the Ultimate Migraine Control exercise.

The Ultimate Migraine Control

If you've been reading this book from the beginning and practicing the exercises as you went along, you have already perfected the ultimate migraine control method. If not, go back to chapter 3 and follow the instructions for increasing your hand temperature.

Migraine headaches come from dilation of the blood vessels in the head. This causes increased pressure in the head and is the cause of the pain. Because you redirect some of your body's blood flow from your head into your hands when you raise their temperature, you reduce the pressure in the head. By reducing the pressure, you eliminate the cause of the pain.

This procedure takes a little longer, and you need to find a place where you won't be interrupted for 25-30 minutes, but it is almost universally successful.

Some Other Avenues

There are now many pain clinics which devote appreciable resources to headache and migraine pain. Some are having reasonable success. But the major success seems to be coming from behavioral approaches. Biofeedback is one prime example. You are taught how to do things like increase your hand temperature. Sound familiar? Go back to chapter 3. Do not pass go. Do not spend $200, at least, to learn this!

Acupuncture is a technique that boasts an appreciable success rate. Your author found it very effective. It is inconvenient to have to get to the acupuncturist when you have the migraine but well worth the trip if you have no other recourse.

Herbal remedies have helped many migraine sufferers. Feverfew has a great deal of evidence to support its use.

There are also some new medications coming on the market. These are just being announced and are not yet in widespread use. There may or may not be something here. You'll need to watch their progress.

Chapter 31

Eliminating Aches and Pains

*"Pain dies quickly, and lets her weary prisoners go;
the fiercest agonies have shortest reign."*
WILLIAM CULLEN BRYANT

A Word Of Caution

Remember, pain is a signal. When we feel pain, it is there to warn us that something has gone wrong. Aches and pains are the feedback we need to point our attention where it is needed. Sometimes the things that have gone wrong are physical; sometimes they are emotional. It is good practice to identify the source and rule out, or properly care for, any physical cause before you begin working on eliminating the signal. So if you are experiencing acute or chronic pain, a visit to your physician may be advisable. Sometimes this can eliminate the pain without any further effort on your part. It is as though we could tell the pain its message was received and we are taking care of whatever needs to be taken care of. We don't need the signal any longer.

But, if your physical pain stems from emotional sources, we suggest you work with chapter 5 at the same time you are doing the exercises in this chapter. That also acknowledges that you have received the signal and are now taking care of the thing(s) that need to be attended to.

However, there are times when we already know what the signal represents. We may even be taking all the appropriate actions to treat the situation. Yet, we might still have pain to deal with until we eliminate or completely correct its source. For example, how can you lessen or eliminate the pains of arthritis or bursitis? What do you do to manage the discomfort of a toothache until the dentist can see you? How can you find relief from the chronic back pain millions suffer from, without any identifiable cause or effective treatment? What can you do in case of an accident, a broken bone, a nasty cut or other mishap to reduce or stop the pain until help arrives or you can get to an emergency room? And how do you control the physical pain that can accompany an emotional issue while you resolve that emotional issue?

Pain, Pain, Go Away

One of the most important realizations in the management and/or control of pain is that, unknowingly, we already do it quite frequently. Did you ever notice a bruise on your hands, knees, or feet and have no idea how you got the injury? When and how did you injure yourself? You just don't know! Very often, the first time you feel any pain associated with the injury is when you discover the bruise. Somehow, you have controlled the pain until then.

Many of us have experienced another classic example of unrecognized pain control. Haven't you noticed that, while you are sitting in the waiting room at the dentist's or doctor's office, or even in the emergency room, the pain that brought you there in the first place goes away? And that it goes away before any treatment is received?

How Can That Be?

The simple explanation for the above is that our thoughts were elsewhere and, without our awareness, we tuned out the pain. Pain almost always requires some cooperation from us, either consciously or unconsciously, in order to be noticeable. By placing our attention elsewhere, we unknowingly tune out the discomfort. For example, in the case of a toothache, most people in the midst of a busy day don't notice the throbbing pain they are experiencing. But as soon as they stop everything and, for example, try to go to sleep, the aching tooth has no trouble communicating that attention is needed to correct the situation.

There is a physical reason we can do this. Our brains manufacture powerful pain-suppressing chemicals, known as endorphins. You have probably heard of them before. It seems as though our brains have the ability to secrete these chemicals at will, and often do exactly this when we are focused on something we want or need to do. It is as if our minds tell our brains we haven't got time for the pain right now so do something to stop it. And our brains obediently comply.

Doing It Intentionally

How then can we *knowingly* use our ability to tune out aches and pains which will be cared for at another time? The key, of course, is shifting into a Quantum state and then putting your attention elsewhere.

Pain Management Exercise 1
Floating Away

First, decide if your pain would prefer to float away or drop off. Then, after deciding, use the appropriate visualization to bring this into reality. We actually recommend you use both methods and then decide which works better for you.

Pick a comfortable spot and lie down. Now shift into a Quantum Focused state and make contact with your body as a whole. Feel what it feels like. Picture it in your mind. Listen to the sounds it makes. You may even get an idea of odors and tastes. Use whatever comes to you.

Now, specifically locate the area of pain. Picture, hear and sense the pain. Notice how it is like, and how it is different from your body as a whole. Mentally surround the pain with a colored light which matches the intensity of the pain, e.g. red for searing pain, black for throbbing pain, etc. Let the colored light contain the sounds and the sensations (feelings, smells and/or tastes) of the pain. Let the color take on a harsh, or sharp, or throbbing, or searing, or whatever shape.

Now, mentally change this colored light into a brilliant white light. Watch the change as it occurs. You may notice that, first the sounds, then the sensations of the pain also change as the color changes; other times the changes in sensations will precede the sounds. You may even see the color change shape into a more comfortable shape several full seconds before the pain subsides. The feelings of pain turn into mild discomfort as they begin to leave your body.

Then, see the package of brilliant white light simply floating up and out of your body, taking the residual discomfort with it. See the discomfort floating in the light, going farther and farther away. Listen to the sounds as they fade into the distance. Notice how the smell or taste fades away. Feel the increasing comfort filling in the space left for it.

Again, imagine your body as a whole. Notice how the picture has changed. Listen to the more comfortable sounds it now makes. And, most importantly, feel how much better it feels.

The Pain That Wasn't There

This particular approach has demonstrated marvelous results in many instances. Here is what happened with one reluctant individual, Henry, whose wife brought him into the office. Henry was an amputee who lost his left leg below the knee to diabetes. It had been seven months since his operation, but he was experiencing severe cramps in his missing left foot. He had been assured that there was nothing wrong with his operation. He had an artificial leg that he was learning to use and was surprisingly comfortable with it very quickly. Yet, he had these cramps and no foot to massage in order to relieve them.

There was no place in the office for Henry to lie down so he was helped into a Quantum state and guided through the above exercise while sitting in his wheelchair. His remarks afterward are typical.

"I didn't think this would work. I went along with your instructions just to get out of here.

"In the beginning, I felt foolish. But then the most amazing thing happened. I didn't realize it happened until after you finished. I was picturing the color change and enjoying the look of it. I was so engrossed I forgot about my foot. When we were done, I went back to my foot, expecting to find the pain again. It was completely gone."

Pain Management Exercise 2
Dropping Off

Pick a comfortable spot and lie down. Now shift into a Quantum Focused state and make contact with your body as a whole. Picture your body in your mind. Feel what it feels like. Listen to the sounds it makes.

Now, specifically locate the area of pain. Picture, hear and sense the pain. Notice how it is like, and how it is different from your body as a whole. Mentally surround it with a very heavy cover.

Now imagine that, enclosed in this covering, the whole package of pain — its appearance, its sound, its smell, its taste and its feeling — is sinking through your body and into the floor. That's it . . . just sinking right through your body, through whatever you are lying on, and right on through the floor. Sinking deeper and deeper into the floor. Watch the cover as it slips away until it is completely out of sight.

When you no longer feel the pain you may get up and leave any remaining discomfort behind you.

Results with this approach have been every bit as amazing as with floating away. One client who had bursitis but loved to play tennis said that what she liked best about it was that she could modify it and use it "anywhere and anytime". She liked being able to lie down and really concentrate on the exercise. But, in her words, "It works just as well if I imagine I am lying down".

Laugh It Off

We often hear about the healing power of laughter. Pain management is one of its most immediately noticeable results. Norman Cousins, fighting to overcome a progressive, debilitating and painful disease of the spine, used to watch old Marx Brothers' movies. He stated that a good belly laugh could give him up to two hours of essentially complete freedom from pain. We have seen this work for others too.

Aside from deliberately finding funny things in your life, or putting funny things into your life, you can enhance this result further by imagining the pain being laughed off in your mind's eye too. This makes a good Power Image for emergency use. Funny thing, though. Some people have started laughing out loud from the impact of their "Power Image".

Chapter 32

Painless Childbirth

"Bravery is the capacity to perform properly even when scared half to death."
GENERAL OMAR BRADLEY

A Private Battlefield...

You may think it odd to begin a section on childbirth with a quote describing battlefield conditions. But many women have suggested to us they would sooner go to war and take their chances on death and dismemberment than go through childbirth. So while this chapter is for all women who are contemplating having a family, it is especially for those women who are afraid of the process.

...Or A Personal Hell?

Childbirth is a natural physiological function for human females. Yet, it has come to be approached, in contemporary society, with emotional responses ranging from apprehension to stark terror. As both your authors are male, we have taken the liberty of incorporating the experiences of several women, with whom we have worked, who have had one or more children using the techniques we shall describe. You will discover that, contrary to the mental conditioning and programming you have received since childhood, pain is NOT a necessary part of giving birth. To quote one woman who has had children both by conventional methods and the following techniques, the latter experience was, "like the greatest orgasm you could imagine".

Would You Say That Again?

Descriptions like that begin to change your expectations, don't they? That's great because you too can experience this wonderful event in a very positive, pain-free way.

The first step is to master your Quantum Focused state; that is, to become proficient at entering it at will. Once you have attained this ability, the following exercises will teach you to mentally induce anesthesia instantaneously. This means more than just painless childbirth. It means you can reduce, or altogether avoid exposing both you and your baby to drugs. These drugs can affect the baby, depressing its respiration for example. Studies indicate that babies born without exposure to drugs are healthier and more contented, they feed better and cry less. There are many women who undergo "natural childbirth" *without* mental conditioning just to achieve this for their infant.

You Can Be Fully There . . .

Plus, with Quantum Focused childbirth, you are there, awake and alert, for the birth of your child. All the positive aspects, the joy, happiness, fulfillment, and so forth are there for you to revel in . . . unfiltered by sensation-numbing drugs. The only thing "missing" is the discomfort, reduced or eliminated by your mental anesthesia ability.

. . . And Go Home Sooner

Evidence also indicates that recovery time for the mother is faster, with less bleeding and more rapid healing. Still other statistics demonstrate a shorter time in labor. And, unlike drugs which wear off much sooner than most women would like, you can maintain your state of comfort for several days until you no longer need it.

And now, on to the exercises that enable you to *enjoy* the birth of your child. As you want to master your Quantum Focusing ability before you move on to these exercises, it is suggested that you begin the process early in your pregnancy. This will provide additional benefits as you can control other potential side effects of pregnancy, such as morning sickness, with your Focusing practice. When you have mastered Focusing, then incorporate the exercise below.

Painless Childbirth Exercise

Enter your Quantum Focused State and repeat the following suggestions to yourself. You might even want to record these on a tape recorder and then play them back.

"I am going to have a baby. This is perfectly natural and normal, and I am going to enjoy this experience. I will be free from any pain or discomfort. The only physical sensations I have, related to my contractions, are feelings of pressure or tugging or pulling. These will not be uncomfortable. They will just be pressure or tugging or pulling.

I will be pain-free. If someone asks me about the contractions and uses the word 'pain', this will deepen my anesthesia. I will hear the word 'pain' and become immediately more comfortable.

There may be other women around the delivery room who are without my training. They help me, even without knowing it. If any of these women use the word 'pain', I go deeper every time they use it. If any of these women otherwise indicate any discomfort, I am unaware of it. Any shouting or yelling or screaming makes me relax more, go deeper, and become more comfortable.

I will be deeply relaxed yet awake and alert. The birth of my baby is a joyous occasion, one I will always remember fondly. The birth happens easily. I am always comfortable. It is almost as though I am watching someone else give birth. I have all the emotional enjoyment, but my body is somewhere else.

I induce anesthesia easily and on my own command. Every time I say the words 'blue rose' to myself or aloud, my abdomen will go deeper asleep. I can sense only pressure or tugging or pulling. I take deep breaths and concentrate on my feelings of well-being. The words 'blue rose' make any and all uncomfortable sensations associated with my delivery numb whenever I repeat them.

I am having a child. This is a joyful experience. I am confident and relaxed. My body cooperates with all the requests made by my doctors and nurses. This is as natural and easy as eating and breathing. I breathe easily. I pay attention to my breathing. The process is automatic. My body automatically does exactly what it needs to do.

It becomes numb when this is helpful to me. I am as numb as I want or need to be. The words 'blue rose' make my body number in any place that is useful during my delivery. My body remains numb for any procedures that my doctors and nurses carry out around my delivery. My body remains as numb as it needs to for me to be comfortable after delivery.

I heal quickly. In the unlikely event any cutting or stitching is required, my body cooperates fully. The blood moves away from any area it needs to for my quick healing. Any stitches heal rapidly. My skin heals more rapidly than my doctors can believe. They marvel over how rapidly I heal. I heal exceptionally fast even for the rapid healer that I am. The parts of my body that need to remain numb during my healing do so. I am comfortable in every aspect of my child's birth.

The time I am in labor is surprisingly short. My contractions feel only like pressure. They are rhythmic and effective. I deliver my baby quickly and easily. My baby is perfectly healthy. My baby is strong. My baby is beautiful.

I am healthy and strong. I am beautiful. I am calm and relaxed. The whole birth is easy, rapid, joyous and natural. My body completely returns to normal as I heal rapidly. The words 'blue rose' are always available to me for another child if I so desire in a conscious, joyous and comfortable manner."

Congratulations, Mom! You can now experience one of life's greatest joys in a state of peace, comfort, wonderment and full appreciation and enjoyment.

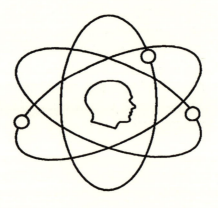

Chapter 33

Overcoming Allergies

"My allergy tests suggest that I may have been intended for some other planet."
WALT WETTERBERG

A Common Affliction

Allergies may well cause more discomfort to more people than any other physical affliction. Originally, we thought of allergies only as those common irritants, from ragweed to cats, that made physically susceptible people sneeze and wheeze. Today we have to count in the food allergies which give rise to a completely different set of symptoms, from headaches to mood alterations. In fact, allergies are so common that even the allergists don't really know how many people suffer from them.

More importantly, they don't know how many people *don't* suffer from them. For there is a large mental component to allergic reactions. Under stress, for example, allergic reactions in people who are physically allergic to some specific stimulus are stronger than when these people are not stressed. And there are cases of multiple personality disorders (the so-called "split personalities") where there are severe allergies in one personality and no reaction to the same substance in another personality. And this has been shown in the laboratory. We have some degree of mental control over the release of histamine and other allergy-related compounds in the body, so there may be people who are "physically" allergic to something, but simply don't know it because their mental beliefs have prevented the allergies from reacting. We wonder how many of these people would demonstrate allergic reactions if they were told they were allergic to something.

A Specific Example

One of the authors gave his daughter, Andrea, who demonstrated allergies to almost everything in the laboratory tests, a gram of vitamin C, along with the advice that this was a special form of vitamin C that had super-powerful antihistamine effects that would give her about six hours of complete relief. Her nose was already running, her eyes tearing and she generally looked uncomfortable when she took the vitamin. A short while later, we left for a state park near us. An hour passed from the time she took the vitamin C to the time we reached our destination.

Once there, we went hiking in the woods. It was a time of the year when Andrea "should" have been incapacitated by the allergens in the environment, but while she did sniffle occasionally, and even blew her nose once or twice, she was able to enjoy several hours of hiking through some beautiful terrain. We covered five or six miles, up and down the sides of mountains, through woods, along the banks of streams and around waterfalls, through all kinds of meadows with a variety of vegetation. During this entire hike, there was no obvious allergic reaction. In fact, Andrea was much more comfortable during this time than she had been in the air-conditioned and filtered environment before we left. And she was more comfortable when we returned . . . her comfort lasted for about six hours after she took the vitamin.

What Caused It?

Now we should point out that vitamin C does have some antihistamine effect. But she had previously taken vitamin C routinely without this relief. Why? Because nobody had ever told her before that it would do this. Hmmmm?!

Overcoming Allergy Attacks Exercise

Find a comfortable place and enter your Quantum Focus state. If you are combating a debilitating allergy that is excessively irritating you at this moment, take several extra minutes to relax yourself completely. You will feel the allergy easing just by doing this.

Now imagine yourself in some wonderful place, perhaps your special place where you've been so many times before. Choose a place where you will be free from whatever allergens have annoyed you in the past. Just enjoy being here for several minutes, breathing free and easy, head clear and free from discomfort or pain, your mood excellent and balanced. You're in the allergy-free environment of your Quantum Focus state. Notice that you are already feeling better.

As you continue to relax, tell yourself over and over that you are in this allergen-free environment. Remind yourself that you have cleared all the allergens from your body. Feel the progressive relief occurring in your mind and body.

Now project yourself inside of your own brain. Walk through the halls until you come to the door marked "control room". Open the door and walk in.

As you look around, you are probably impressed by the complexity of the controls that keep your body running smoothly. You may even be in awe of the sophistication of the systems and dials you see. But somehow you know exactly how to interact with all this in order to enter your own instructions into the system.

Each of us has a different interface. You may have workers running the controls. You may find it all computerized. It may be run in any other way that makes sense to you. But, regardless, you know how to enter your instructions now. Either into a computer, or telling them to a worker, or doing whatever you have to do to enter these instructions.

1. Turn off excessive histamine release throughout my body. Restrict it only to the places and times when it is needed for my well-being.
2. Clear out any offending substances around my body. Eliminate them through natural and healthy channels so as to be virtually unnoticed except by their absence.
3. Program new responses into my body parts so I tolerate these substances that used to irritate my cells and tissues. Program responses that protect my body without disturbing me.

When you have completed entering your instructions, project yourself back to your safe and comfortable environment. Then, return to your normal state of consciousness.

Chapter 34

A Better Sex Life

"Sex lies at the root of life, and we can never learn to reverence life until we know how to understand sex."
HAVELOCK ELLIS

Not Too Loud!

Without a doubt there is more mystification and taboo surrounding healthy sexual expression than any other human endeavor. The vital nature of our sexual drives is both suppressed and exploited at the same time. In the Victorian era, sex was treated by pretending it didn't exist. Although we have come a long way since then, in just one generation current sex myths have gone from "sex can make you *mad*" to "sex can kill you".

The new symbols of sexuality — money, power and protection — play havoc with the natural signals which communicate sexual desirability. Instead, they set up false criteria which doom human contact and mutual pleasuring. So how is a person to improve their sex life? Quite simply, the secret to a better sex life is simply being in the moment and being there with a healthy attitude.

Good Sex Versus Great Sex

Good sex results from the pure physicality of sexual contact. Great sex results when this physicality is combined with the spiritual and emotional meeting and joining of two people. The exchange is highly energetic and results in a total discharge of the sexual/emotional/spiritual tensions built up prior to and during the act.

As far as we are concerned, the difference between "great sex" and "just sex" lies in the feelings one has about self and others. If you do not love yourself, and you do not have feelings of love for your partner, you are missing out on great sex. No matter how much you enjoy sex now, there is still far more pleasure available to the experience, including loving the contact between you and your partner — this is essential to great sex.

Children Play Better Than Adults

Another way to enhance the sexual experience is bring your inner child to mind and explore the sensual and sexual contact through the eyes of your inner child. Explore your partner's body, touching and kissing every part and saving the genitals for last.

Then, in your mind, become aware of a magnetic attraction pulling your bodies into each other so your hearts beat as one. Allow your pelvis to take charge of the pace and motion as you and your partner release the wonderful tension and melt into bliss.

Deep inside us, we all have very powerful natural impulses. Tapping into them always results in the release of sexual energy and excitation. The ancients saw a connection between enlightenment and the conscious experience of this energy rising from the bottom of one's spine to the top of one's head.

Keeping this in mind, we created the following exercise.

Better Sex Exercise

Shift into a peaceful, easy Quantum Focus state... and focus your attention on your spine. Every breath you take, every beat of your heart, gives you the sense that your spine is ever so softly beginning to glow. Starting from the base of your spine, and moving ever so slowly upward, it is glowing. See your spine glowing... ever so slowly moving upwards.

Now imagine this light generating a very warm sensation moving up from the base of your spine. Feel and enjoy the warmth at the base of your spine. It feels so very good; a very pleasant warmth.

Now imagine there is a serpent who is happy to wake up and see the light. The warmth energizes the serpent and it too begins to move up your spine. As this very special serpent winds its way up your spine, you see flashes of lights and feel the most erotic impulse running up your spine and exploding into excitation and pleasurable feelings. Feel the tingling inside you and notice it as it moves through your skin so you can feel its amazing tingling now, both inside and outside of you.

Now focus your attention on your spine and draw an imaginary connection to the part of your body that is between your anus and your vagina or scrotum. Begin to make a strong mental connection between that part of your body and the muscle you use to turn off your urine flow while urinating. That's right... tense that muscle and put your tongue on the roof of your mouth just behind your upper teeth.

You have created a psychoneuro bridge which directs increased blood flow into your genitals and heightened sensitivity into your nerve endings. It is very interesting, is it not, how you can center? And now bring yourself back into your waking consciousness and into the moment.

Setting The Stage

Candlelit evenings with soft music and joyful expectation of loving sexual contact and pleasure go a long way towards promoting the mood. Good conversation can also set the stage for an exciting and fulfilling sexual experience. Flowers and kind words also promote the feelings and the setting and are heartily recommended. Just **remember**: the greatest gift you can share with your lover is your total, undivided attention. So light the fires and stay in the moment.

Getting In The Mood

When love is added to sexuality, or sexuality is added to love, the results are always enhanced. The song says, "I'm in the mood for love", but the word love used this way is most often understood as, "I'm in the mood for sex". More often than not, people forget to include love in the mix.

Chapter 8 deals with increasing love for self and others. We recommend you add these feelings to your sexual experiences. If you don't truly love the person you are having sex with, then love the feelings and sensations you are willfully sharing with this person.

When you are able to generate high-voltage sexual excitement by imaging you and your lover enjoying the mood with great mental clarity, you can shift into the moment and share the flow with your lover. You're in the mood and in the moment. Your blood is flowing . . . and so is the Quantum life force you both share. It's only natural to get in "sync" with each other and really tune in, turn on and let go.

You and your lover are in for a better sex life — far better than you ever dreamed possible. By all means, ENJOY IT!

Chapter 35

Overcoming Frigidity

"Sex is a flame which uncontrolled may scorch; properly guided, it will light the torch of eternity."
JOSEPH FETTERMAN

Can You Be Too Cool?

One of the textbook problems occurring around sexuality is the failure to become sexually aroused. In women, this is known technically as "frigidity", while in men it is called "impotence". Thus, the inability of some women to let go and enjoy sexual contact has been medicalized and presented as a treatable medical/psychological disorder. The concept is quite cruel, as it suggests normal women are hot and if you're not . . . you have a medical/psychological disorder. Many women think of themselves as cold as ice. They get down on themselves, because they buy into the belief that they are unable to turn on, heat up, melt and respond the way "normal" women do. If you buy into that rot and consider yourself frigid, please read on.

We do not accept the concept of "frigidity". We believe that the key to determining whether or not you need help is your answer to the following question: Do you feel your ability to respond sexually is limited or frustrated?

It's Your Decision

If you wish to enhance your sexual response, the imagery found in chapters 34 and 38 can help you get back in touch with your sexuality in a very positive way.

The Exercise

Put your hand on the bottom of your vagina and find the area between your anus and your vagina. Now mentally tense the muscles in this area. (For purposes of this exercise, we will call this the "S" spot.) Now put your tongue on the roof of your mouth just behind your upper teeth, and imagine a very special link between sexual energy and this physical act. Imagine that sexual energies are moving up and down this pathway between these two parts of your body-mind.

If you are out of touch with your sexuality, you could practice this exercise while walking, sitting, standing up and lying down. Imagine that you are a channel for sexual energy and that every time you practice this exercise you are becoming a clearer channel and experiencing an explosion of excitement and pleasureable feeling as more and more sexual energy is running up and down your spine. As you practice, just think about sexual energy running through your body and mentally feel this energy inside you, and outside you on the surface of your skin.

Affirmations and Quantum Focus Imagery

The following affirmations are to be said out loud when your situation permits you to do so, or mentally to yourself, when your situation suggests this would be better, while you are in a deeply peaceful Quantum Focused state. Repeat the following affirmations seven times each, at least three times a day for about a month. After repeating the affirmations, do the above exercise and finish this healing experience by thinking about something in your past that really turned you on. If you can't recall something from your past experience, make something up . . . take it step by step . . . see, hear, and feel yourself become sexually turned on. The exercise, affirmations and imagery work synergistically and thus are far more powerful when applied together.

Your affirmations are:

- Sexual pleasure is a healthy and natural human state.
- I am open and receptive to my natural ability for sexual arousal.
- I joyfully surrender to my sensual and sexual awakenings.
- I am brimming with sexual excitement.
- When I give myself over to sex all other thoughts fade away.
- I feel very good about myself.
- I am ready, willing, and able to have great sex!

Have patience with yourself. Be loving and forgiving. It will happen surprisingly quickly, so relax, let go and enjoy yourself!

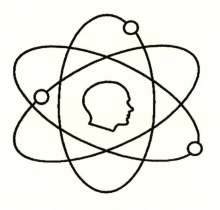

Chapter 36

Overcoming Impotence

"Man is a reasoning rather than a reasonable animal."
ALEXANDER HAMILTON

While It's No Big Thing . . .

The inability of a man to complete a sexual act is medically called impotence. In its common usage, the term is generally understood to mean the inability to achieve and maintain an erection during sexual contact.

Most men experience this problem in their lifetime and, more often than not, it is self-limiting. It is more common than premature ejaculation, the second most frequent complaint about sex. But for premature ejaculation, mere rest and relaxation often remedy this temporary condition.

Impotence can be caused by medication, injury or disease . . . although the major cause is most often psychological. So, the first step to take, if you are experiencing impotence that doesn't just disappear spontaneously (and quickly), should be a complete physical examination and consultation with your health care provider.

... And Can Be Depressing

Impotence is often very emotionally painful and plays havoc with a man's self-esteem. Most often the psychological problems are the hardest to relieve because the person gets caught up in a spiral of increasing pressure. He develops the expectation of failure, becomes more concerned about failing, puts more pressure on himself not to fail, thus increasing the likelihood of failure, and this leads him to a self-fulfilling chronic problem.

... You Can't Keep A Good Man Down

This chapter is designed to help you assist your doctor in helping you, or to help you self-heal this problem if no physical causes are found. The imagery and affirmations also complement working with a sex therapist if you so choose.

In our experience, the problem is most often simply misunderstood and then, as mentioned above, psychologically amplified by incorrectly perceived worries, self-doubts, and challenges to one's manhood. Most of the men we know who had this problem were not aware of the many unrelated worries and doubts they had on their minds. Financial security, problems on the job and relationship problems were the most commonly reported ones, so a part of them was not even turned on, though other parts seemed to be.

We have found that when we teach these clients to Quantum Focus their attention in the moment and put all their unwanted thoughts on hold — violá, no more problem. It is just this simple!

The Exercise

We highly recommend you incorporate the Magic Smile experience found in chapter 8 and work the affirmations and imagery found in chapter 34 into your daily practice. In your Quantum Focused state, add the following affirmations to the affirmations in chapter 8 and visualize yourself having great, satisfying sex with your partner. The affirmations were designed to quickly neutralize doubts and increase your sexual confidence and performance.

- I tune in and turn on.
- All worries and concerns are put on hold. They quickly fade away.
- I am in the moment; I feel excited and sensual.
- Sexual pleasure is my natural birthright; I deserve to enjoy this.
- I feel sexy and alive. I am turned on.
- My penis knows what to do.
- My penis is becoming aroused.
- My penis is throbbing with excitement.
- I am ready, willing and able to have great, satisfying sex.

Power Image

Your Power Image is especially well-suited to this challenge. Create one in which you can see yourself going from the present "what is" to the future "what is" that you are now making the present "what is." Use this whenever you feel it will help, even if it's only for five to ten seconds at the appropriate time.

A Word About Exercise

Exercise is a two-fold help in overcoming impotence. First, it is a great de-stressor, getting rid of some of the built-up blocks to good sex. Second, it improves your self-image. This can also translate directly into better sex.

And A Word About Premature Ejaculation

The approach used to overcome impotence is also very useful when applied to premature ejaculation. Simply make your affirmations more appropriate to the situation. Your Power Image is absolutely dynamite here!

Chapter 37

Enhancing Creativity

"Ideas are the root of creation."
ERNEST DIMNET

At Times, We All Believe It

Have you ever been in a position where you've said, even to yourself, "I wish I were more creative" or "I'm just not a creative person". Of course you have. We all have, usually when faced with something that is not even that important to our lives. One of us remembers struggling for days over what costume to wear to a masquerade party. "And the costume I eventually devised wasn't very creative, despite my agonizing over it for so long. I also recall wracking my brain to find a theme for a party which, again, was okay but not spectacular when I chose it. Oh how I wish I had known then what I know now!"

Who Is Creative?

Researchers (from Alex Osborn's pioneering work half a century ago right up through Edward de Bono and the University of Buffalo's Sidney Parnes) study creativity and its prevalence in the population. They measure creativity in numerous ways and look for correlations with other traits. Their studies find a wide range of demonstrated creative ability. Interestingly, creativity does not seem to be associated with any other measurable characteristics. It is found equally in males and females. It has no relationship to intelligence scores and, in general, defies attempts to characterize who will be creative and who will not. The most common results of these studies are usually just descriptions of a range of creative ability across the population. They consistently tell us that, like it or not, some of us are very creative while others of us have essentially no creative abilities at all. We know from our experience that this conclusion is ridiculous!

A Natural Ability

In investigating creativity, the root of the problem is that the researchers can only measure creativity *as it is demonstrated by their subjects during the study*. They cannot measure the innate ability of each subject to be creative. This would require that they first train the subjects to be creative by reopening their natural abilities, which would then invalidate their findings about how creative we are.

We are certain that creativity, like all talents, comes in a wide range of abilities. As noted above, according to the research done, the generally accepted idea is that this range goes from very creative to totally non-creative. However, when we have worked with supposedly "non-creative" people to reawaken their natural abilities, we have found that they become quite creative. It is our position that the range of innate creative ability actually goes from "very creative" through "more creative" and up to "incredibly creative". *There are no non-creative people*, just people with their creative abilities asleep or undeveloped.

Beware Of Others' Beliefs . . .

We all have creative abilities deep within us. We are born with them. Like so many other things we learn in life as we grow up, we often learn that we are not creative. More correctly, we actually learn that we "should not be" creative, for creativity stems from imagination. . .and imagination is usually discouraged by our parents, teachers and so on.

It is not that they mean to make us unimaginative. It is that our imagination appears outwardly to others like we are not doing anything. They cannot see our thoughts. They only see us staring off into space with a blank look on our faces which they cannot understand. "Stop daydreaming! Go do something useful with your time". Or, often more directly, "If you've got nothing to do, go clean up your room". If you are told often enough that imagination is a "waste of your time", you eventually learn not to imagine. Some of us have just been luckier than others in that we had the right encouragement, either from our parents, teachers or friends, or even from our own inner knowing, and we kept the imaginative, creative process awake.

We see this daily in the practice of hypnotherapy. Many people who come to us for help have had their imaginations almost totally closed down during their upbringing. Yet, with a little coaching, encouragement and practice, they prove to be very creative. The long and short of it is, if you are a typical individual, YOU HAVE A GREATER CREATIVE ABILITY THAN YOU'VE EVER IMAGINED! Which just proves the point. If your imagination were running at its full capacity, you would already have imagined how creative you are. You would already know that you are creative. The mere fact that you might consider yourself limited in creative ability proves how much more you still have within.

... And Make Our Own Unlimited

The key to unleashing your full creative power is to unlearn how you've already learned to think. It is our rigorous rules for how to think that act like brakes on our creative accelerator. We want to be creative, but we unconsciously limit ourselves because of the way we think. It is time to train ourselves to think differently — more creatively if you wish.

One of us concluded, "This was the main reason my attempts at a costume and a party theme went awry. I tried to be creative by thinking the way I always had. I just tried to do it harder!" This won't work. Yet, it is usually our first response. For example, imagine a pencil. How big is it? What color is it? What valuable uses does it have? For most of us, there is a rather short and fairly well-defined list of answers that come to mind when we ask ourselves those questions.

The exercise below is designed to help you reawaken your ability to think expansively about any issue. It uses that pencil as an example. But as you practice, you will want to substitute other items and ideas. You won't be able to help doing so as your creative abilities continue to revitalize themselves and begin to take over the exercise. Pretty soon, you'll be thinking in creative ways without even thinking about it.

Creativity Enhancement Exercise

Find a comfortable place and enter your Quantum Focus state. Take several extra minutes to relax yourself completely. Mentally watch and sense your muscles relaxing sequentially from the scalp at the top of your head all the way down to the tips of your toes. As you imagine all the stress, all the tension, all the strain just draining out through your toes, you will feel your creative juices begin to pulse.

Now imagine yourself in some wonderful place, perhaps your special place where you've been so many times before. Choose a place where you will be free from any restrictions placed on you by your everyday world. Just enjoy being here for several minutes, breathing free and easy, body and mind clear and free from discomfort or distraction, your mood excellent and balanced.

Notice that you already feel an increase in the intensity of your creative flow. This may be the only time during your day that you fully realize you are much more creative when you relax, when you don't work hard at thinking.

As you continue to relax, remind yourself that you can always take twenty minutes to relax; to feel good; to center and balance yourself. And while you do this, creativity just naturally flows. Your unconscious mind will do the "working harder" part of the task, without you paying any conscious attention to the effort or consciously putting in the effort.

In this relaxed, creative environment, your only "task" is to enjoy your thoughts of peace and comfort while you permit your mind to be creative all by itself. Remember to forget about thinking consciously and forget about remembering to consciously think. Just be.

Allow the image of a pencil to come into your thoughts. How big is it? Make it bigger. Bigger still. Move it outdoors if you have to and make it bigger yet. Now, you could push the pointed end easily into the ground and use it for a telephone pole. Make it bigger still. Even bigger. Imagine it with a hollowed-out space running up through the middle. In this space is a spiral stairway which is the way for someone to get up to the eraser and turn it on. See the top rotating. Watch the eraser-light blink on and off. What a novel way to build a lighthouse.

What color is your lighthouse? Change it to white with red trim. Now red with white trim. Now red with blue trim. Blue with white. And several more combinations of your choosing. Now make it smaller again. Still smaller. Small enough to be a pencil again. With the light, you can now use pencil in the dark. But make it still smaller. Smaller and smaller.

Attach a piece of line to the front end and mentally insert it into a vein of a person with clogged arteries. The light makes it easy to navigate through the circulatory system, and when you encounter any plaque on the arterial walls, erase it. See the person healthier and happier because of your pencil.

Again make it the usual pencil size, if you can remember what that is. Add a pleasant scent to the graphite core (the "lead") of your pencil. Write with it. As you write, the scent is vaporized and you have a room deodorizer. Neat, huh? Change the scent. Use vanilla, then sandlewood, then pine, orange or lemon. Describe the color of each scent. Which do you enjoy the most?

Give yourself permission to allow other changes to your object, changes in size, color, composition, texture, and so on. It was once a pencil. What is it now? (Pause) And now? (Pause) And now? Take your time and have fun with your object.

By now, you feel the glimmerings of your own creative abilities as they have gotten involved so easily with this process. Let these abilities "run wild" for two or three minutes of clock time while they automatically strengthen themselves and relax you even deeper.

Then, permit yourself to reorient to the outside world with the great anticipation of modifying this exercise appropriately each time you do it (even more easily) in the future.

When you have returned to your normal waking state of consciousness, take a moment to reflect on how much fun this is.

As with all the exercises in this book, repetition makes them more powerful. But this one has some special powers of its own. Somehow, you will sense the joy in it very quickly. It seems to directly arouse the imaginative, creative process the very first time you do it. This exercise is more play than exercise. It is simply fun to do, and you will find yourself substituting, first, all kinds of objects, and then more abstract thoughts, as you permit your creativity to take it over for you.

Choose Your Time

To some extent, we are subject to our biorhythms. While it is possible to overcome the natural high and low parts of our days, why not use the highs and circumvent the lows when we can? If the situation arises when you need to perform at your best while you are not at your biorhythmic best, do it! You can alter your biorhythm with your Quantum Focus practice.

But nature created those rhythms for a reason. They are part of the universal energies and their balance. Remember back in chapter 29 (page 255) you learned that you can have too much of a good thing. So work with your own rhythm when you have the option.

Determining Your Peak Time

There are two ways to determine the peak part(s) of the day for you. First is the mechanical approach. Simply take your temperature several times each day for several days. The part of the day when your body temperature is highest will be your peak hours for performance, physical and mental.

The other way is to listen to your inner guidance. You will soon be able to tell when your peak hours occur. Sometimes it's fun to determine your peak period this way first. Then measure your temperature if you want to confirm how well you are mentally attuned to yourself.

And A Couple More Ideas

One of the best ways to increase your creativity is to try new things. The more new things you get involved with, the more chances you have to be creative. The more chances you have, the more creative you'll be.

Keeping a journal is another aid to increasing your creativity. Looking back over things you have done, from the perspective of greater experience, is often a source of insight. Something that was elusive then may be very clear now.

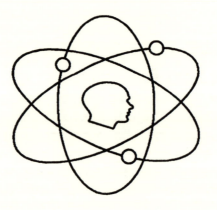

Chapter 38

Inner Child Care

*"Our remedies oft in ourselves do lie,
which we ascribe to Heaven."*
WILLIAM SHAKESPEARE

The Unanimous Decision

It is often said, "If you think you can, you can". This is only true, in our opinion, when the person has no inner conflicts or doubts. Thinking you can is not enough! There must be total agreement!

Millions of mental viruses that develop into unconscious fears and doubts can limit and weaken our creative powers. Many of these infections occur during childhood and remain hidden inside us. When a person is so divided, "thinking you can" is never enough. When a person thinks, "I can," and another part of them thinks, "Oh NO I can't!", the result is always failure. They cannot!

We call this the Ellner-Jamison Law. In such a conflict, the doubts and fears always win. But with total inner agreement, it is our opinion that outcomes are easily predictable. You can do anything you think you can! When you are in agreement in body/mind/spirit, you can! This, too, is part of the Ellner-Jamison Law. If you think you can, and you are in agreement with your inner child that you can, we truly believe you can do just about anything.

An Old And Proven Concept

This simple healing concept has been, and is, used by many healers, counselors and therapists to help a person achieve total inner agreement. Your "Inner Child" can be a powerful ally. In fact, we created a very special Quantum Focus exercise which contains a powerful mental ritual for use anytime you wish a renewed sense of peace and inner well-being. We call this exercise the Quantum Focus Magic Smile, and invite you now to experience our healing ceremony.

The Magic Smile Exercise

Please shift into a Quantum Focused state and begin to imagine that you are in your personal paradise. You are secure, happy and at peace. Now very gently turn your attention to your heart. Imagine that every beat of your heart is now taking you deeper and deeper inside yourself as you now begin to notice your inner child taking shape in your mind's eye. Your surroundings disappear from your awareness and you become engrossed with your inner child's manifestation.

You are now seeing your inner child's face clear as a bell. As you continue to view your inner child's face . . . tell your inner child that you are happy to give "as much unconditional love as is necessary" in order for both of you to release painful memories and limiting beliefs.

Love and imagination are the best medicine in caring for your inner child . . . unconditional love and forgiveness clear your energy fields and restore your psychospiritual health. You can feel this happening and you easily drift deeper and deeper into this healing experience. This is a good time to mentally review your most personal resolutions and goals.

Your inner child is very interested in your wildest dreams and, as if by magic, your inner child begins to share your visions and dreams. Your inner child begins to believe in your dreams. You are now feeling waves of youthful joy and desire. It is one of the most powerful feelings in the universe! These are the kind of wonderful feelings that turbocharge people and empower them to make their dreams come true. Enjoy it. Let it turbocharge and empower you.

Very good, now once again focus on your inner child's face. This time imagine that the face of your inner child is the size of a movie screen. Notice a magical smile starting in your inner child's eyes and slowly moving across its whole face. This powerful image is now planted deep within your being. Whenever you call it to mind, the smile transforms you . . . you feel a smile deep within your being and it spreads rapidly into every cell in your body . . . radiating a mystical sensation which moves in and around you.

You feel an inner freedom when you feel centered and deeply connected to the moment. You feel ready for anything and deeply confident as you become aware that your inner smile is about to reveal itself to the world by communicating through your now smiling eyes and the smile moving across your face. Feel the smile inside you, moving the muscles in your eyes and mouth into a healing and psychospiritual nourishing smile.

Now, as you begin to shift back into your waking state, mentally flash on your inner child's smiling face and remember, when you are in total agreement, you can do anything! Now open your eyelids; your eyes want to smile.

We recommend you use this basic imagery as follows:

Upon awakening, before getting out of bed, recall your inner child's face and imagine that the smile in your inner child's eyes are again releasing those feel-good mystical sensations that make every cell in your body want to smile. Just for today, begin your day with a big smile.

Allow 3 minutes for a mental recess midday. This time, take a deep breath and allow your eyes to go out of focus but remain open. Recall your inner child's smiling eyes in your mind's eye. Feel those mystical sensations that make every cell in your body want to smile. Now return to your waking consciousness (to the moment) and give the world a big smile.

Upon retiring for the night, gently relax your body and recall your inner child. Now ask your inner child to help you resolve all the stuff that is on your mind, knowing full well that if you and your inner child sleep on it and work together, anything is possible. Now give yourself over to a restful, healing sleep.

Good Night, sleep loose.

Chapter 39

Learning Faster

"The secret of education lies in respecting the pupil."
RALPH WALDO EMERSON

Are Those Old Beliefs Back Again?

Were you ever told that you just couldn't do some particular thing right? How about that you simply have no aptitude for some specific activity? Maybe you heard, "Can't you do anything right?" One of us was told he had done something "stupid" by more than one teacher during his education. This generally happened when he had found a different solution to a problem than the one they favored. At one time or another, we've all been told something unflattering and indicative of the fact that we just were unteachable or incapable of learning.

Many of these negative experiences occurred in school, but many others happened outside of the "educational institutions". One of us remembers long ago when a then coworker had made an error in something new he had been told to do. "I vividly remember the boss telling him, 'I want you to send a letter to your major professor in college. And I want you to tell him that he is an idiot . . . because he trained you and *you* are an idiot!' He said this in a very loud voice and in front of about a dozen employees."

Who Is Really At Fault?

Remember how many times you've heard a parent, perhaps even one of your own parents, suggest something similar to a child. Or heard "friends" tell one another about all the things they couldn't learn to do. No wonder learning is a word that makes many of us feel very uncomfortable when we think we are the ones who have something to learn. There is a part of us that wants to avoid getting into any position where anything like the above examples could happen again. The truth of the matter is, our ability to learn was not at fault. The fault lay in their lack of teaching skill.

We Learn Differently . . .

We each learn in different ways. Consider this. Your teenager constantly receives poor grades in history or language at school. Seems they cannot remember dates or vocabulary. Maybe they cannot remember anything else for that matter, for when you have asked him or her to do something for you around the house, they have conveniently forgotten. Yet, he or she knows all the words to every song played on MTV or their favorite rock station. And they learn (i.e. remember) the words to the new songs after hearing them only a few times. Can't be the memory that doesn't work, can it?

. . . And Exhibit Fantastic Abilities

But despite this innate ability to learn that we all have, we somehow get to the point of beginning to believe that we cannot learn. Notice how, before we were age two or three — before we had taken on board that we could not learn — we had managed to learn to walk, talk and perform many other acts and basic social skills. Researchers still wonder how we do all this. Once we begin to believe that we cannot learn this or that, however, our mind sets up the conditions to "keep us honest" and makes it difficult or impossible for us to achieve that goal.

... Until We Give Up

Is this hopeless? Suppose that, faced with balancing your checkbook and managing your personal budget, you believe:

- I can't do math.
- I can't figure this out.
- I never know how to handle these situations.
- I need someone to tell me how to do this.
- I'm not smart, or "smart enough", or even "too stupid" to do this.

Does this mean you are beyond help? ABSOLUTELY NOT! It may mean you have to get some short-term help in order to learn now the things you didn't learn earlier, but you can do it. You need three things to be successful. First, the desire to do whatever it is. You probably wouldn't be reading this chapter without that desire so we can assume you already have the first requirement. Then, second, you need to believe that you can do it. This chapter is designed to attain that requirement. Third, you need a method to put the first two requirements together.

And for that, you have one of the most powerful methods — Quantum Focus — in your hands right now.

So Let's Get Learning!

What are you waiting for? What is it you would like to learn? Not "learn" the way you used to think of the word, but learn by a new, faster, easier method. Lessons for school? A new method for doing something around the house? How to use your new computer? To read faster or retain more of what you read? To have a better memory in general? To concentrate better? To get along with people better? It makes no difference what you want to learn. If you can find the knowledge somewhere, in a book, or with someone else who knows what you want to learn, you can learn it too!

Despite how well this works, it is not magic. It works by releasing powers and abilities you already have but are not using to their fullest potential. Once you take off the brakes, you'll be astounded by how fast your mental engine can run. So, let's take off the brakes.

There is one bit of preparation you must do other than the exercise that follows. Find a source for the knowledge or know-how you want to learn. While this may come in many formats, all entail one or more of the following: reading, watching, hearing and experimenting. We will work with all of these in the exercise below. Feel free to modify the exercise appropriately if you want to work with only one or two of them.

Faster Learning Exercise
Phase One

This phase of increasing your learning ability is to be done daily during the period that you are actively acquiring your new knowledge.

With the intention of becoming deeply relaxed, sit or lie down, gently close your eyelids and take two or three long, deep, calming breaths. Feel yourself drawing in peacefulness with each relaxing breath in, and exhaling all your problems, worries and concerns with each breath out. Permit yourself to slip quietly and comfortably into your Quantum Focused state.

Realize that your inner mind will very quickly take over this experience for you as you mentally allow your body to fade out of your awareness. You may feel a sense of being in a favorite place where you are relaxed. Perhaps it will appear as a warm tropical isle; maybe it will feel like a cool green forest; or maybe just the sound of soothing music lights up your relaxed mind. Or, perhaps it is the new awareness of the presence of nothingness that fills your mind with its pleasant emptiness. Sit and enjoy that for a while.

Now imagine yourself about to learn something new. Instruct yourself exactly as follows, using all the phrases that apply to what you are going to do.

A) "I am about to read how to (insert what you are going to learn). I am interested in this. It is important and valuable to me and will make my life better. I will read this material easily, in a relaxed manner, and will retain all I need to know in order to accomplish my objective."

B) "I am about to watch a demonstration of a way to (insert your objective). I am interested in this. It is important and valuable to me and will make my life better. As I watch this example, I will remain relaxed and see all that I need to see in order to do this procedure. I will understand and remember all I need to be successful at (insert your objective)."

C) "I am about to listen to a lecture on (insert the topic). I am interested in this. It is important and valuable to me and will make my life better. I will listen in a relaxed manner, allowing all the knowledge I need to enter my mind freely. I will retain all I need to accomplish my goal."

D) "I am about to do (insert the task) for the first time. I am interested in doing this. It is important and valuable to me and will make my life better. As I work at this, effective and efficient ways to accomplish it become obvious to me. I learn easily from every move I make, retain all the useful methods for repeated use whenever I need them, and enjoy relaxed success."

Now imagine yourself going through whatever learning experience you will go through. See yourself absorbing the knowledge — actually watch it drifting through the air and into your mind. Then, see yourself becoming proficient at whatever it is you have learned.

As you drift and drift, you become more and more aware of new possibilities. Allow yourself to bask in the good feelings and sensations and you begin to open to a whole new way of seeing yourself and the world you live in. Feel the excitement and peace that can bring.

And now, very slowly, permit your attention to gently return to a fully conscious and aware state. Let your inner mind guide you back to the present; to the here and now . . . feeling at peace, energized and completely alert.

Faster Learning Exercise
Phase Two

This phase is to be done immediately before you go into the learning experience in the "real world" (i.e. just before going to the lecture or before beginning to assemble that new unit at work). Just prior to beginning, take 15 seconds, close your eyes if you can do so without causing any undue attention or danger[3], permit your Quantum Focused state to take control, and mentally say to yourself whichever of the following is appropriate.

A) "I am about to read how to (insert what you are going to learn). I am interested in this. It is important and valuable to me and will make my life

---

3. Obviously, don't close your eyes if this creates a dangerous situation. For example, if you are learning to drive, it is perfectly okay to close your eyes before you take control of the car. It would be very foolish to close them after you have taken control. Use good judgment about this.

better. I will read this material easily, in a relaxed manner, and retain all that I need to know in order to accomplish my objective."

B) "I am about to watch a demonstration of a way to (insert your objective). I am interested in this. It is important and valuable to me and will make my life better. As I watch this example, I will remain relaxed and see all that I need to see in order to do this procedure. I will understand and remember all that I need to be successful at (insert your objective)."

C) "I am about to listen to a lecture on (insert the topic). I am interested in this. It is important and valuable to me and will make my life better. I will listen in a relaxed manner, allowing all the knowledge I need to enter my mind freely. I will retain all I need to accomplish my goal."

D) "I am about to do (insert the task) for the first time. I am interested in doing this. It is important and valuable to me and will make my life better. As I work with this, effective and efficient ways to accomplish it become obvious to me. I learn easily from every move I make, retain all the useful ones for repeated use whenever I need them, and enjoy relaxed success."

Then, open your eyes (if they were closed) and go about doing whatever it is you're doing. This will have triggered your mind to accept whatever follows in the "real world" exactly as it did in your practice during phase one.

When you finish doing whatever it is you have done, again take 15 seconds, slip into your Quantum Focused state and say to yourself:

"I have just completed (reading/watching/listening/doing whatever it was). I am interested in this. It is important and valuable to me and will make my life better. I have now learned and will retain all I need."

Open your eyes, returning to your usual state of alertness, and trust you have now gained new knowledge more easily than you ever did before.

Other Things To Do

Here are a few other ways to have a positive influence on our ability to learn. Pick and choose those you like, or use them all. You will quickly find the best combination to maximize the results of your learning style.

Music

There is extensive evidence that music, especially classical music, speeds learning. There appears to be something magical about classical music. For example, University of California (Irvine) researchers found that playing Mozart in the background improved learning ability, memory, and I.Q. To date, most studies on the effect of music and learning have been conducted using either classical or rock music and most of the results have shown that classical music improves learning, while hard rock diminishes it.

This appears to be more attributable to the attention-grabbing capacity of the music rather than the class to which it belongs. All music speeds learning, probably because of its ability to stimulate "whole brain" functioning. When we use our whole brain, we learn better. Soft, relaxing music (classical, New Age and so on) seems to speed learning more than other forms because it is background music. It does not distract attention from the subject you want to learn. Whole brain stimulation plus attention to the subject yields great results.

Hard rock has more of a tendency to attract attention away from the apparent object of learning. But its ability to enhance the act of learning itself is evident when you consider that those who use rock while studying may not learn the target subject as well as those who use softer music, but they do know all the lyrics. You just have to wonder where their attention really was while studying. It would be interesting to compare results using the 1812 Overture turned up high.

Work Your Peak Hours

Taking on challenges, mental or physical, is always easiest when we work during our peak period of the day. Chapter 37 included instructions for determining when your peak time occurs. Using this time will multiply all your other efforts and increase the speed with which you obtain results.

Smart Pills . . .

There is an old joke (probably several) about smart pills. It concerned a not particularly bright guy who was having trouble with a girl he really liked. She was not interested in him in any way, shape or fashion. No matter how he approached her, she always refused to give him the time of day. He was heartbroken, but undaunted. He would simply keep trying until she said yes.

Another fellow, who knew exactly how much this first fellow wanted to hook this woman, came to him and said, "Do you know that the trouble you're having with her is easy to solve? You just haven't got the brains to figure it out. But I can help you to get around that little obstacle."

"Oh," said the first guy. "I'd be very grateful if that is true. Tell me how you can do it?"

"It's very easy. I have a box of smart pills. You take three of these every morning and you will become very, very smart . . . smart enough to win her hand. I have to tell you that they are rare and difficult to get so they are very expensive."

"How much are they?" asked the first man.

"Five dollars apiece. And I only have this one bottle of 100 pills."

"That's fine," said man number one. "Give me the whole bottle."

He had to go to a nearby money machine to get that much money. He did and paid the second man $500 for the bottle, not knowing that the bottle, from which the label had been removed, contained only a common pain reliever. He took the bottle and went home, extremely anxious to start taking them the next day so he could become smart . . . smart enough to win his woman.

Well, he took three pills the next morning, and was rejected again when he approached the object of his affection. He took three more the next day, with the same result. And so it went for the next two weeks. That day, he encountered the man who sold him the pills. He went up to him and said, "Say, I've been taking those pills you sold me every day for two weeks. Nothing is happening. I don't think they work and I think you cheated me."

"I didn't cheat you," said the second man. "Look. You're already smarter than you were two weeks ago!"

. . . Or Are They?

It is never as easy as this example to determine the impact of chemicals on intelligence. However, unlike the story above, there is an increasing amount of evidence to indicate that what we eat has an impact on how well we think. High-protein-containing foods have an arousing effect, improving our alertness and probably our basic capacity to think. Carbohydrate-rich foods have a tendency to be calming and dulling, both physically and mentally.

There is also mounting evidence that some supplements positively impact our ability to think, reason, learn and remember. The scope of this subject is much too broad for us to discuss fully here. We want to provide you with the basic information to let you know it exists so those of you who might have an interest in the effect of nutrition on mental acuity can follow up this line of research on your own.

Several B vitamins have been shown to improve mental abilities. Thiamin in particular has received frequent accolades and choline has been touted to improve neurotransmitter function within the brain. Vitamin B^{12} has also been shown to help mental functioning. However, B vitamins should be balanced to work effectively, so if you decide to supplement some of them, supplement them all. Vitamin C has been given high marks too.

Some herbs have also been credited with improving mental function. Ginkgo Biloba, for example, is claimed to increase circulation to the brain. (Increased oxygenation seems to be the mechanism through which exercise provides its mental benefits too.) We know one 55-year-old individual who demonstrated dramatic improvement in memory after beginning regular daily Ginkgo use. Impressive results have also been claimed for Gotu Kola and Ginseng.

Minerals have also received some attention. Zinc, for instance, has been useful in improving learning abilities in experiments with monkeys. This may or may not be directly applicable to man, but there is an appreciable percentage of the population who is, at best, only marginally well-fed as far as zinc is concerned.

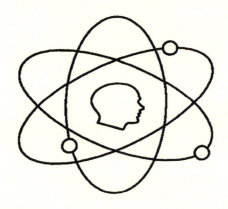

Chapter 40

Remembering More

Do you remember?
(Or, as the song said, "Memories are made of this")

What Was That Again?

Do you remember the last time you forgot something? Perhaps it was a phone number or a loved one's birthday. Or are you one of the many people who never forgets a face but often can't remember the name that goes with it? The exercises and affirmations that follow, when combined with the imagery found in chapter 38, will help you remember more . . . and make *you* very easy to remember! That's right, one of the most wonderful benefits to be found in developing your Quantum Focus skills is that the daily practice will greatly enhance the impression you make on the world.

Remember This!

This may be a good time to remind you that the goals of Quantum Focus are *to help you increase your innate creative skills and abilities and to introduce you to optimal levels of functioning*.

As you practice and develop your innate creative skills and abilities and begin to live in the moment, you are tapping into your spirituality and providing yourself your daily requirement of *this essential nutrient*. You are also processing information at optimal levels. As you begin to experience the power and bliss found in the moment, you will also discover the many lessons to be found only in the now. Your skills at this will heighten your awareness of every gesture you make, every step you take. The exercises are engineered to help develop your concentration and focusing skill. Again, when combined with the imagery found in chapter 38, your memory will become fine-tuned and help you make a memorable impression.

But first the affirmations. You remember, we use affirmations to deprogram any self-limiting beliefs that may hide out in our psyche. In the case of memory, many people think, "I'm not good with names.", "I'm terrible with numbers." or "I can never remember to . . ." How much of a role do these suggestions play in our remembering or not remembering?

The Memory Conditioner

We begin these exercises by memorizing the affirmations below and shifting into a Quantum state of bodymindspirit.
(REPEAT 3 TIMES MENTALLY AND 3 TIMES OUT LOUD)

- My memory is razor sharp and clear.
- My memory is getting better every day.
- I can remember names and I do.
- I can remember anything I want to.

Now, before you begin Exercise 1, come back into the moment. In the Far East, tea ceremonies are a very special teaching experience. The serving of the tea is treated as a sacred act. Everything is done with the precision that is only found in being in the moment. The student puts his/her total attention into the serving of the tea.

Treat the experience of Exercise 1 as if it were a tea ceremony. That is, give it the blessing of your full and undivided attention. Remain in the moment, aware of every step you take, aware of every movement you make, and set up the chair and candle you will need.

The Memory Conditioner
Exercise 1

(You will need a watch with a second hand and a candle for this exercise.)

Place the candle approximately 15 feet away from where you will be sitting and light it. Sit down, take a deep calming breath and gently focus your full attention on the candle's flame. Be aware of sitting in the chair, of the air on your skin, and any and all feelings that arise from sitting and watching the candle.

Create a line of vision between you and the flame and give your full attention to the flame, but first note the time. Note the elapsed time every time your attention shifts. Are you able to focus on the flame for 30 seconds, 60 seconds, 120 seconds? With practice you will soon be able to focus on the flame for 1, 2 or 5 minutes without any physical or emotional complaint or effort.

Tonight, when brushing your teeth, treat it as if it were a tea ceremony and give it your full focused attention. Keep this focused attention on everything between now and falling asleep.

The Memory Conditioner
Exercise 2

This exercise will combine your skill in dialing a phone number and committing it to memory within the tip of your dialing finger. We call this exercise the "magic" finger. Do it as if it were a tea ceremony.

During the next several weeks, every time you dial a phone number be in the moment. Focus on your dialing finger tapping out the number dialed, as if the memory is going to reside in your finger. Do this with phone numbers you are committing to memory and with numbers you already know. Pass the numbers you know on to your fingers. With practice you will be able to really let your fingers do the dialing.

The Memory Conditioner
Exercise 3

During the next several days, whenever you meet someone treat the meeting as if it were a tea ceremony. Give whomever you are greeting your total undivided attention. Be aware of being deeply centered and calm and turn your full attention to this person. Just be with the person.

This will greatly improve both the experience and your overall memory. It will help you to develop a computer-like memory and remember names, faces, numbers with ease.

Some Additional Help

Check out the hints at the end of chapter 39 on faster learning. These apply to our memory skills too. After all, learning is made up of understanding, remembering and then being able to apply the material we have acquired.

Chapter 41

Better Golf

*"Let me get this straight: The less I hit the ball,
the better I am doing . . . Then why do it at all?"*

Johnny Hart (in "BC")

Applying Quantum Focus to sports is one of the most visible ways to appreciate the ability and effectiveness of releasing your inner mind's power. Here is an opportunity to measure something tangible, not a feeling or an attitude, which will impress and convince even the most skeptical of people.

Different Strokes For Different Folks

We begin with improving a game of golf, and continue with tennis and bowling in the next two chapters. Please understand, though, that the technique we are using is applicable to any sport you wish to pursue. Golf, tennis and bowling were selected based on their popularity. We have worked with people in many kinds of sports: runners, triathletes, softball players, card players (*they* insisted it was a sport), gymnasts, swimmers and jugglers, to name just a few. These people demonstrate the wide applicability and flexibility of Quantum Focus techniques.

It's Amazing What They Study In High School

A basketball foul-shooting study done at the University of Chicago with some high school kids helps demonstrate the power of this technique. A class was divided into three groups. Each group took a number of foul shots to establish a baseline. The three groups were essentially equal in ability.

One group was told to come back in six weeks. They were not to touch a basketball in the meantime. They were not to watch basketball games. They were not even to think about basketball. Just show up in six weeks!

The second group practiced shooting foul shots 30 minutes every day for that six week period. To motivate them to take this practice seriously, it was intimated that they would be rewarded for their improvement.

The third group didn't touch a basketball again until the end of the experiment. But, they practiced mentally (i.e., visualized) for 30 minutes each day during the six week period. They were instructed to see themselves always making the shot. They were to be so good that they never missed.

How They Did

At the end of the six weeks, the three groups were brought together for testing. Each group shot a series of foul shots. The results are telling.

Group one, who did nothing for six weeks, equaled their earlier percentage of shots made. Group two, who practiced for 30 minutes each day, improved by 24 percent. Group three, who practiced only in their minds, improved by 23 percent.

The difference between groups two and three is not statistically significant. In essence, those who practiced only in their minds improved as much as those who stood out on the court every day to practice. It would have been interesting to see what a fourth group, one assigned to practice both mentally and physically, would have done!

Practice Makes Perfect?

The improvement that occurs in all sports is due to the following underlying principle. The mind cannot distinguish between vividly imagined and real events. At your Quantum Focused level, vividly imaging yourself playing your favorite sport creates an unconscious set of impulses to the muscles (sometimes called muscle memory) involved in that sport and unconscious patterns of thought that occur during playing. These become tendencies to move and think in those ways, which means you will perform the programmed actions in consistent, set ways. You tip the balance toward perfection and get better and better.

These same muscle and thought patterns are created while you actually play the game. This is the reason for practice! You keep doing it over until you can create the muscle memory and thought patterns that let you do it perfectly. So what's the difference between physical practice and mental practice?

Perfect Practice Makes Perfect!

In a nutshell, these thought and muscle patterns are created during practice by the actual motions you go through. When you play perfectly, you are forming these unconscious patterns to play perfectly. But when you play at some level other than perfect, you form patterns to play at this lesser level.

However, when you practice on your "inner field", that is in your mind in a Quantum Focused state, you *always* play perfectly! Remember the High School foul-shooting experiment. The third group was told to see themselves playing perfectly. They never missed. If you do not see yourself playing perfectly when you visualize your game, then CHANGE THE VISUALIZATION SO THAT YOU DO!!!

A question that comes up frequently is, "If I visualize that I play perfectly, then I should be able to play (run, swim, etc.) perfectly. This means that I will simply continue to form patterns for perfect performance every time I play". While various athletes have days when they perform "perfectly", they are not always perfect. Why are there no perfect performers?

The flaw in that argument lies in the premise, not in the conclusion. Remember, we are creating tendencies towards perfection. While these tendencies go a long way towards improving our physical performance and move us in the direction of perfect play, they may not take us all the way to perfection.[4]

Theoretically, if we could perform any action perfectly in a consistent manner, we would only get better. But first we have to achieve that consistent perfection. Then we could expect to show consistent perfect performance. If, on the other hand, we have occasional imperfect days, we are setting up imperfect tendencies. There is always a kind of tug-of-war between tendencies to do it perfectly and do it some other way. Actual physical practice is usually well-filled with actions short of perfection.

The reason for the impact of Quantum Focus techniques is that they help add more tendencies toward perfection. By adding more weight to this side of the balance, you get better and better. The key: always play perfectly in your Quantum Focus sessions!

Better Golf Exercise

Enter a Quantum Focused state and take your mind to a day at a favorite golf course. It may be one you play regularly, or one you have seen, or even one you have only dreamt about playing on.

---

4. We are speaking of perfection here in terms of sporting performance. Keep in mind that we are human and human is perfect just for being. Our perfection does not rely on anything being done at any specified level. Sports are something we add to our lives for pleasure and entertainment. Even the professional athletes derive some sense of pleasure from their sport, even if it's only a huge paycheck! But the absence of perfection in sports ability has no bearing on our being perfect human beings.

The day is perfect for golf. The temperature is just where you like it to be. There is exactly the amount of sunshine you feel is perfect for a great day on the links. There is almost no wind; only a mild, refreshing breeze that arises in-between shots. It keeps you comfortable while never interfering with your ball's true flight.

Despite the perfect day, the course is almost deserted except for you. If you feel like being alone, you can play the course all by yourself. If you enjoy the company of others, bring along those people who make up your ideal twosome, threesome or foursome. You can bring friends, loved ones, regular partners, or superstars. After all, you are so good at this game, they all want an opportunity to play with you and learn how they can improve!

Now take your time and actually play the course. Watch first as if you were watching a movie. See yourself teeing up the ball, swinging with a textbook style, and driving the ball straight and true down the fairway. It may land on the green; it may even be a hole-in-one. Usually, it is more fun to sink some beautiful putts during the game rather than just teeing off and picking your ball up out of the cup.

It is also useful to imagine yourself playing from some tougher positions, perhaps blasting out of a bunker up onto the green. Of course, the only way your ball could ever have wound up in a hazard is through some fluke event. Perhaps it hit a bird in flight which diverted its otherwise perfect trajectory, or maybe a mischievous squirrel picked it up and ran with it. But you accept these misfortunes gracefully and play the ball from these challenges perfectly.

Now change your perspective. Step into the picture and be the golfer. See the ball and the course as they look when you are on the course. Look at the ball as you step up to address it, feel the power and rhythm of your swing, hear the contact with the ball, watch it sail into the blue sky and come back down in a perfect line, right to where you intended to hit it.

Feel how the warmth of the sunshine and the cooling breeze in-between your shots is keeping you comfortable as you go around the course. Notice how easily you can read the breaks in the green, and how adeptly and perfectly you putt into the cup.

Take as much time as you want and need to enjoy this game of golf, maybe the best game you've ever played. At this same time, you are improving your ability to physically perform all of these shots you are playing perfectly in your mind right now. When you are finished, you might want to stop in at the nineteenth hole for a cooling glass of that special refreshing punch they serve on this course. You remember the one, the special one that helps to set all these impulses into your physical body so they are more potent the next time you play. Then allow yourself to return to your outer world.

We have two additional comments for your benefit. The first is that you will find this exercise exceptionally effective if you take ten or fifteen minutes to do it just before you go out onto the course. If you cannot do this in the clubhouse, then find a shady spot outside. Of course, if you would rather not let your regular golf companions in on the secret of your improved game, you may want to do the exercise before you leave home.

Second, as you step up to the ball on the course, simply close your eyes for a few seconds and picture in your mind exactly how you want to hit the ball and where you want to see it land. Then open your eyes and do it.

Other Approaches

Getting the best equipment is a prerequisite to playing your best game in any sport. Second-rate equipment will always keep you playing somewhere below the level at which you could be playing.

Consider, too, paying a professional instructor to help you straighten out any technical flaws you may have. Knowing how to do it right will help you to see yourself doing it right in your imaging.

Stay in the moment, using any of the Quantum Focus techniques you find most rapid and comfortable. This will keep you from letting previous shots or upcoming potential traps interfere with doing what you want to do *now*.

You can demonstrate the results of getting out of the moment and interfering with the unconscious muscle and thought patterns you are working to establish. This is a dirty trick, so we can't advise that you actually do it. We will only tell you about it to help solidify our point. The next time you're playing golf with someone who, on the back nine, holds a slight margin over you, watch the impact of the mind on their play when you say something like this.

"I've been admiring your ability to drive off the tee so consistently well. While I've been studying you, I've observed that most of your technique is obvious. There is one thing I would still like to know, though. Just when in your backswing do you inhale?"

Listen to the answer if you get one. Then step back and watch the fun. Although you may have been given some reply other than, "I don't know", it's a good bet he or she doesn't know. And now, for the rest of the round, he or she will be trying to figure it out while in the process . . . out of the moment and disrupting the unconscious flow they had been using before. You could easily win today's round.

Note: We advised you against putting this into practice. We must also advise you that it works repeatedly with the same person. Also, we will disavow any association with you, or knowledge of this, if your companion reads this book too.

Chapter 42

Better Tennis

"We have fun—that's what I like about bowling. You can have fun even if you stink, unlike in, say, tennis. Every decade or so, I attempt to play tennis, and it always consists of thirty-seven seconds of actually hitting the ball and two hours of yelling, 'Where did the ball go?' 'Over that condominium!' Etc. With bowling, once you let go of the ball, it's no longer your legal responsibility. They have these wonderful machines that find it for you and send it right back."

DAVE BARRY

If your tennis game resembles the one described above, use your Quantum Focus state and skills to dramatically change that. The exercise below can do wonders for your game. (See chapter 41 for a explanation of how and why this is so.)

Better Tennis Exercise

Begin by entering your Quantum Focused state and getting mentally ready for a great game of tennis. Start by imagining yourself in the stands waiting to see you play on the center court. It's the day of that big tournament and you're obviously excited and anxious to get going. The weather is cooperating by being perfect for the tournament. And the crowd is made up of many important celebrities who have come to watch you play. Everyone is impressed by what they already know of your abilities.

And then you see you and your opponent take the court. Your opponent can be anyone you wish. Graf? Nastase? Seles? Agassi? Bjorg? Riggs? King? Conners? Navratilova? McEnroe? Or a close friend with whom you love to play? You decide and play against whomever you wish.

Watch as the match begins. See how powerfully you serve the ball. Wow! An ace! Next serve. Again powerfully and well placed. This time the ball is returned and you play it back again and charge the net. Your opponent just gets to your shot and hits it back. You reach out and drop it just over the net and cross court. Your point again.

After you've watched you play for a while, noticing how well you recover from each shot you make to an advantageous position on the court. Watch and admire how perfectly you execute your serve, forehand and backhand.

Now step into that you on the court. Change the perspective so that you see the match through your eyes while you're on the court.

Continue to play your superb game. Feel the toss when you serve, and then feel the ball on the sweet spot of your racquet. Hear the sound of their meeting at the power point of your serve. Feel the perfect swing that delivers your serve into the opposite court in perfect position. You make your opponent work hard to return those serves that he or she can return at all.

Sense your cat-like balance as you spring from position to position, always poised to move quickly and gracefully. Feel your anticipation leading you in the right direction even before your opponent has hit the ball. Enjoy the way you can not only get to the ball, but also control exactly where and how you want to hit it. When you hit the ball, it is almost as though it knows just where it should go.

Keep mental track of the score: points, sets, whatever you enjoy. Have a great time. When you've finished, know that you have just improved your physical game, as well as your day, with this marvelous performance you turned in. When you're ready, return to your outer consciousness with a smile.

Have a great time with your new-found skills. As we recommended at the conclusion of the preceding chapter, you might find there is an even greater impact if you do this exercise just before you play. Unlike golf, you do not have time to visualize during a volley. By the time you open your eyes, the ball could be behind you. But you do have the time and opportunity to close your eyes for an instant to visualize just before you serve. Doing this will help improve your serve.

Your Power Image is ideal for use as a quick supercharger here.

Add Ons

See the comments on equipment, professional instruction and staying in the moment at the end of chapter 41. To help stay in the moment while you're playing, do this in-between volleys. (You know the time we mean, when you're usually replaying the last volley in your head while you're walking back to the service line for the next point.) While walking, put your Quantum attention on the feel of each foot's contacting the ground as you walk. Pay complete attention to that contact until you get back to position, then transfer it to the game.

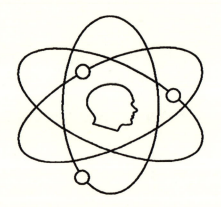

Chapter 43

Better Bowling

"We have fun—that's what I like about bowling. You can have fun even if you stink, unlike in, say, tennis. Every decade or so, I attempt to play tennis, and it always consists of thirty-seven seconds of actually hitting the ball and two hours of yelling, 'Where did the ball go?' 'Over that condominium!' Etc. With bowling, once you let go of the ball, it's no longer your legal responsibility. They have these wonderful machines that find it for you and send it right back."

DAVE BARRY

No, you didn't lose your place. We repeated chapter 42's opening story because it was applicable to this chapter too. You can improve your bowling just as easily as you can improve your tennis (or any other sport for that matter, as we noted in chapter 41).

If you haven't read chapter 41, you might wish to do that now. It explains how and why this Quantum Focus exercise works. After you've read it (or not, if you don't care how and why it works), do the exercise below to help your bowling improve.

Better Bowling Exercise

Enter a Quantum Focus state and get ready to go bowling in your mind. Imagine yourself at some beautiful bowling alley. It's a rather new place, and they keep it meticulously maintained. The alleys are true. There are no high boards. They are cleaned, oiled and buffed just right each morning so your ball always runs true.

Imagine yourself sitting at the scoring table watching you bowl. Watch your form as you make your approach. Notice how every move is perfectly coordinated. See how well you keep your shoulders parallel to the floor, never dropping your shoulder or forcing the ball. Walk up to the next alley and watch you from the side. Smooth approach. Good rhythm, not too fast and not too slow. Gentle slide to the foul line, stopping just before it. Clean release. The ball moves up to the pocket and — good hit, good mix, and it cleans the pins off the alley.

Now step inside the bowling you. See the alley and pins through your eyes. If you're a spot bowler, make a mental note of your spot. Adjust your mindset for a perfect ball. As you turn to pick up your ball from the return, you hardly even notice the others present.

Make sure your hand is dry. Pick up your ball and slide your fingers into it. Take your position on the approach. Check briefly over your shoulder to see that there is no one beginning in the next lane. And now get ready. Feel the surge of coordination pass through your body. Fix your target, spot or pins, whichever you use, in your sight and your mind. Let that target translate to your body. Now begin . . . step, step, step, slide, release. Great! Watch your ball going down the lane exactly as you had planned, into the pocket, good mix and clear the alley. Yes!

Enjoy as much mental bowling as you have time for. Bowl with or against anyone you wish. Keep seeing that consistent, perfect form . . . and the consistent results.

Now and then, you might want to see yourself converting spares. Even if you have to have them specially set up for you. If 7 or 10 pins have given you trouble before, convert a number of these, using your same perfect form and the appropriate release point on the alley. You may even want to show off with some 5-7 or 5-10 split conversions in your make-it-look-easy style.

Keep bowling until you are content with your achievements for the day. Then return to your outer consciousness, again secure in the knowledge that you have improved your physical game a little more.

Have a good time when you do the above exercise. Let yourself feel the excitement and the joy. We recommend bowling many 200 and 250 games, but avoiding too many 300's. The repeated 300 games begin to make the game too easy. There is always the danger of the lack of challenge creating boredom with the game and this could lead to letting your concentration slip.

When you are going bowling, do this exercise shortly before you leave. Then, you might take five seconds or so, just before you begin your approach, to visualize your completing that particular approach exactly as you plan, with the ball carrying the pins completely off the alley. If it doesn't, visualize converting the spare before you actually shoot it. You'll be amazed by how quickly you add pins to your average.

Some Extra Pointers

See the comments on equipment, professional instruction and staying in the moment at the end of chapter 41. In addition, use your Quantum Focus before you roll your first ball. See the ball coming up into the pocket perfectly. STRIKE!

If you should get the opportunity to roll a second ball, see the spare being converted. Watch the ball running exactly where you want it to run. You can easily convert twice as many spares, especially some of the more challenging ones like 5,7's and 5,10's.

Chapter 44

Better Relationships

"The way to love anything is to realize that it might be lost."
GILBERT K. CHESTERTON

If you use this book for nothing other than this chapter, it will still be well worth your investment in time, energy and money. Relationships are both important and fragile. You can help strengthen yours to make it durable and rewarding.

Relationships Can Be Tough . . .

Half of all marriages happening today are winding up in divorce. This says nothing about other relationships, many with far lower commitment than marriage. But it is possible, make that probable, to avoid revolving door relationships.

We speak here of all kinds of relationships. Romantic ones are high on our list. But other relationships need nourishment also. Family, friends, work-related, and community relationships can all benefit from the exercise below.

. . . But You Can Make Them Easier

Relationships, all relationships, *seem* to take place on the conscious level. In fact, the majority of what actually goes on, mentally and emotionally, occurs at an unconscious level. By identifying these subconscious thoughts, feelings and beliefs — and by understanding and communicating them — we can begin to make larger and larger parts of our relationships conscious. That is, we can begin to know and understand what is actually happening in them.

The value of this is, we can then begin to consciously choose how we react to any given situation rather than reacting from the unconscious. We can choose to act and react specifically to what is happening right in front of us, leaving out our history and its associated baggage. We can choose to take actions that promote the intimacy, harmony and cooperative aspects of relationships while decreasing or eliminating those actions which foster disharmony and other counterproductive outcomes.

... And More Fulfilling

This does not mean your giving up those things you hold dear in order to preserve the peace. In fact, once you begin to become familiar with what is transpiring in your unconscious mind, you will be better able to distinguish those things that are truly important to you from those which are not . . . but which have sometimes seemed important in the past. You will find that you can communicate your true needs and desires better and thus receive many more of the things you really want and need than you ever did before. And you will be able to do this in a way that enhances all your relationships so that both you and the other parties benefit. This is one of the most truly win-win situations you can imagine or attain.

... And They Pay You Back Even More

One of the factors in good health is healthy relationships. Open and intimate relationships with loved ones are obviously rewarding emotionally, but people in these kinds of relationships resist stress better too. They tend to keep their health better and live longer . . . and fuller, as they enjoy living more. But even social relationships can have a protective effect.

Clean Living?

During an epidemiological study on heart disease, Stuart Wolf, M.D., at Temple University's School of Medicine, discovered a group of people with an exceptionally low rate of this illness. Researchers felt they must be living a very healthful lifestyle, at least according to what they knew to be healthy, to help prevent heart disease. So they went to Roseto, PA, to see first hand.

What they discovered was quite unexpected. The group was overweight, eating a lot of fats and oils; it was sedentary and had generally what the researchers judged to be poor health habits. Yet, they had a very low incidence of heart disease. They also had a very close-knit and socially supportive community. Somehow, it appeared that this wonderful, supportive social system had conferred protection on them, even to the extent that it had negated the other high-risk behaviors in which they were engaged. This finding has been confirmed now in many additional instances.

A Rabbit Test

How widespread is this phenomenon in the animal kingdom? Surely only humans respond this way.

If you believe this, then consider another experiment designed to induce and promote heart disease in rabbits by feeding them very high fat diets. (This sounds cruel, but that's how many of the diseases are studied in the laboratory. You can't deliberately induce heart disease in man, but he does a pretty good job of this himself, doesn't he?)

In this study, Dr's. R.M. Nerem, and M.J. Levesque and J.F. Cornhill found one group of rabbits that did not develop heart disease like all the rest. A search began to discover why. The genetic background was checked. Food was checked. Time of feeding was checked. Right on down the line, one factor after another was determined to be identical to all the other rabbits. Then a breakthrough occurred. It was discovered that it was the rabbits in the bottom row of cages which were staying healthy.

Now, lighting conditions were checked. Cage temperatures were checked. Air flow, and so on. No differences. Except this. The attendant who fed these rabbits was taking them out of their cages and petting them . . . showing them love. But, she wasn't tall enough to do this with any rabbits other than those on the bottom row, so she simply reached up and fed and watered the upper cages.

What are your conclusions?

Love Is A Many Skilled Thing

There are many skills involved in strengthening and enhancing relationships. Communication ability is always counted as one of, if not *the*, most important skill of all. It is for this reason that the next chapter is on communication. But there is one skill you must have in order to use your communication ability. You MUST KNOW WHAT IT IS YOU NEED IN ORDER TO COMMUNICATE IT! It is precisely this understanding and self-awareness that the following exercise is designed to bring you.

Better Relationships Exercise

Enter a Quantum Focus state and decide which of your relationships you want to improve. It may be romantic, family, social, work-related or any other relationship. They all lend themselves to the clarification you will generate during the next ten to fifteen minutes.

Select one to work on today. Save the rest for other days when you will do this exercise again. Focus for one minute on your chosen relationship. See the other person(s) involved. Hear their voices. Feel your reactions to them.

Now focus on yourself. Mentally imagine your body merely as a place where you live . . . like living in your house. The real you is not the body any more than you are the house in which you live. Feel the real you slipping deeper and deeper away from the scene. Down and down, deeper and deeper within. To a place which looks strangely familiar to you even if you haven't been here before.

It's a natural place, with trees and water, in which you feel very safe and very peaceful. As you look around at the landscape, you notice a rather rocky trail leading up the side of a mountain near where you stand. The gray rocks are in stark contrast to the green grass and blue sky. Yet, it is an interesting trail and you begin to climb it.

It is strange how, as you climb higher and higher, you go deeper and deeper into your Quantum Focused state. Climb higher . . . go deeper. Climb higher . . . go deeper. Deeper and deeper . . . higher and higher. Until you get to exactly the right level for what is about to occur.

You see a small house. It is rather primitive and looks like it may be thousands of years old. Yet, it somehow seems to be contemporary too. Walk up to the door and knock twice, three times. Wait for an invitation before entering.

A wise old man, who can tell how old, lives within. He is known as "The Sage". He has been around for so long that he seems to know the answers to all questions and puzzles of life. He learns more every day so that his knowledge is remarkable, if not magical. About ten seconds after you knock, the Sage invites you in.

He never asked who was there. He already knew. We can only wonder about the limits of his knowledge. So far, no one has exceeded them. Enter and greet this wise old man with respect.

The Sage offers you a seat. It feels as if you already know this old man. Maybe you have met before. Now, he offers you the chance to sit and talk with him for as long as you wish over the next five minutes of clock time. He indicates he knows why you are here, but wants you to ask him the questions that are on your mind. This will help you to formulate them, and see new ones, and understand the answers you will discuss with him.

Take all the time you need to discuss the relationship you want to enhance. Ask about anything you wish. You may have questions about what to do, how to do it, why you even want to preserve or improve this relationship. Take your time and listen carefully to what you both say . . . both with words and without.

When you are through conversing with the Sage, bid him farewell for now. He says he hopes you come back to see him again. Then imagine in your mind the next time you encounter the object of the relationship you discussed with the Sage. See and hear your interchange with this person. Feel the feelings that arise in each of you. Using the new knowledge you have gained, watch as you automatically say and do the most appropriate things to achieve your goals. You don't need to stop and think about them, they just seem to happen as they come from your unconscious mind in perfect form.

Enjoy this interchange for a while. Notice how the feelings in each of you are becoming more and more aligned. You can sense the relationship improving from both your own and the other person's perspective. It is almost as though everything you say and do somehow magically transmits exactly the right thoughts and ideas to the other person. They respond positively, and return these same transmissions to you.

After you have completed your encounter with this person, slowly return to your usual waking state of consciousness. Sit quietly for a few minutes and reflect on what you have just learned so your conscious mind can also absorb this lesson.

Other Help

One fundamental relationship rule that is becoming more commonly recognized and appreciated is, "Neither of you is the property of the other". While this appears to be most applicable to romantic relationships (it is already being printed on West Virginia and Kansas marriage licenses), it is every bit as useful to remember it in all your relationships. Its use in family relationships is easy to understand. But when you carry it into other relationships, such as at work where some "bosses" act as if they owned their employees, it will help you to always treat others respectfully. This is a big step toward making any relationship better.

Can Money Buy Happiness?

Today there is so much available information on techniques that make relationships work (books, workshops, tapes, even products available through infomercials) that we need only allude to them. These techniques are generally useful, when we use them.

Your Quantum Focus practice will make using any of them much easier and more consistent. You could say there is a relationship between how much these techniques can do for your relationship and how much you actually use them. And there is also a relationship between doing your Quantum Focusing and using the techniques. It's in your hands (head, heart and spirit) now.

Most of these programs deal extensively with communication, so check out the next chapter while it's only a page away.

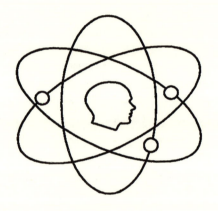

Chapter 45

Better Communication

"Kind words are the music of the world."
F. W. FABER

Do They Hear What We Say? . . .

We define mis✪communication as any unsuccessfully transferred thought, idea, feeling or attitude. We may imagine we have successfully conveyed our message to the other person, but the message they received is significantly different from that which we thought we sent.

Mis✪communication can ruin personal relationships. Mis✪communication can ruin professional relationships. In fact, mis✪communication can end relationships before they even get started.

. . . Or Do We Not Say What We Mean?

Most people are unaware that they have serious communications problems. We all know what it feels like to be misunderstood. We are all familiar with the value placed on meaning what one says. On the other hand, almost everyone has met, or knows of someone who met, a total stranger who instantly felt like an old friend. This is what we call "love at first communication" and, like "love at first sight", it can lead to highly valued relationships.

The Three B's

In this chapter we will introduce you to the three B's of meaningful communication. In our experience, the three B's are foolproof. When applied they insure that you, and the person or people you are communicating with, have the opportunity to really communicate. So what are these three B's that improve communication?

1. Be present and in the moment.
2. Be attentive to the speaker.
3. Be open to the communication.

Sounds almost too easy, doesn't it? But it really is just this simple. Here's how and why the three B's of meaningful communication work.

Be Present And In The Moment

Nothing alienates people more than feeling that the person speaking to them is not really there mentally. Far too many communications take place while the communicator's thoughts are somewhere else. And then people wonder why they are misunderstood. So the next chance you have to communicate with someone, turn your attention inward and very quickly become centered and peaceful. Then quickly extend your attention outward and remain in the moment. You are now ready to communicate.

Be Attentive To The Speaker

People truly enjoy total attention. Treat the communication as if it was the most important conversation in your life. Listen carefully and non-judgmentally. More often than not, the tone of voice and the expression on a person's face are just at important as the words being used to communicate. So pay attention.

Be Open To The Communication

Take everything in and be with it before responding. Most miscommunication occurs because people react rather than act when communicating. In other words, listen to the other person rather than forming your own response while the person is talking. Let the person have his/her say and just be with the information before commenting. It is perfectly all right to pause after they finish speaking before you respond. Actually, it helps the speaker realize you are paying very serious attention to what was said. After all, you thought about it before you responded.

More Tips To Better Communication

1. People often want and need you to listen rather than give them advice. Many communications fail because the message is not the communication. Many times people just want to think out loud and get things off their chest. Giving the person an opportunity to do so often results in the person resolving their own problems. (And many of these people will thank you for your advice anyway . . . even though you know you didn't offer any. You offered them the opportunity to see their own way out.)

2. If you are not sure you understand the communication, say so. You can always say something like, "I hear you saying," or "If I understand you correctly, you mean," and then repeat the person's communication as you think you understand it in your own words. When you finish, ask, "Is that right?" Paraphrasing in this way not only clarifies meanings, it also tells the person you care enough to be sure you understand the communication.

3. Whenever possible, let the person know you relate to what is being said. "I can imagine how that might feel", "That would make me feel great too", "I am aware that could be very painful" or "Could you use a hug?" are just some examples of relating to what is being shared. You may not have reacted to the event being described by the speaker in exactly the same way they did.

Keep in mind, though, that they are as entitled to their feelings — whether you agree with them or not — as you are to yours.

By verbally responding in the manner described, you are acknowledging and validating those feelings for them. And this process forces you to pay attention and try on the situation in order for you to feel your own reactions in any way whatsoever.

4. Eye contact is important to good communication (if local customs allow eye contact).

5. Whenever appropriate, SMILE!!!

6. If appropriate, a gentle, *respectful* touch can enhance communication. But be careful here. Respectful is the operational word. Cultural patterns differ greatly in regard to touching. And some people are not comfortable being touched at all.

7. If you are not clear about the communication, ask open-ended questions. "What do you think you should do?" " What would you like the result to be?" " How would you like me to help?"

Using the three B's and the above tips can turn you into an instant Master Communicator. Practice being in the moment during all your communications. Pay attention and keep an open and non-judgmental attitude. The benefits will speak for themselves.

Better Communication Exercise

If you desire an exercise to help you begin to put all the above into practice, simply slip easily into a Quantum Focused state and imagine yourself speaking with others. You can have intimate, private mental conversations with a loved one; you can hold mental business conversations with colleagues; you may even enjoy mental social interchange with friends; or you can practice whatever other communication situations you desire. Just remember to imagine yourself naturally following all the guidelines above, with poise, ease, grace and comfort.

Some Other Avenues

At the end of the previous chapter we commented on the wealth of books, tapes, workshops and other programs that are available for relationship building. Most of these work extensively on communication. You might do well to investigate some of them for yourself.

And, as we pointed out in that section, your Quantum Focus practice will help you use all the techniques you learn, whether here or elsewhere, on a more regular and consistent basis. This will then make them that much more effective.

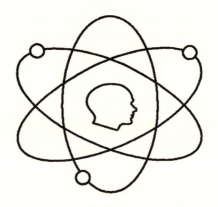

Chapter 46

Your Quantum Future...
Inner Peace & Bliss

"All the world's a stage..."
WILLIAM SHAKESPEARE

Congratulations. You are on your very own pathway to inner peace and bliss. You discovered that the practice of Quantum Focus meditation and focusing your imagination and attention is the only key you need for self-regulation and empowerment. Your future is now, and you have everything you need for a full, happy, meaningful life. We will end this chapter and book with imagery and affirmations for living fully in the moment.

Pre-read the exercise and enter a profound state of complete ease and calmness. Imagine for a few moments that Life is a stage, and you are one very special player. Now mentally repeat, "I AM IN THE MOMENT. I AM ACTING FOR LOVE AND LIFE. I AM HERE, NOW, AND MY ATTENTION IS WHERE I AM." Imagine that when you shift back into the moment, you are to receive an intuitive call from "Cosmic casting", and that the actual happening you are part of is the very stage life unfolds on.

Open your attention wide and focus your senses keenly and sharply on everything happening in the moment. Let all your actions stem from this immediate situation, and stay in the moment. This is your optimal level of functioning, and the moment has everything you need to enjoy the role you assume in your life. In fact, the moment often provides even more meaningful and enjoyable roles for you to assume.

Once again, the key to self-empowerment is practice, practice, practice. Throughout the day, make it a habit to stay in the moment. Thinking about the past or the future is not being in the moment. The ideal time to think about the past or future is during Quantum Focus meditation, and we have provided you with imagery and affirmations for healing your past, or creating your future.

All the rest of your waking time spent entertaining worrisome thoughts about the past or future are a waste of time and should be considered toxic. By learning how much time you spend thinking about other stuff and not being in the moment, you are moved to spend as much time in the present as possible.

We recommend that you start and end your day shifting into Quantum Focus meditative states. Center yourself, come back into the moment and give whatever you are doing the blessing of your full attention. Act as if everything you do is so important that your full undivided attention is required. So if you start your day with a shower, move into the moment and give your full attention to the sensations of the water . . . the feel and smell of the soap and shampoo.

After you finish the shower, shift into a Quantum Focus meditative state and center again. As you come back into the moment, give your full attention and enthusiasm to drying off. Treat drying off as if was the most important act of the day. Use the same technique for every activity in your day, that is, give great importance to what you are doing and put your undivided attention into the doing.

Everyone will notice the difference. Your work and play will be greatly enhanced. Your presence will be recognized and appreciated. Remember everyone enjoys undivided attention and every act you make is greatly enhanced when you put your full attention into it. This is your road map for a life filled with all the rewards and benefits found only in the moment.

The next exercise is taught in many "mystery and truth" schools for the purpose of fine-tuning their students' attention and senses. It simply involves putting your full attention inside and then moving your attention outside while remaining in a waking meditative state.

This practice will round out your Quantum Focus training and make you the best you can be. We recommend that you practice this in many different settings, for instance practice both indoors and outdoors. Practice in quiet and noisy places. The important thing is widening your senses and sharpening your awareness.

Let's Practice

The key to this practice is to sit in a given situation and open your senses to all the sights, smells, tastes and sensations in that moment. So all you need is to develop the habit of doing this practice between activities. The practice is as follows:

> While sitting, take a deep breath and open your mind to all the sensations of sitting in a chair. Scan your body and allow your whole body to release any tensions and relax.
>
> Now open your sense of hearing. Allow yourself to tune in to all the sounds happening in the moment. Hear the sounds, first separately, and then tune in on the whole of the sound.

Now allow your eyelids to open and look out directly ahead, and without focusing your eyes just let them take in everything in front of you.

Now focus your attention on your skin. Be aware of your skin and feel everything touching your skin. Feel your clothes. Feel the air on your skin.

Become aware of your feet on the ground, feel the weight of your body on the chair.

Now open your attention to any tastes in the moment. Do you have any sense of taste in this experience?

Now shift your attention back to your eyes and begin to focus your attention on all the colors in front of you.

Now bring your attention back to your body, re-scan yourself and again focus your attention on the moment. Remind yourself, you are driving the machine, and give your full, undivided attention to your next activity.

PLEASE USE YOUR NEW POWERS OF ATTENTION AND IMAGINATION EVERY CHANCE YOU GET... YOUR QUANTUM FUTURE IS AWAITING YOU.

Appendix A
Overcoming Insomnia

The obvious solutions to insomnia are suggested by examining the factors which disturb sleep. If we cut out alcohol in the evening, avoid drugs, begin to wind down from the day before going to bed, so as to remove the high level of mental activity, and stop worrying, we can eliminate (or at least drastically reduce) our exposure to the major sleep-disturbing factors. The first three of these are easy to do. The last, turning off worry, takes a little effort and some training. We shall return to the use of Quantum Focus in overcoming worry later.

A Worthwhile Life

Always remember that one of the necessities for awakening refreshed, renewed and raring to go is awakening to a life worth living. If life is awful, if we do not want to go do whatever it is we have to do that day and there is no relief in sight, if there is no meaning or challenge in life, then all the techniques in the world for sleeping better will not get you up "bright-eyed and bushy-tailed" in the morning. In fact, you may wind up sleeping more and more, and feeling only worse for it.

If, on the other hand, you have a purpose to your life, if life is stimulating and challenging, you can get up every morning with a vigor you only dreamed of before . . . even when you don't seem to have gotten sufficient sleep.

Of course, you can run on this borrowed energy for just so long before the crash occurs. You must still get a certain amount of restful, rejuvenating sleep. But without a purpose to life, no amount of sleep seems to be enough. So, before you invest in the following exercises, reread Chapter 7 and use your Quantum Focusing ability to discover and follow your life's purpose.

Getting A Good Night's Sleep

Once you have done the simple things, like slowing down before you go to bed, and reduced or eliminated the use of substances which can interfere with a natural, refreshing sleep, you are still faced with letting go of worry. Quantum Focus gives you the means to let go; it permits you the peace of mind needed to face all your problems and see them as challenges which motivate you to new peaks of performance in every aspect of life.

As you learned in chapter 10, applying the Quantum state to specific worries (e.g. the bills) can bring you new ways to solve these specific concerns (e.g. innovative ideas for making money which use your unique skills and abilities). By focusing your attention in the Quantum state, you access resources you never before even realized you had.

By using the follow technique when you begin to learn how to use Quantum Focus for sleeping, you can make the process even easier and solve several of life's other challenges at the same time. Once you have mastered the Quantum Focus technique, you can simply begin with the procedure as described in "Tape Instructions" in chapter 13.

The Technique

Start by writing down the major worries that concern you. Put as many things on the list as you can think of. It doesn't matter if they are big or small. Write them all down. sometimes it's the small stuff that gives us the biggest challenges.

Your list may look something like:

- Paying the mortgage
- Keeping the job
- Providing for the family
- Sending the kids to college
- Getting the kids into college
- Recent fighting with the spouse
- Deadlines at work

- Deadlines at home
- Repairing the roof
- Keeping the cars running
- The children's emotional well-being
- Susie's new punk boyfriend
- John's biker friends
- Bill's poor grades
- Favorite TV show canceled
- Nuclear war in the Mideast
- Earthquakes, etc., etc.

Now, break the list down into categories:

Things Money Can Solve	Things Money Can't Solve
Paying the mortgage	Keeping your job
Providing for the family	Getting the kids into college
Sending the kids to college	Fighting with spouse
	Deadlines at work
Repairing the roof	Deadlines at home
Keeping the cars running	Children's emotional well-being
TV show canceled	Nuclear war
	Earthquakes

You may have put some of the things on the *Money Can Solve* list that we have listed under the *Money Can't Solve* category. For example, having money cannot guarantee your job, but enough money might mean you no longer care about this particular job. There may be something else you'd rather do, something that adds purpose to your life. You have to decide for yourself where each item belongs.

Now break the *Money Can't Solve* list into two lists:

Things I Can Directly Impact	Things I Cannot Directly Impact
Keeping job	Nuclear war
Getting kids into college	
Fighting with spouse	Earthquakes
The deadlines I can affect	The deadlines I cannot impact
Children's emotional well-being	

(We would argue that, through Quantum Focus, we can impact every item on each list. But for now, assume that the above is the result of your dividing the items.)

You now have three categories to work with: *Things Money Can Solve, Things I Can Directly Impact* and *Things I Cannot Directly Impact.*

Here you can use Quantum Focus is three separate ways: First, to find unique or innovative ways to improve your financial situation by capitalizing on powers and abilities you already have and thus eliminating the first category of worries (chapter 10); second, to discover the most effective ways to improve the situations you already know you can affect (see chapters 6, 11, 37, 38, 44 & 45 for example); and, third, by discovering ways to let go of the things you cannot change and replace them with feelings of harmony and peace (chapter 46). In all of these, you make contact with levels of intelligence far superior to any you have invoked before, and your results will be far superior to those you have achieved previously.

What Will Happen

You have now prepared your mind for reprogramming an expectancy of sleep. With practice, you will find that this expectancy has become so strong that the above preliminary procedure becomes completely unnecessary.

By this time, sleep will become automatic. As you lie down on your bed, it will almost seem as though you were lying at some resort with gentle winds blowing across your body, carrying all your disturbing thoughts away. You will find it is not only easier to fall asleep, but also easy to sleep soundly and awaken feeling like the proverbial new person.

Side B of your tape was specifically designed to guide you into the ideal state of mind for sleep. In fact, the Quantum Challenge is to try and stay awake for the full 15 minutes of tape play. The amazing thing will be that, as you practice, you will begin to fall asleep sooner and sooner during the tape, and your sleep will become more and more restful and energizing.

Using Your Tape

As you have learned, rolling your eyes upward and shifting your attention to the peaceful realms within you is your gateway to the Quantum State, and focusing your imagination while it is in the Quantum State is the key to Quantum Focus. Tonight, when you are ready for bed, start side B of your Quantum Focus tape, move into the Quantum State and let's meet the sandman. Remember, if possible, try to stay awake during the tape.

SWEET DREAMS!

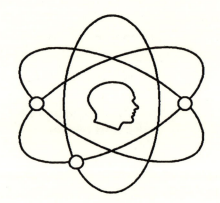

Appendix B
Remembering Your Dreams

Virtually everybody dreams, although many people are unaware of it. In many native cultures, dreaming is a very major part of the psychospiritual lives of the society. Even the children are taught to value and manipulate their dreams.

One easy and powerful way to develop control over your dreams is simply to remember the following three points:

1. *Intention*. Think about remembering tonight's dreams many times during your waking hours. Each time you think about remembering them, repeat to yourself, "I will remember tonight's dreams when I awaken tomorrow." In short, create and acknowledge the *intention* to remember your dreams.

2. *Action*. Put a pad near your bed so you can write down your dream(s) immediately after awakening. Sometimes you will awaken in the middle of the night and remember a dream you just had. If you write down even a few key words, this will be sufficient to remind you of the dream and the details will most often return with it.

3. *More Action*. Upon awakening, lie in bed and think about what you were dreaming. Let yourself just drift, as if you were going back to sleep, and rejoin your dream. As you pick up on last night's dream(s), write down whatever comes into your mind.

Repeat this exercise for a few weeks, and before you know it you will be aware of dreaming and will begin to awaken with fresh memories. Continue to write them down and they will continue to become easier and easier to remember. Within two or three months, you will have trained yourself to remember your dreams vividly, and will be ready to use them for purposes other than mere amusement.

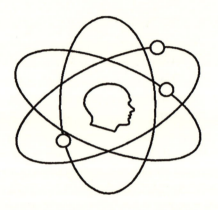

About the Authors

Michael Ellner, Ph.D.

The Reverend Dr. Michael Ellner has a degree of Doctor of Philosophy in Religion, conferred on him by the Universal Life Church. He is a driving force in holistic healing who has earned international recognition as the President of HEAL (Health Education AIDS Liaison, Inc.). Also a leading consultant, his hallmark contribution is to the legion of people with AIDS-related fears and concerns whom he has helped to take charge of their lives.

Dr. Ellner is certified as a Medical Hypnotherapist, a NYS HIV Counselor, an Ordained Spiritual Counselor, Reiki Master, NLP Trainer, Psychoneurogenics Practitioner, Clinical Practices, and an Innate Learning Facilitator. He is a member of the National Institute of Health's Complementary Therapies Working Group and also serves on the Boards of Advisors for The International Medical and Dental Hypnotherapy Association, the New York State Hypnotherapists Association, the New York Chapter of the National Guild of Hypnotists and The World Institute of Cognitive Sciences.

Dr. Ellner's awards include the National Guild of Hypnotists' Hypnosis Humanities Award (1989 and 1994) and Hypnosis Educator of the Year Award (1995), the 1990 International Medical and Dental Hypnotherapy Association's Founder's Award, the 1991 Mind-Body-Spirit Award of the International Association of Counselors and Therapists, and a Doctor of Divinity (1994). In 1995, he was inducted into the Hypnosis Hall of Fame.

Richard Jamison, Ph.D.

Richard Jamison is the President of Productivity Enhancement Inc. of Rutherford, N.J., a member of the Management Faculty for Fairleigh Dickinson University's MBA program and the College of Natural Sciences' faculty at Westbrook University. He has been an advisor to the African National Congress, the Costa Rican and Israeli governments, and was recently invited to participate in the Citizen Ambassador Program to China.

Dr. Jamison has a doctorate in Biology and an M.B.A. in management/motivation and serves on the Board of Advisors for The World Institute of Cognitive Sciences. He has had extensive empowerment training and has also trained with several leaders in the holistic health field (*i.e.*, Bernie Siegel, Lawrence LeShan, *et al.*).

Dr. Jamison is an expert on harnessing the subconscious mind's power, particularly for making sudden, extensive and permanent transformation. He appears in print and on radio and television, and regularly leads seminars and addresses business and community groups. He is the author of *The Maxichem Nutritional System,* co-author of *The Relationship Journal,* and appears in *Who's Who of Seminar Leaders.*

Index

abundance, 52-53, 58, 99, 107, 112
aches and pains, 263
    eliminating, 281-283
acupuncture, 255, 280
agoraphobia, 145-147
    overcoming, method one exercise, 148
    overcoming, method two exercise, 149
AIDS, 19, 265-267
Allah, 53
allergies, 71, 77, 78, 92
    common irritants, 293
    food allergies, 293
    mental beliefs, 92, 294
    mental component, 92, 293-294
    overcoming, 71, 293-296
    overcoming allergy attacks exercise, 295-296
    stress, 293
    symptoms, 293
anger, 23, 92, 103
    arthritis, 92
    cancer, 92
    forgiving one's self, 103-104
    forgiving others, 103-104
    heart disease, 92
anxiety, 17-18, 62, 76, 80, 92, 115-123, 146, 253
    additional aids to being calm, 120
    anti-anxiety exercise, 117-119
    approaching deadline effect, 120
    being late, 120
    caffeine, 121
    conquering, 80, 115
    hobbies, 122
    hot bath, 120-121, 123
    hypertension, 92
    intellectual pursuits, 122
    music, 120, 122
    phobias, 146
    physical activities, 122
    procrastination, 120
    sense of control, 117
    sex, 123
    sources of caffeine, 121
    the solution, 116
    trust, 116
    what is, 115
    worry, 115
aromatherapy, 80, 83, 136
    and sleep, 136
art of the state, 36
attitudes, 62, 249-250, 253, 297, 337, 361, 364
    stress-related diseases, 92
audiotape, 12-13, 33-34, 46-47, 123
    insomnia, 131-132, 372, 375
auto-pilot, 21-23, 25, 64, 80

basic exercise, 19, 25, 31, 34-38, 45-46, 60, 78
being in the moment, 24, 25, 31, 40-41, 43, 60, 63, 71, 76, 95, 97, 164, 169, 207, 209-210, 297, 300, 306, 307, 333-334, 336, 343, 347, 362, 364, 367-370
beliefs, 20, 23, 25, 61-65, 71, 78, 93-96, 99, 104, 109, 161, 164, 181, 224, 240, 249-250, 253, 257-258, 265, 269, 294, 301, 310, 318, 321, 334, 354
    learning and, 321-322, 334
Benson, Herbert, 42, 45, 73
bliss, 32, 86, 259, 298, 334, 367
body, 18, 32-35, 37, 41-43, 45-48, 52, 70-73, 75, 101, 121, 133-134, 146, 162, 185, 224, 231-234, 238-239, 254-255, 269-270, 279, 284, 294, 298-299, 315, 342, 357
bodymind, 41, 76, 117, 118, 119
bodymindspirit, 37, 46, 65, 210, 334
Borysenko
    Joan, 45
    Myrin, 45
brotherhood, 21
Byrd, Randolph, 57

caffeine, 150, 187
    chocolate, 121
    headache medications, 121
    soda, 121, 136
    tea, 121
    withdrawal symptoms, 121

cancer, 19, 62, 71-74, 223-224, 249, 264-265, 267-268
    accelerated decline, 61
    anger, 92
    depressive feelings, 92
    helplessness, 92
    hopelessness, 92
    loneliness, 92
change, 21, 24-25, 31-32, 38, 45, 56, 70, 72, 75, 77-78, 101, 128, 142, 149, 168, 215-217, 220-221, 230, 258, 266-267, 288, 374
changing your past, 32
childbirth, 287-291
    changing expectations, 288
    drugs, 288
    emotional responses, 287
    fulfillment, 288
    happiness, 288
    joy, 288
    mental anesthesia, 288
    mental conditioning, 287
    natural physiological function, 287
    pain in, 288
    painless, 287
    painless childbirth exercise, 289-291
    programming, 287
choosing your path, 20-21, 28, 86-90, 130, 218, 367
chronic health problems, 61
clarity, 81, 300
claustrophobia, 151-152, 177
    desensitization exercise, 152
    dispelling past life origins, 153
    origin, 151
    past lives, 152

Index

power image, 153
cleansing sleep exercise, 67
comfort zone, 217
comfortable feelings, 53, 76, 101, 110, 117, 119, 159, 165, 179, 183, 195, 202, 217, 221, 234
communication, 52, 96, 207, 247, 283, 297, 319, 354, 356, 361
   be attentive, 362
   be open, 363
   be present, 362
   better communication exercise, 364-365
   better relationships, 356
   in the moment, 362
   mis✣communication, 361
   the three B's, 362
   tips, 363-365
confidence, 61, 75, 78, 81, 92, 117, 253, 265, 307
consciousness, 18, 19, 21, 32, 38, 41, 52-53, 66, 77, 97
   quantum consciousness, 32, 75, 80, 104, 252
   states of, 32, 42, 45, 60, 75, 97, 140
controlling your body, 45
Cousins, Norman, 286
creativity, 39, 42, 109, 135, 207, 309-315, 333
   beliefs affecting, 310-311
   biorhythms, 315
   descriptions of, 310
   enhancement exercise, 312-314
   exercise, 312
   innate ability, 310
   measurable characteristics, 310
   peak time, 315
   unconscious fears and doubts, 317
cultural trances, 59

de Bono, Edward, 309
depression, 17, 18, 70, 77
diet, 121, 231, 238, 253, 268, 270-271, 355
disease, 61-62, 66, 71, 73, 103, 161, 223, 239, 249, 251-257, 269, 272, 286, 305, 355
   stress-related, 66, 71, 73-74, 92, 273
dis✣stress
   relieving, 69
dreams, 32, 42, 135, 139-140, 194, 202, 212, 220
   claustrophobia exercise, 154
   exercise, 141
   fear, 142
   fear of change exercise, 220
   fear of driving exercise, 158-159
   fear of failure exercise, 194-195
   fear of public speaking exercise, 212-213
   fear of success exercise, 202-204
   lucid dreaming, 141
   programming, 139, 202-204
   remembering, 377
   seeding, 149, 153
   the supercharger, 139
   waking up inside, 141
Duarte, Alex, 137

Dunne, Brenda, 28

Eastern teachings, 23, 162, 167
Ellner-Jamison Law, 317
Ellner's rule, 23, 25
emotional processes, 179-181
emotional baggage, 62-63,
emotional stability, 59, 64, 75
   emotional stability exercise, 65-66
emotional well-being, 25, 40, 64, 237
emotions, 59, 67, 80, 96, 162, 236, 287
   cancer, 61
   disease, 66, 92-93, 254
   healing, 40, 61, 66, 261-262, 290, 298
   negative, 66, 91-92, 244-245, 281-282
   toxic, 61-62, 66, 91-93, 257
empowerment, 24, 26, 80, 170, 206, 207, 367-368
end-of-dis✪stress exercise, 75
energy, 55-56, 61, 65, 77-78, 82, 87, 89, 207, 233, 255, 264, 298, 302, 318, 371
enhanced consciousness, 18, 31-32, 60, 66, 80, 140
enthusiasm, 61, 109, 207
entranced, 32, 59
essential oils, 82-83
   arousing/aphrodisiac, 82
   calming, 82
   sedative, 82
   sensual/euphoric, 82
   stimulant, 82
exercise, 80, 122, 232, 233, 239, 253-255, 268, 269-270, 307

expectation, 18, 21-23, 27-28, 33, 40, 89, 253, 288, 300, 306
   doing your part, 29
failure, 189-192, 197-198, 301, 306, 317
familiar zone, 217
fear of change, 215
   desensitization exercise, 218
   dream exercise, 220
   overcoming, 215
fear of crowds, 177
fear of death, 161, 206, 255-256
   an Eastern view, 162
   breaking the hex, 162
   eternal source exercise, 163
   overcoming, 161, 164-165
   power image, 165
fear of doctors, 92
fear of driving, 155
   desensitization exercise, 156-157
   dream exercise, 158-159
   overcoming, 155
   power image, 157
   road to mastery, 156
fear of failure, 189
   dream exercise, 194-195
   exercises, 192-195
   if I wanted to, 190
   learning experiences, 191
   no more failure exercise, 192-193
   overcoming, 189
   producing better results, 191
   reprogramming, 190
   the first step, 191
fear of flying, 177
   additional things to do, 186
   choices, 180-181
   hypnotists, 181

I can fly exercise, 181-185
    overcoming, 177
    power image, 186
fear of heights, 167
    exercise, 169
    overcoming, 167
    power image, 170
fear of public speaking, 205
    exercise, 210-211
    most common fear, 206
    overcoming, 205, 210-211
fear of success, 197
    arbitrary limits, 199
    dream exercise, 202
    exercise, 201
    overcoming, 197
    pattern, 198
fear of the unknown, 217
fear of water, 173
    exercise, 173
    overcoming, 173
    water exercises, 174
fears, 62
    dreams, 142
    inborn, 216
feelings
    toxic, 66
Fillmore, Lowell, 210
finance, 107
    healthier finances exercise, 110-112
flow state, 44, 312, 343
Friedman, Meyer, 73
frigidity, 301
    affirmations, 302-303
    overcoming, 301
    the exercise, 302
future focusing, 26, 43
Glaser, Ronald, 73-74

goals, 20, 26-27, 87, 110, 125-127, 129, 141, 318, 333
    starting point, 129
    goal setting exercise, 127-128
    happiness, 127
    money, 127
    obtaining, 125, 141, 358
    relationships, 127
    setting, 125
    subgoals, 130
    unconscious mind, 128-129
    written, 126-128
God, 21, 53-54
grief, 92
groaning, 66, 67
guided meditation, 32
guilt, 92

happiness, 27, 52, 63, 72, 86, 99, 107, 127, 190, 254, 288, 359
hate, 92
headaches, 121, 275, 293
headaches and migraines, 275-280
    abscesses, 277
    acupuncture, 280
    biofeedback, 280
    cavities, 277
    common headache cure/relief exercise, 277
    controlling, 276
    eliminating, 275
    feverfew, 280
    herbal remedies, 280
    migraine headache control, 278-279
    pain clinics, 280
    possible sources, 277
    stress, 277

tension, 277
TMJ, 277
toxic fumes, 277
ultimate migraine control, 279-280
heal time, 32, 41-43
healing, 19-20, 39-44, 60, 62, 96, 162, 256, 288, 318, 368
   buried emotions and feelings, 25, 80-82, 96, 103-104, 318
healing power of laughter, 286
healing process, 19, 60, 62, 66, 75, 80, 96, 102, 162, 251
   breaking the hex, 161-162
   inner consciousness, 19, 318
   stages, 162
healing system, 251-252
   natural killer cells, 74, 252
health, 52, 61, 63, 249, 355
   AIDS, 265
   allergies, 293
   attitudes, 62, 249-250
   basic assumptions, 251
   beliefs, 249-250, 253, 258
   cancer, 269
   consciousness changing, 252
   diabetes, 269
   diet, 270-271
   disease, 269
   every day in every way exercise, 263-264
   exercise, 253-255, 269
   heart disease, 269, 355
   HIV, 265-266
   holistic model, 251
   hypertension, 71, 92, 269
   immune system, 249
   inner child work, 256
   life-threatening issues, 258
   longevity, 269
   mental makeover, 253
   mind/body/spirit, 252-254
   models, 256
   nutritional supplements, 271
   overweight, 269
   perpetual healing exercise, 261-263
   principles, 253
   quantum focus shake, 252
   quantum focus shake exercise, 255
   RDA's, 272
   relationships, 253, 255, 355
   responsibility for, 251
   staying healthy, 249
   stress, 69-70, 253
   stress management, 273
   the hidden traps, 253
   toxic emotions, 256, 257
   toxic thinking, 264
   unconscious mind, 252
   vitamins and minerals, 80, 239, 253, 272, 330-331
   weight, 229-242, 253, 269-271
   young old age exercise, 259-260
   your best weight, 269
healthier finances exercise, 110
heart disease
   anger and, 92
   grief and, 92
   hostility and, 92
   never enough time and, 92
helpless and unloved
   arthritis, 92
helplessness
   cancer, 92

Index 387

Heraclitus, 59
higher power, 20, 41, 53, 58, 64
higher self, 21, 53
HIV, 265-266
hope, 62, 72
hopelessness, 92
    cancer, 92
hostility
    heart disease, 92
hurts, 62
    forgiveness, 103-105, 318
hypertension, 71, 269
    anxiety, 92
    fear of doctors, 92
    insecurity, 92
hypnosis, 32, 57, 140
    of social conditioning, 250

I can fly exercise, 181-185
illness, 11, 19, 20, 53, 61, 72, 96, 161, 162, 250, 252, 256, 265, 355
impotence, 305
    affirmations, 306-307
    exercise, 306-307
    expectation, 306
    imagery, 306
    major cause, 305
    overcoming, 305
    power image, 307
    self-doubt, 306
    self-esteem, 306
    worries, 306
in the moment, 25, 60, 71, 95, 97, 169, 297, 300, 367
    a clean slate, 97
    bliss, 367-368
    conscious living, 140-141
    inner peace, 367-368
    memory, 333
    secret to a better sex life, 297
    sports, 343
    total, undivided attention, 300
in the zone, 44
increasing hand temperature, 47
influence your future, 32
inner awareness, 168
inner child, 256, 317
    Ellner-Jamison Law, 317
    healing concept, 318
    inner agreement, 318
    the magic smile exercise, 318-319
    unconditional love, 318
    unconscious fears and doubts, 317
inner landscape, 63
inner oasis, 161
inner peace, 32, 55, 63, 86, 99, 169, 367
inner terrain, 63-64
inner wisdom, 53
insecurities, 62
    hypertension, 92
insomnia, 131, 371
    alcohol in, 371
    caffeine, 136
    drugs, 371
    expectancy of sleep, 375
    mental activity, 371
    overcoming, 371
    sleeping better, 371-372
    stimulants, 135
    stop worrying technique, 372-374
    stress, 71
    worrying, 371
inspiration, 81, 265, 268
irrational fears, 164

agoraphobia, 145
claustrophobia, 151
fear of failure, 189
fear of flying, 177
fear of success, 197
origin, 151

Jahn, Robert, 28
Jamison's law, 22
Jehovah, 53
joy, 59, 80, 107, 164, 171, 314
    childbirth, 288, 290-291

Kieclot-Glaser, Janice, 73-74
knowledge, 51, 52, 168, 191, 240
Kubler-Ross, Elisabeth, 256

lack of confidence
    allergies, 92
learning, 321
    and what we eat, 330-331
    beliefs, 321-323
    faster learning exercise, 324-328
    influences on, 328
    music, 328
    peak hours, 329
    we learn differently, 322
Lee, Bruce, 167
Levi, Peretz, 137
life's purpose, 85
limitations, 32. 171, 213
    breaking through, 32, 40
limiting beliefs
    Henry Ford, 113
    money, 109
    universal abundance, 112
Lincoln, Abraham, 64
listening to your symptoms, 96

loneliness
    cancer, 92

magic smile, 100, 318
mastering the moment, 60
mastery, 31
McGill, Ormond, 140
meditation, 21, 32, 57, 74, 140, 206, 264, 367
memory, 333
    affirmations, 333
    conditioner, 334
    exercises, 335-336
    imagery, 333
    remembering more, 333
mental aspects of living
    importance in reaching goals, 26
    improving our lives, 26
    self-sabotage, 26
metaphysical tenets of quantum focus, 41
migraines, 275
    characteristics, 276
    the Type A personality, 276
mind, 19-29, 31, 33, 37, 41-42, 46, 51-54, 109, 122, 132, 140, 254
    limiting programming, 52, 95, 107, 109, 240-242, 250, 258
    unconscious, 13, 41-42, 53, 62, 95, 109, 126, 128-129, 142, 152-154, 179, 185, 187, 192, 194, 198, 202, 212, 220, 224, 225, 238-239, 242, 253, 278, 313, 315, 339, 354

user's manual for, 13, 327, 358
money, 28, 29, 93, 107, 186, 199, 200, 297, 329, 353,
   creating a monopoly, 109
   do whatever you do best, 109
   happiness, 107
   healthier finances exercise, 110
   identify a talent, 109
   mental, physical and spiritual balance, 107
   negative thoughts and beliefs, 109
   success formula, 110

nail-biting, 243
   freedom from nail-biting exercise, 246-248
   preparation for quitting, 244-246
   removing the underlying desire, 244
   the physical habit, 244
natural balance, 96
nutritional supplements, 271
   RDA's, 272

oneness, 21
opinions, 62
Osborn, Alex, 309

pain, 277, 281
   arthritis, 282
   as a signal, 281
   broken bone, 282
   bursitis, 282
   childbirth, 287-8
   control of, 282
   emotional sources, 281
   endorphins, 283
   from accidents, 282
   laugh it off, 286
   management, 282
   pain management exercises, 283-286
   power image, 286
   toothache, 282
   unconscious mind, 283
painless childbirth, 287
panic attacks
   caffeine, 150
   first aid, 150
   panic attack reaction, 146
   physiological cycle, 146
   self-limiting, 146
   vicious circle, 146
Parnes, Sidney, 309
past lives, 152, 256
   claustrophobia, 152-154
   phobias, 152-154
peace, 52, 207, 367
   inner child, 318
perception, 25
perfect human beings, 94
personal consciousness, 52-53
phobias
   agoraphobia, 147
   caffeine, 150
   claustrophobia, 151
   desensitization, 150
   drugs, 146
   major classes of, 146
   panic attacks, 146
   treating, 150
physiological changes in enhanced states, 32
poisoned emotions, 60
   antidote, 60
   resentment, 60

to detoxify, 61
worry, 60
poverty, 53, 63
power image, 38-40, 80, 149, 265, 347
   claustrophobia, 153
   fear of death, 165
   fear of driving, 157
   fear of flying, 186
   fear of heights, 170
   freedom from pain, 286
   impotence, 307
   premature ejaculation, 308
   public speaking, 209
   stress, 77, 80
   weight management, 242
prayer, 56-57
   cardiac arrests, 58
   deaths, 58
   for people, 57-58
   pain medication, 58
   seeds, 57
   Spindrift, 57
presence of mind, 31
procrastination, 120, 218
psychospiritual viruses, 61
public speaking, 205
   keys to overcoming, 207
   mastering, 207
   power image, 209
   the 3 B's, 207-208, 362

Qi Gong, 255
quantum fluctuation, 27
quantum focus
   advantages, 57
   audio tape, 12-13, 34, 46, 47, 132, 375
   automatic, 33, 41
   basic exercise, 34, 36-37
   blast, 42-43
   creating life situations, 23
   defined, 11-12
   do your part, 28
   emotions, 60
   enhanced consciousness, 31
   getting started, 33
   influences on, 15
   mastery, 31
   mental martial art, 21
   music, 33
   peace of mind, 23-24
   personal empowerment, 24
   physiological changes, 45
   power image, 38-40
   practicing, 33
   prayer, 57
   right/left-brain activity, 46
   self-healing, 41
   self-improvement, 24
   shuffle, 42
   spirit of, 26
   stress, 39, 75
   use, 20
quantum focus challenge, 132
quantum focus hike, 80
quantum focus shake, 252
   exercise, 255-256
quantum future, 367
   exercise, 369-370
   inner peace, 368-369
quantum moments, 21, 63

real time, 32, 41-42
reality, 53, 75, 77, 141, 147, 168, 192, 201, 210, 283
reconnecting with the spirit, 49
reconnecting with the spirit exercise, 54
Reiki, 255

Index

relationships, 353
   beliefs about, 354
   better relationships exercise, 356-359
   can money buy happiness?, 359
   communication in, 354
   community, 353
   family, 353
   friends, 353
   good health, 354-355
   romantic, 353
   unconscious aspects, 353-354
   work-related, 353
relaxation, 34, 37, 47, 73, 81, 117, 122, 185, 263, 264, 305
relieving dis✧stress, 69
religion, 20, 50-53
remembering your dreams, 377
   action, 377
   intention, 377
   more action, 377
resentments, 60-62
Rosenman, Ray, 73

secret to better sex, 297
self-esteem, 32, 61, 91-97, 253, 306
   become a volunteer, 102
   exercise A, 97-99
   exercise B, 99-100
   I love myself, 101
   ideas that will help, 101
   increasing, 91, 97-100
   lack of, 91, 97
   low, 91-93, 306
   psychological pathogens, 91
   rate yourself, 101
   the mirror, 101
   toxic feelings, emotions and beliefs, 91
   wounded, 97
self-forgiveness, 103-105
self-hypnosis, 32
self-improvement, 20, 24, 97, 143, 156, 164, 191, 209, 212, 224, 253, 362, 374
self-sabotage, 95, 109, 198, 200, 204, 213
self-worth, 93, 227, 237, 241
sensuality, 81
sex, 80, 83, 123, 297, 301, 305
   beliefs, 301
   better, 83, 297
   better sex exercise, 299-300
   candlelight evenings, 300
   conversation, 300
   desirability, 297
   enlightenment, 298
   feelings, 300
   flowers, 300
   frigidity, 301
   getting into the mood, 83, 300
   good sex, 298
   great sex, 298
   impotence, 301, 305-307
   inner child, 298
   joyful expectation, 300
   kind words, 300
   love, 298, 300
   natural signals, 297
   physicality, 298
   premature ejaculation, 305
   problems, 301
   secret to a better sex life, 297
   sexuality, 81, 297, 300, 302
   soft music, 300

spiritual and emotional
     meeting, 298
symbols of sexuality, 297
taboos surrounding, 297
total, undivided attention,
     300
shame, 92, 104
sigh a day, 66
sleep, 32, 66-67, 82, 131, 149,
     153-154, 158-159, 162,
     186, 194-195, 202-203,
     212-213, 220-221, 320,
     371-375
  a life worth living, 132
  additional aids, 135
  aromatherapy, 82, 136
  energizing, 131
  exercise one, 133
  exercise three, 134
  exercise two, 133-134
  high carbohydrate foods, 136
  lavender, 82, 136
  melatonin, 137
  quantum sleeping, 132-134,
       153-154, 194-195,
       202-203, 212-213,
       220-221
  restful, 66, 67, 131
  tryptophan, 136
  tryptophan-containing
       foods, 136
sleep disorders, 131
smoking, 223
  affirmations, 225
  belief, 224
  desire to stop, 224
  finally stopping, 224
  imagery, 225
  ready and willing to stop, 224

stop smoking exercise one,
     225-226
stop smoking exercise two,
     226-227
what to do first, 225
why haven't I quit?, 224
why should I quit?, 223
willpower, 224
spirit, 18, 19, 51-52, 162
  essential aspects, 51, 162-163
  infinite and timeless, 51-52,
       54
  sense of connection, 51
  unbounded and eternal, 51-
       54
spiritual malnutrition, 49-50, 162
spirituality, 20, 25, 32, 40, 45, 50-
     51, 53-54, 65, 95-97, 107,
     162, 183, 208, 251-254,
     298, 318, 333
  definition, 51
  sense of connection to other,
       52
sports, 174, 270, 337
  mental practice, 337-339, 343
  bowling, 337, 349
  bowling exercise, 350-351
  equipment, 174, 343
  golf, 270, 337-340, 343
  golf exercise, 340-342
  improvement, 270, 339
  muscle memory, 339
  physical performance, 270,
       340
  physical practice, 339
  professional instructor, 343
  reason for practice, 339
  staying in the moment, 343
  tennis, 286, 337, 345
  tennis exercise, 345-347

the technique, 337
visualization, 339, 347, 351
Star Wars, 64
staying healthy, 249
stress, 39, 57, 69-72, 77-80, 123, 182, 251, 253, 275-277, 293
  adrenaline, 70
  allergies, 71, 293-294
  autoimmune conditions, 71
  B complex, 80
  bronchitis, 71
  cancer, 71-72, 74, 92
  danger of, 69
  decrease in immune function, 72
  deeply-held beliefs, 71, 92
  diabetes, 71
  disease, 66, 74, 92, 273
  endocrine disorders, 71
  feelings of peace, 72, 246
  happiness, 72
  health, 69-70, 73-75, 307
  heart disease, 71
  heartbeat, 70
  hypertension, 71, 92
  immune system, 70, 72, 74
  infections, 71
  insomnia, 71
  internal reactions, 70-72, 275-277
  lethargy, 71
  levels, 72
  magnesium, 80
  meditation, 74
  misconceptions, 70
  natural killer (NK) cells, 74
  neutralizing harmful reactions, 72, 307
  polished stones, 81
  positive factors, 71
  preconditioned responses, 275
  prioritizing daily tasks, 79
  quantum focus, 75
  quantum focus hike, 80
  reactions within the body, 70-73, 75, 275, 277
  reducing the effects, 67, 69, 75, 182, 307, 354
  stressors, 70-72, 91, 244
  things we can do, 67, 69, 71, 307
  thyroid disorders, 71
  truth about, 70
  ulcers, 71
  vitamin C, 80
  well-being, 69
  what is, 70
subconscious addiction, 60
subconscious mind, 19, 27, 62, 95, 107, 109, 225
subconscious programming, 24-25, 354
subgoals
  aligned with your overall goal, 130
  as bridges to final goal, 130
  support your overall mission, 130

The Relaxation Response, 73
thoughts affecting computer output, 28
toxic emotions, 61, 66, 92-93, 256-257
tranquility, 75, 76
truth, 52
turning point in illness, 19, 61
Type A personality, 73, 276

Type B personality, 73

unconscious mind, 19, 22, 27, 53, 71, 109, 126, 128, 140, 142, 152, 158, 179, 185, 187, 192, 198, 224, 238, 239, 253, 258, 311, 313, 317, 339
    goals, 22, 126-129, 194, 202, 212, 220, 242
    level, 93, 94, 252, 278
    maintaining health, 63, 258
    muscle memory, 339, 343
    pain, 278, 283
    past lives, 152-154
    relationships, 353-354
    smoking, 224
unhappiness, 53, 61-64, 107, 216, 238, 243, 245
universal consciousness, 21, 52-53, 57
universal intelligence, 53, 202
universal laws, 41, 93, 208, 315
unresolved tensions
    arthritis, 92

visualization, 32, 225, 226, 283, 339

wealth, 63, 127, 128
weight, 229
    calories, 232
    calories we burn up, 231
    calories we consume, 231
    control over, 229
    cravings, 230, 235-236
    diabetes, 269
    diet math, 231
    effect of exercise, 233
    emotions and eating, 236-237
    heart disease, 269
    hunger, 236
    hypertension, 269
    important factors in, 231
    longevity, 269
    management exercise, 233-237
    metabolism, 232-233
    to gain a few pounds, 238-242
    too heavy, 230
    too thin, 229-230
wellness, 251
Wolf, Stuart, 355
worry, 21, 22, 60, 70, 79, 115, 116, 117, 119, 120, 146, 253, 371
Wurtman, Richard, 137

your life's purpose exercise, 88

zeal time, 32, 43-44